The
Circle
Maker

Draw the
Circle

Resources by Mark Batterson

Be a Circle Maker

The Circle Maker

The Circle Maker Video Curriculum

The Circle Maker Prayer Journal

The Circle Maker, Student Edition

Draw the Circle

In a Pit with a Lion on a Snowy Day

Praying Circles around Your Children

Primal

Soul Print

Wild Goose Chase

The Circle Maker

Praying Circles Around Your
Biggest Dreams and Greatest Fears

Draw the Circle

The 40 Day Prayer Challenge

Mark Batterson

ZONDERVAN

The Circle Maker/ Draw the Circle Compilation
Copyright © 2013 by Mark Batterson

The Circle Maker
Copyright © 2011 by Mark Batterson

Draw the Circle
Copyright © 2012 by Mark Batterson

This title is also available as a Zondervan ebook. Visit www.zondervan.com/ebooks.

This title is also available in a Zondervan audio edition. Visit www.zondervan.fm.

Requests for information should be addressed to:
Zondervan, *Grand Rapids, Michigan* 49530

ISBN 978-0-310-62091-4

Published in association with the literary agency of Fedd & Company, Inc., Post Office Box 341973, Austin, TX 78734.

Cover design: *Extra Credit Projects*
Interior illustration: *iStockPhoto®*
Interior design: *Beth Shagene*

Printed in the United States of America

13 14 15 16 17 18 /DCI/ 20 19 18 17 16 15 14 13 12 11 10 9 8 7 6 5 4 3 2 1

Mark Batterson encourages readers to take their prayer lives to a new level that will honor the mighty power of God. Like the man who made prayer circles for rain, we are to make bold prayers for things that seem impossible. Through the stories of modern-day prayer miracles, you will be inspired to draw prayer circles around your family, friends, and yourself. *The Circle Maker* teaches that God is for you and that the big dreams you claim in your prayers will be reflected in the way you live your life.

> **Pastor Matthew Barnett**, cofounder
> of the Dream Center

Mark Batterson is a master storyteller. His stories illustrate important biblical truths that convict me in my heart and make me hunger for a closer walk with God. *The Circle Maker* is such a story. I have changed the way I pray — longing for a more powerful and effective prayer life. I am now drawing circles.

> **Ruth Graham**, author of
> *Fear Not Tomorrow, God Is Already There*

Mark Batterson is one of the most brilliant and engaging writers on the planet. I love the way he both challenges and encourages his audience through the written word. *The Circle Maker* isn't just a book full of really good ideas and catchy phrases; it's a concept that, if applied, could totally change the way we walk with God.

> **Perry Noble**, senior pastor of NewSpring Church

My friend Mark Batterson has a way of always drawing us close to the heart of God through his writing. In his latest book, *The Circle Maker*, he shows us how through prayer we can enjoy sitting at the table of heaven's boardroom.

> **Pastor Rich Wilkerson**, founder of Peacemakers
> and senior pastor of Trinity Church in Miami, Florida

Mark is one of those favored few who dig a little deeper into the Word, consistently finding truths that are sometimes surprising and always challenging.

> **Frank Wright**, PhD, president and CEO
> of National Religious BroadcastersResources by Mark
> Batterson

Mark Batterson's *The Circle Maker* will have you praying circles around any situation you are facing. You'll be inspired and motivated into a deeper level of prayer and faith.

> Craig Groeschel, senior pastor of LifeChurch.tv
> and author of *Weird: Because Normal Isn't Working*

Honi the circle maker is a longtime legendary figure, and Mark Batterson is well on his way. You will love the freshness of this approach to prayer.

> John Ortberg, pastor at Menlo Park Presbyterian Church in
> Menlo Park, California, and author of *The Me I Want to Be*

Mark Batterson has hit the nail on the head in *The Circle Maker*! He clearly and practically lays out what prayer looks like and the powerful results that come from a bold prayer life.

> Pete Wilson, author of *Plan B*

Without a doubt Mark Batterson is a voice to our generation and one of my favorite authors. *The Circle Maker* will inspire us to dare to pray the kind of prayers that change us and the world around us. When we pray, we move God, and when God is moved, he moves mountains. This book reminds us of the most important key for unlocking the God-dream inside.

> Christine Caine, founder of the A21 Campaign

What's your Jericho? What promise does God want desperately to shower upon you — if you but ask? *The Circle Maker* gives you timeless wisdom for claiming God's promises, pursuing dreams, and changing the world.

> Dr. George O. Wood, general superintendent,
> The General Council of the Assemblies of God

My bookshelves at home are littered with books I intended to read but never finished. Mark doesn't write those kinds of books. Mark writes books that demand a second and even third reading, because there's always something new to find. With *The Circle Maker*, Mark has done it again.

> Jon Acuff, *Wall Street Journal* bestselling author
> of *Quitter* and *Stuff Christians Like*

The
Circle
Maker

To my father-in-law, Bob Schmidgall.
The memory of you kneeling in prayer lives forever,
as do your prayers.

Contents

Chapter 1

The Legend
of the Circle Maker

Young children danced in the downpour like it was the first rain-
fall they'd ever seen. And it was. Parents threw back their heads,
opened their mouths, and caught raindrops like they were libations.
And they were. When it hasn't rained in more than a year, raindrops
are like diamonds falling from the sky.

It would be forever remembered as *the day*. The day thunderclaps
applauded the Almighty. The day puddle jumping became an act of
praise. The day the legend of the circle maker was born.

It was the first century BC, and a devastating drought threatened
to destroy a generation — the generation before Jesus. The last of the
Jewish prophets had died off nearly four centuries before. Miracles
were such a distant memory that they seemed like a false memory.
And God was nowhere to be heard. But there was one man, an eccentric sage who lived outside the walls of Jerusalem, who dared to pray
anyway. His name was Honi. And even if the people could no longer
hear God, he believed that God could still hear them.

When rain is plentiful, it's an afterthought. During a drought, it's
the only thought. And Honi was their only hope. Famous for his ability to pray for rain, it was on this day, *the day*, that Honi would earn
his moniker.

With a six-foot staff in his hand, Honi began to turn like a math
compass. His circular movement was rhythmical and methodical.
Ninety degrees. One hundred eighty degrees. Two hundred seventy
degrees. Three hundred sixty degrees. He never looked up as the

crowd looked on. After what seemed like hours but had only been seconds, Honi stood inside the circle he had drawn. Then he dropped to his knees and raised his hands to heaven. With the authority of the prophet Elijah, who called down fire from heaven, Honi called down rain:

"Lord of the universe, I swear before Your great name that I will not move from this circle until You have shown mercy upon Your children."

The words sent a shudder down the spines of all who were within earshot that day. It wasn't just the volume of his voice; it was the authority of his tone. Not a hint of doubt. This prayer didn't originate in the vocal chords. Like water from an artesian well, the words flowed from the depth of his soul. His prayer was resolute yet humble, confident yet meek, expectant yet unassuming.

Then it happened.

As his prayer ascended to the heavens, raindrops descended to the earth. An audible gasp swept across the thousands of congregants who had encircled Honi. Every head turned heavenward as the first raindrops parachuted from the sky, but Honi's head remained bowed. The people rejoiced over each drop, but Honi wasn't satisfied with a sprinkle. Still kneeling within the circle, Honi lifted his voice over the sounds of celebration:

"Not for such rain have I prayed, but for rain that will fill cisterns, pits, and caverns."

The sprinkle turned into such a torrential downpour that eyewitnesses said no raindrop was smaller than an egg in size. It rained so heavily and so steadily that the people fled to the Temple Mount to escape the flash floods. Honi stayed and prayed inside his protracted circle. Once more he refined his bold request:

"Not for such rain have I prayed, but for rain of Your favor, blessing, and graciousness."

Then, like a well-proportioned sun shower on a hot and humid August afternoon, it began to rain calmly, peacefully. Each raindrop was a tangible token of God's grace. And they didn't just soak the skin; they soaked the spirit with faith. It had been difficult to believe the day before *the day*. The day after *the day*, it was impossible *not* to believe.

Eventually, the dirt turned into mud and back into dirt again. After quenching their thirst, the crowd dispersed. And the rainmaker returned to his humble hovel on the outskirts of Jerusalem. Life returned to normal, but the legend of the circle maker had been born.

Honi was celebrated as a hometown hero by the people whose lives he had saved. But some within the Sanhedrin called the circle maker into question. A faction believed that drawing a circle and demanding rain dishonored God. Maybe it was those same members of the Sanhedrin who would criticize Jesus for healing a man's shriveled hand on the Sabbath a generation later. They threatened Honi with excommunication, but because the miracle could not be repudiated, Honi was ultimately honored for his act of prayerful bravado.

The prayer that saved a generation was deemed one of the most significant prayers in the history of Israel. The circle he drew in the sand became a sacred symbol. And the legend of Honi the circle maker stands forever as a testament to the power of a single prayer to change the course of history.

Chapter 2

Circle Makers

The earth has circled the sun more than two thousand times since *the day* Honi drew his circle in the sand, but God is still looking for circle makers. And the timeless truth secreted within this ancient legend is as true now as it was then: *Bold prayers honor God*, and *God honors bold prayers*. God isn't offended by your biggest dreams or boldest prayers. He is offended by anything less. If your prayers aren't impossible to you, they are insulting to God. Why? Because they don't require divine intervention. But ask God to part the Red Sea or make the sun stand still or float an iron axhead, and God is moved to omnipotent action.

There is nothing God loves more than keeping promises, answering prayers, performing miracles, and fulfilling dreams. That is *who* He is. That is *what* He does. And the bigger the circle we draw, the better, because God gets more glory. The greatest moments in life are the miraculous moments when human impotence and divine omnipotence intersect — and they intersect when we draw a circle around the impossible situations in our lives and invite God to intervene.

I promise you this: God is ready and waiting. So while I have no idea what circumstances you find yourself in, I'm confident that you are only one prayer away from a dream fulfilled, a promise kept, or a miracle performed.

It is absolutely imperative at the outset that you come to terms with this simple yet life-changing truth: *God is for you*. If you don't believe that, then you'll pray small timid prayers; if you do believe it, then you'll pray big audacious prayers. And one way or another, your small timid prayers or big audacious prayers will change the trajectory of your life and turn you into two totally different people. Prayers are prophecies. They are the best predictors of your spiritual future. *Who you become* is determined by *how you pray*. Ultimately, the transcript of your prayers becomes the script of your life.

In the pages that follow, you'll encounter modern-day circle makers who will inspire you to dream big, pray hard, and think long. The golf pro who prayed around the golf course he now runs will inspire you to dream bigger dreams. The government employee who beat out twelve hundred other applicants and landed the dream job he applied for twelve years in a row will challenge you to hold on to the promise God has put in your heart. The parents who prayed for their son and their son's future spouse for twenty-two years and two weeks will inspire you to pray beyond yourself. And the time-defying answer to an evangelist's prayer for a Capitol Hill movie theater in 1960 will inspire you to think long and pray hard.

The Circle Maker will show you how to claim God-given promises, pursue God-sized dreams, and seize God-ordained opportunities. You'll learn how to draw prayer circles around your family, your job, your problems, and your goals. But before I show you *how* to draw prayer circles, it's important to understand *why* it is so important. Drawing prayer circles isn't some magic trick to get what you want from God. God is not a genie in a bottle, and your wish is not His command. His command better be your wish. If it's not, you won't be drawing prayer circles; you'll end up walking in circles.

Drawing prayer circles starts with discerning what God wants, what God wills. And until His sovereign will becomes your sanctified wish, your prayer life will be unplugged from its power supply. Sure, you can apply some of the principles you learn in *The Circle Maker*, and they may help you get what you want, but getting what you want isn't the goal; the goal is glorifying God by drawing circles around the promises, miracles, and dreams He wants for you.

My First Circle

Over the years, I've drawn prayer circles around promises in Scripture and promises the Holy Spirit has conceived in my spirit. I've drawn prayer circles around impossible situations and impossible people. I've drawn prayer circles around everything from life goals to pieces of property. But let me begin at the beginning and retrace the first prayer circle I ever drew.

When I was a twenty-two-year-old seminary student, I tried to plant a church on the north shore of Chicago, but that plant never took root. Six months later, with a failed church plant on my résumé, Lora and I moved from Chicago to Washington, DC. The opportunity to attempt another church plant presented itself, and my knee-jerk reaction was to say no, but God gave me the courage to face my fears, swallow my pride, and try again.

There was nothing easy about our first year of church planting. Our total church income was $2,000 a month, and $1,600 of that went to rent the DC public school cafetorium where we held Sunday services. On a good Sunday, twenty-five people would show up. That's when I learned to close my eyes in worship because it was too depressing to open them. While I had a seminary education, I really had no idea how to lead. That's challenging when you *are* the leader. I felt underqualified and overwhelmed, but that is when God has you right where He wants you. That is how you learn to live in raw dependence — and raw dependence is the raw material out of which God performs His greatest miracles.

One day, as I was dreaming about the church God wanted to establish on Capitol Hill, I felt prompted by the Holy Spirit to do a prayer walk. I would often pace and pray in the spare bedroom in our house that doubled as the church office, but this prompting was different. I was reading through the book of Joshua at the time, and one of the promises jumped off the page and into my spirit.

"I'm giving you every square inch of the land you set your foot on —just as I promised Moses."

As I read that promise given to Joshua, I felt that God wanted me to stake claim to the land He had called us to and pray a perimeter all the way around Capitol Hill. I had a Honi-like confidence that just as this promise had been transferred from Moses to Joshua, God would transfer the promise to me if I had enough faith to circle it. So one hot and humid August morning, I drew what would be my first prayer circle. It still ranks as the longest prayer walk I've ever done and the biggest prayer circle I've ever drawn.

Starting at the front door of our row house on Capitol Hill, I walked east on F Street and turned south on 8th Street. I crossed East Capitol, the street that bisects the NE and SE quadrants of the city, and turned west on M Street SE. I then completed the circle, which was actually more of a square, by heading north on South Capitol Street. I paused to pray in front of the Capitol for a few minutes. Then I completed the 4.7-mile circle by taking a right turn at Union Station and heading home.

It's hard to describe what I felt when I finished drawing that circle. My feet were sore, but my spirit soared. I felt the same kind of holy confidence the Israelites must have felt when they crossed the Jordan River on dry ground and stepped foot in the Promised Land for the first time. I couldn't wait to see the way God would honor that prayer. That prayer circle had taken nearly three hours to complete because my prayer pace is slower than my normal pace, but God has been answering that three-hour prayer for the past fifteen years.

Since *the day* I drew that prayer circle around Capitol Hill, National Community Church has grown into one church with seven locations around the metro DC area. We're on the verge of launching our first international campus in Berlin, Germany. And God has given us the privilege of influencing tens of thousands of people over the last decade and a half.

All Bets Are Off

As I look over my shoulder, I'm grateful for the miracles God has done, and I'm keenly aware of the fact that every miracle has a genealogy. If you trace those miracles all the way back to their origin, you'll find a prayer circle. Miracles are the by-product of prayers that were prayed *by you* or *for you*. And that should be all the motivation you need to pray.

God has determined that certain expressions of His power will only be exercised in response to prayer. Simply put, God won't do it unless you pray for it. We have not because we ask not, or maybe I should say, we have not because we circle not. The greatest tragedy in life is the prayers that go unanswered because they go unasked.

Now here's the good news: If you do pray, all bets are off. You can live with holy anticipation because you never know how or when or where God is going to answer, but I promise you this: He will answer. And His answers are not limited by your requests. We pray out of our ignorance, but God answers out of His omniscience. We pray out of our impotence, but God answers out of His omnipotence. God has the ability to answer the prayers we should have prayed but lacked the knowledge or ability to even ask.

During my prayer walk around Capitol Hill, I drew circles around things I didn't even know how to ask for. Without even knowing it, I drew prayer circles around people who would one day come to faith in Jesus Christ at our coffeehouse on Capitol Hill that wasn't even an idea yet. Without even knowing it, I walked right by a piece of property at 8th Street and Virginia Avenue SE that we would purchase thirteen years later as a result of a $3 million gift that wasn't even a prayer yet. Without even knowing it, I walked right under a theater marquee on Barracks Row, the main street of Capitol Hill, that we would renovate and reopen as our seventh location fifteen years later.

Those answers are a testament to the power of God and a reminder that if you draw prayer circles, God will answer those prayers somehow, someway, sometime. God has been answering that prayer for fifteen years, and He'll keep answering it forever. Like Honi, your prayers have the potential to change the course of history. It's time to start circling.

Chapter 3

The Jericho Miracle

Every book has a backstory. There is a moment when an idea is conceived in the imagination of an author and this idea is destined to become a book. And because I believe the backstory will help you appreciate the story, let me share the genesis of *The Circle Maker*.

During my senior year of college, I developed a voracious appetite for reading. I spent all of my spare cash and spare time on books. Since then, I've read thousands of books on topics ranging from spirituality to neurology to biography to astronomy. Not only are my bookshelves filled to maximum capacity; I have books stacked on top of my shelves as high as I can reach, and books stacked on my floor in precarious piles that look like the Leaning Tower of Pisa. I ran out of shelf space a few years ago, which means that not every book "makes the shelf." I do have one shelf, however, that contains only my favorites, a few dozen of them. One of them is titled *The Book of Legends*.

A collection of stories from the Talmud and Midrash, *The Book of Legends* contains the teachings of Jewish rabbis passed down from generation to generation. Because it contains more than a millennium's worth of wisdom, reading *The Book of Legends* feels like an archaeological dig. I had dug down 202 pages when I stumbled across a story that may as well have been a buried treasure. It was the legend of Honi the circle maker. And it forever changed the way I pray.

I've always believed in the power of prayer. In fact, prayer is the spiritual inheritance I received from my grandparents. I had a grandfather who would kneel by his bedside at night, take off his hearing aid, and pray for his family. He couldn't hear himself without his hearing aid on, but everyone else in the house could. Few things leave as lasting an impression as hearing someone genuinely intercede for you. And even though he died when I was six, his prayers did not. Our prayers never die. There have been moments in my life when the Spirit of God has whispered to my spirit, *Mark, the prayers of your grandfather are being answered in your life right now.* Those moments rank as the most humbling moments of my life. And after discovering the legend of Honi the circle maker, I realized that my grandfather had been praying circles around me before I was even born.

The legend of Honi the circle maker was like a revelation of the power of prayer. It gave me a new vocabulary, a new imagery, a new methodology. It not only inspired me to pray bold prayers but also helped me pray with more perseverance. I started circling everyone and everything in prayer. I drew particular inspiration from the march around Jericho, when God delivered on a four-hundred-year-old promise by providing the first victory in the Promised Land. While the story doesn't explicitly mention the people taking up positions of prayer, I have no doubt that the Israelites were praying as they circled the city. Isn't that what you instinctively do when you face a challenge that is way beyond your ability? The image of the Israelites circling Jericho for seven days is a moving picture of what drawing prayer circles looks like. It's also the backdrop for this book.

Jericho March

The first glimpse of Jericho was both awe-inspiring and frightening. While wandering in the wilderness for forty years, the Israelites had never seen anything approximating the skyline of Jericho. The closer they got, the smaller they felt. They finally understood why the generation before them felt like grasshoppers and failed to enter the Promised Land because of fear.

A six-foot-wide lower wall and fifty-foot-high upper wall encircled the ancient metropolis. The mud-brick walls were so thick and tall that the twelve-acre city appeared to be an impregnable fortress. It seemed like God had promised something impossible, and His battle plan seemed nonsensical: *Your entire army is to march around the city once a day for six days. On the seventh day you are to march around the city seven times.*

Every soldier in the army had to have wondered why. Why not use a battering ram? Why not scale the walls? Why not cut off the water supply or shoot flaming arrows over the walls? Instead, God told the Israelite army to silently circle the city. And He promised, after they circled thirteen times over seven days, the wall would fall.

The first time around, the soldiers must have felt a little foolish. But with each circle, their stride grew longer and stronger. With each circle, a holy confidence was building pressure inside their souls. By the seventh day, their faith was ready to pop. They arose before dawn and started circling at six o'clock in the morning. At three miles per hour, each mile-and-a-half march around the city took a half hour. By nine o'clock, they began their final lap. In keeping with God's command, they hadn't said a word in six days. They just silently circled the promise. Then the priests sounded their horns, and a simultaneous shout followed. Six hundred thousand Israelites raised a holy roar that registered on the Richter scale, and the walls came tumbling down.

After seven days of circling Jericho, God delivered on a four-hundred-year-old promise. He proved, once again, that His promises don't have expiration dates. And Jericho stands, and falls, as a testament to this simple truth: If you keep circling the promise, God will ultimately deliver on it.

What Is Your Jericho?

This miracle is a microcosm.

It not only reveals the way God performed this particular miracle; it also establishes a pattern to follow. It challenges us to confidently circle the promises God has given to us. And it begs the question: What is your Jericho?

For the Israelites, Jericho symbolized the fulfillment of a dream that originated with Abraham. It was the first step in claiming the Promised Land. It was the miracle they had been hoping for and waiting for their entire lives.

What is your Jericho?

What promise are you praying around? What miracle are you marching around? What dream does your life revolve around?

Drawing prayer circles starts with identifying your Jericho. You've got to define the promises God wants you to stake claim to, the miracles God wants you to believe for, and the dreams God wants you to pursue. Then you need to keep circling until God gives you what He wants and He wills. That's the goal. Now here's the problem: Most of us don't get what we want simply because we don't know what we want. We've never circled any of God's promises. We've never written down a list of life goals. We've never defined success for ourselves. And our dreams are as nebulous as cumulus clouds.

Instead of drawing circles, we draw blanks.

Circling Jericho

More than a thousand years after the Jericho miracle, another miracle happened in the exact same place. Jesus is on His way out of Jericho when two blind men hail Him like a taxi: "Lord, Son of David, have mercy on us!" The disciples see it as a human interruption. Jesus sees it as a divine appointment. So He stops and responds with a pointed question: "What do you want me to do for you?"

Seriously? Is that question even necessary? Isn't it obvious what they want? They're blind. Yet Jesus forced them to define exactly what they wanted from Him. Jesus made them verbalize their desire. He made them spell it out, but it wasn't because Jesus didn't know what they wanted; He wanted to make sure *they knew* what they wanted. And that is where drawing prayer circles begins: knowing what to circle.

What if Jesus were to ask you this very same question: *What do you want me to do for you?* Would you be able to spell out the promises, miracles, and dreams God has put in your heart? I'm afraid many of us would be dumbfounded. We have no idea what we want God to do for us. And the great irony, of course, is that if we can't answer this question, then we're as blind spiritually as these blind men were physically.

So while God is for us, most of us have no idea what we want God to do for us. And that's why our prayers aren't just boring to us; they are uninspiring to God. If faith is being sure of what we hope for, then being unsure of what we hope for is the antithesis of faith, isn't it? Well-developed faith results in well-defined prayers, and well-defined prayers result in a well-lived life.

If you read this book without answering this question, you will have missed the point. Like the two blind men outside Jericho, you need an encounter with the Son of God. You need an answer to the question He is still asking: What do you want me to do for you?

Obviously, the answer to this question changes over time. We need different miracles during different seasons of life. We pursue different dreams during different stages of life. We stake claim to different promises in different situations. It's a moving target, but you have to start somewhere. Why not right here, right now?

Don't just read the Bible. Start circling the promises.

Don't just make a wish. Write down a list of God-glorifying life goals.

Don't just pray. Keep a prayer journal.

Define your dream.

Claim your promise.

Spell your miracle.

Spell It Out

Jericho is spelled many different ways. If you have cancer, it's spelled *healing*. If your child is far from God, it's spelled *salvation*. If your marriage is falling apart, it's spelled *reconciliation*. If you have a vision beyond your resources, it's spelled *provision*. But whatever it is, you have to spell it out. Sometimes Jericho is spelled without letters. It's a zip code you're called to or a dollar figure that will get you out of debt. And sometimes Jericho has the same spelling as someone's name. For me, Jericho has three different spellings: Parker, Summer, and Josiah.

When my friend Wayne and his wife, Diane, were expecting their first child, they started praying for their baby. They believed prayer was their primary parental responsibility, so why wait till their baby was born? Every evening, Wayne would lay hands on Diane's stomach and pray the promises in Scripture that they had circled for their baby. During the early stages of pregnancy, they came across a book that said it was never too early to start praying for their baby's future spouse. At first it seemed odd praying for a spouse before they even knew the gender of their baby, but they prayed for their baby and their baby's spouse day after day until their due date.

Wayne and Diane decided to wait until birth to discover their baby's gender, but they prayed that God would reveal what the baby's name should be. In October 1983, the Lord gave them a girl's name. It was spelled Jessica. Then in December, the Lord gave them a boy's name, and they started praying for Timothy. They weren't sure why God had given them two different names, but they prayed circles around both Jessica and Timothy until Diane gave birth.

On May 5, 1984, God answered their prayers, and the answer was spelled Timothy. Wayne and Diane continued to circle their son in prayer, but they also kept praying for the girl that he would one day marry. Twenty-two years and two weeks of accumulated prayers culminated on May 19, 2006 — the day Timothy's bride walked down the aisle. Her name? Jessica.

Here's the rest of the story.

Their future daughter-in-law was born on October 19, 1983, the same month that God gave them the name Jessica. A thousand miles away, Wayne and Diane were praying for her by name. They thought Jessica would be their daughter, not their daughter-in-law, but God always has a surprise up His sovereign sleeve. For Wayne and Diane, Jericho has two spellings — Timothy and Jessica — but the same last name.

In case you're wondering, Timothy was allowed to date girls who weren't named Jessica! Wayne and Diane didn't even tell Timothy that God had given them the name of his future spouse before he was born until after he was engaged.

I have the joy of serving as Timothy and Jessica's pastor. So while Timothy and Jessica are the primary beneficiaries of their parents' prayers, I'm a secondary beneficiary. They have been a huge blessing to National Community Church as small group leaders, and like every blessing, it traces back to a prayer circle.

Vague Prayers

A few years ago, I read one sentence that changed the way I pray. The author, pastor of one of the largest churches in Seoul, Korea, wrote, "God does not answer vague prayers." When I read that statement, I was immediately convicted by how vague my prayers were. Some of them were so vague that there was no way of knowing whether God had answered them or not.

It was during this spiritual season, when God was challenging me to spell out my prayers with greater specificity, that I embarked on a ten-day Pentecost fast. Just like the 120 believers who prayed in an upper room for ten days, I felt led to fast and pray for ten days leading up to the day of Pentecost. My rationale was pretty simple: If we do what they did in the Bible, we might experience what they experienced. You can't manufacture a miracle like Pentecost, but if you pray for ten days, a miracle like Pentecost might just happen.

During that ten-day Pentecost fast, I was teaching a series at our church on miracles, and we had just experienced one. We miraculously purchased a piece of Promised Land that we had circled in prayer for more than five years. We took stones that had been laid in the foundation and gave one to everyone as tangible tokens of the corporate miracle God had performed for National Community Church. Drawing on that corporate faith, we challenged people to personalize the question Jesus posed to the two blind men outside of Jericho: What do you want me to do for you? Then we wrote down our holy desires on those stones. I spelled out seven miracles and started circling them in prayer.

In the spirit of full disclosure, not all seven of the miracles I asked for have happened. In fact, one of them even seemed to backfire. I asked God to give us the movie theaters at Union Station where our church met for more than a decade, but instead of giving us the theaters, He took them away. The theaters were unexpectedly closed down, and we were given less than one week's notice to vacate. It was extremely disappointing and disorienting at the time, but I have to admit that this apparent "anti-miracle" was the catalyst for some bigger and better miracles that have happened in its wake. What seemed like the wrong answer turned out to be the best answer. So not every prayer will be answered the way we script it, but I'm convinced of this: The miracles that have happened would not have happened if I hadn't drawn a circle around them in the first place.

The more faith you have, the more specific your prayers will be. And the more specific your prayers are, the more glory God receives. Like Honi, who prayed for a specific type of rain, nuanced prayers give God an opportunity to reveal more shades of His sovereignty. If our prayers aren't specific, however, God gets robbed of the glory that He deserves because we second-guess whether or not He actually answered them. We never know if the answers were the result of specific prayer or general coincidences that would have happened anyway.

That stone with seven miracles written on it sits on a shelf in my office. Occasionally I'll pick it up and hold it in my hand while I pray. There isn't anything magical about it, but it acts as prayer insurance. It insures that I don't forget what I'm praying for. It also insures that God gets the glory when the miracles happen. When you spell out your prayers with specificity, it will eventually spell God's glory.

The Ladder of Success

It's easy to get so busy climbing the ladder of success that we fail to realize that the ladder is not leaning against the wall of Jericho. We lose sight of our God-ordained goals. Our eternal priorities get subjugated to our temporal responsibilities. And we pawn our God-given dream for the American dream. So instead of circling Jericho, we end up wandering in the wilderness for forty years.

A few years ago, I enjoyed a rare day with no agenda. I had just dropped off my family at LAX after a wonderful spring break in southern California. I stayed behind to speak at a leadership conference, but I had one day in between with nowhere to go and nothing to do, so I found a Starbucks along the Third Street Promenade in Santa Monica and spent the day circling Jericho.

That margin, along with a little California sunshine, made room for an epiphany. As I sipped my White Chocolate Mocha, it dawned on me that I had never really defined success for myself. I had written a couple books and started traveling on the speaking circuit, but neither of those goals was as fulfilling as I thought they would be. I often felt excitement mixed with a profound sadness as I scrambled through airport security on my way to whatever speaking destination was next. My life reminded me of the joke I would sometimes tell about the airline pilot who came over the intercom and said, "I have good news and bad news. The bad news is we're lost; the good news is we're making great time." That's what my life felt like, but it wasn't a joke.

I've never met anyone who doesn't want to be successful, but very few people have actually spelled out success for themselves. We inherit a family definition or adopt a cultural definition. But if you don't spell it out for yourself, you have no way of knowing if you've achieved it. You might achieve your goals only to realize that they should not have been your goals in the first place. You circle the wrong city. You climb the wrong ladder.

Variant Spellings

As window-shoppers strolled up and down the promenade, I scribbled a personal definition of success on a napkin. That napkin may as well have been a stone tablet inscribed by the finger of God on Mount Sinai. God redefined success and spelled it out for me on that napkin. Like definitions in the dictionary that capture different dimensions of a word, I jotted down three variant spellings.

The first definition may sound generic, but it's specific to any and every situation:

1. Do the best you can with what you have where you are. Success is not circumstantial. We usually focus on what we're doing or where we're going, but God's primary concern is *who we're becoming* in the process. We talk about "doing" the will of God, but the will of God has much more to do with "being" than "doing." It's not about being in the right place at the right time; it's about being the right person, even if you find yourself in the wrong circumstances. Success has nothing to do with how gifted or how resourced you are; it has everything to do with glorifying God in any and every situation by making the most of it. Success is spelled stewardship, and stewardship is spelled success.

The second definition I wrote down captures my calling. Whether I'm writing or preaching or parenting, this is the driving passion of my life:

2. *Help people maximize their God-given potential.* Potential is God's gift to us; what we do with it is our gift back to God. Helping people maximize their God-given potential is why God put me on this planet. That is what gets me up early and keeps me up late. Nothing is more exhilarating to me than seeing people grow into their God-given giftedness.

The third definition reveals the deepest desire of my heart:

3. *My desire is that the people who know me the best respect me the most.* Success is not measured by how many people I pastor or how many books I sell; success is living life with such authentic integrity that those who know me best actually respect me most. I couldn't care less about fame or fortune. I want to be famous in my home. That is the greatest fortune.

If you don't have a personal definition of success, chances are you will succeed at the wrong thing. You'll get to the end of your life and realize that you spelled success wrong. And if you spell it wrong, you'll get it wrong.

You need to circle the goals God wants you to go after, the promises God wants you to claim, and the dreams God wants you to pursue. And once you spell Jericho, you need to circle it in prayer. Then you need to keep circling until the walls come tumbling down.

Get Outside the Walls

Circling Jericho gave the Israelites a 360-degree perspective of the walled promise. It helped them wrap their spirits around the mud-brick miracle. It gave definition to the fifty-foot-high dream. That is precisely what prayer does. It helps you get outside the problem. It helps you circle the miracle. It helps you see all the way around the situation.

Don't read this book without finding a time and finding a place to circle Jericho. Take a prayer retreat. Take a prayer journal. And take off. Get alone with God, or if you're wired for interpersonal processing over personal processing, then take some friends with you. They can form a prayer circle around you.

If you can, go someplace that inspires you. A change in scenery often translates into a change of perspective. A change in routine often results in revelation. In formulaic terms, change of pace + change of place = change of perspective.

I've always subscribed to Arthur McKinsey's method of problem solving. I think of it as *prayer solving*.

> If you think of a problem as being like a medieval walled city, then a lot of people will attack it head-on, like a battering ram. They will storm the gates and try to smash through the defenses with sheer intellectual power and brilliance. I just camp outside the city. I wait. And I think. Until one day — maybe after I've turned to a completely different problem — the drawbridge comes down and the defenders say, "We surrender." The answer to the problem comes all at once.

The Israelites didn't conquer Jericho because of a brilliant military strategy or brute force. They learned how to let the Lord fight their battles for them. Drawing prayer circles is far more powerful than any battering ram. It doesn't just knock down doors; it fells fifty-foot walls.

When I retrace the miracles in my own life, I'm amazed at how many of them happened outside the city walls. They didn't happen during a planning meeting; they happened during a prayer meeting. It wasn't problem solving that won the day; it was prayer solving. I got outside the city walls and marched around the promise, around the problem, around the situation. And when you do that, it won't just be the drawbridge that drops; the wall will fall.

Chapter 4

Praying Through

Before there was a Mother Teresa there was a Mother Dabney. In 1925, Elizabeth J. Dabney and her husband went to work for a mission in the City of Brotherly Love, but there wasn't much love in her neighborhood. It was a hellhole. Her husband was called to preach. Her portfolio was prayer, but she didn't just pray; she *prayed through*.

One afternoon as she was thinking about a bad situation in their North Philly neighborhood, she asked God if He would give them a spiritual victory if she covenanted with Him to pray. He promised that He would, and she felt the Lord prompting her to meet Him the next morning at the Schuylkill River at 7:30 a.m. sharp. Mother Dabney was so nervous about missing her prayer appointment that she stayed up all night crocheting.

The next morning she went down to the river outside the city walls, and the Lord said, "This is the place." The presence of God overshadowed her. And she drew a circle in the sand:

> Lord, if You will bless my husband in the place You sent him to establish Your name, if You will break the bonds and destroy the middle wall of partition, if You will give him a church and congregation — a credit to Your people and all Christendom — I will walk with You for three years in prayer, both day and night. I will meet You every morning at 9:00 a.m. sharp; You will never have to wait for me; I will be there to greet You. I will stay there all day; I will devote all of my time to You.
>
> Furthermore, if You will listen to the voice of my supplication and break through in that wicked neighborhood and bless my

husband, I will fast seventy-two hours each week for two years. While I am going through the fast, I will not go home to sleep in my bed. I will stay in church, and if I get sleepy, I'll rest on newspapers and carpet.

As soon as she made that prayer covenant, it was like a cloudburst. God's glory fell from heaven like the raindrops that drenched Honi on *the day* he drew his circle in the sand. Every morning at 9:00 a.m., Mother Dabney greeted the Lord with a hearty, "Good morning, Jesus." She wore the skin off her numb knees, but God extended His powerful right arm. She fasted seventy-two hours each week, but the Holy Spirit was her direct supply.

Soon the mission was too small to accommodate the people. Her husband asked her to pray for another meeting place nearby. She prayed, and a man who had been in business for twenty-five years closed up shop so they could rent the building. Mother Dabney would not be denied. She was a circle maker, and circle makers have a sanctified stubborn streak.

Mother Dabney was more comfortable in the presence of God than the presence of people. As it was with Honi, some even criticized the way she prayed. Well-meaning friends begged her to take a break or take a bite, but she held on to the horns of the altar. And the more she prayed through, the more God came through.

Mother Dabney's prayer legacy would be a long-forgotten footnote if it weren't for one headline. The *Pentecostal Evangel* published her testimony under the title "What It Means to Pray Through." That one article sparked a prayer movement all around the world. Mother Dabney received more than three million letters from people who wanted to know how to pray through.

Counterfactual Theory

Circle makers are history makers.

In the grand scheme of God's story, there is a footnote behind every headline. The footnote is prayer. And if you focus on the footnotes, God will write the headlines. It's your prayers that change the eternal plotline. Just like Honi's prayer that saved a generation, your prayers can change the course of His-story.

I love history, and in particular, a branch of history called counterfactual theory. Counterfactual theorists ask the *what if* questions. For example, what if the American Revolution had failed? Or what if Hitler had been victorious in World War II? How would history have unfolded? What would that alternate reality look like? And what are the key footnotes that would have or could have changed the headlines of history?

Reading biblical history like a counterfactual theorist is an interesting exercise. And the Jericho miracle is a great example. What if the Israelites had stopped circling on the sixth day? The answer is obvious. They would have forfeited the miracle right before it happened. If they had stopped circling after twelve round trips, they would have done a lot of walking for nothing. Like the generation before them, they would have defaulted on the promise. And the same is true for us.

I've already stated our primary problem: Most of us don't get what we want because we don't know what we want. Here's our secondary problem: *Most of us don't get what we want because we quit circling.*

We give up too easily. We give up too soon. We quit praying right before the miracle happens.

Praying for versus Praying through

Our generation desperately needs to rediscover the difference between *praying for* and *praying through*. There are certainly circumstances where praying for something will get the job done. I believe in short prayers before meals because, quite frankly, I believe in eating food while it's still hot. But there are also situations where you need to grab hold of the horns of the altar and refuse to let go until God answers. Like Honi, you refuse to move from the circle until God moves. You intercede until God intervenes.

Praying through is all about consistency. It's circling Jericho so many times it makes you dizzy. Like the story Jesus told about the persistent widow who drove the judge crazy with her relentless requests, praying through won't take no for an answer. Circle makers know that it's always too soon to quit praying because you never know when the wall is about to fall. You are always only one prayer away from a miracle.

Praying through is all about intensity. It's not quantitative; it's qualitative. Drawing prayer circles involves more than words; it's gut-wrenching groans and heartbreaking tears. Praying through doesn't just bend God's ear; it touches the heart of your heavenly Father.

I recently attended the president's Easter prayer breakfast at the White House, along with a couple hundred religious leaders from across the country. Before breakfast, a seventy-six-year-old African-American preacher who served alongside Martin Luther King Jr. in the civil rights movement said a prayer. I could barely hear his words, but his faith was loud and clear. He prayed with such a familiarity with the Father that it was convicting. It's like his words were deep-fried in the faithfulness of God. After he said amen, I turned to my pastor-friends, Andy Stanley and Louie Giglio, and said, "I feel like I've never prayed before." I felt like he knew God in a way that I didn't, and it challenged me to get closer to God. I wonder if that's how the disciples felt when they asked Jesus to teach them to pray. His prayers were so qualitatively different that they felt like they had never prayed before.

When was the last time you found yourself flat on your face before the Almighty? When was the last time you cut off your circulation kneeling before the Lord? When was the last time you pulled an all-nighter in prayer?

There are higher heights and deeper depths in prayer, and God wants to take you there. He wants to take you places you have never been before. There are new dialects. There are new dimensions. But if you want God to do something new in your life, you can't do the same old thing. It will involve more sacrifice, but if you are willing to go there, you'll realize that you didn't sacrifice anything at all. It will involve more risk, but if you are willing to go there, you'll realize that you didn't risk anything at all.

Make the sacrifice.

Take the risk.

Draw the circle.

The Last Piece of Property
on Capitol Hill

After the seeming anti-miracle of the movie theaters at Union Station closing, our church began pursuing property on Capitol Hill to build an urban campus that would include a coffeehouse, performance theater, and centralized offices for our multisite staff. With a going price of $14 million an acre and the relative scarcity of developable properties on the Hill, I wondered if we were looking for something that didn't exist. After an exhaustive search, we only found one piece of property that met our specifications, so we dubbed it "the last piece of property on Capitol Hill." Strategically situated where Capitol Hill, the Navy Yard, and Riverfront communities intersect, the location was absolutely perfect. And the front of the property faced the I-295/395 expressway that is the main artery running through the heart of DC, giving it unbeatable visibility and accessibility.

The first time I set foot on that property at the corner of 8th Street and Virginia Avenue SE, I felt like I was standing on Promised Land. For several weeks, I silently circled that city block in prayer like the soldiers who marched around Jericho. Then, just before making an official offer, our executive leadership team met our realtor at the property for one last look. We were filled with excitement as we dreamed about the possibilities, but our dreams were dashed less than twenty minutes later when our realtor called to inform me that a real estate developer had put a contract on the property *as we had been standing on it.*

I was deeply disappointed because I had already envisioned our new campus on that site. I was deeply confused because I felt like it was where God wanted us. But we should praise God for disappointment because it drives us to our knees. Disappointment is like dream defibrillation. If we respond to it the right way, disappointment can actually restore our prayer rhythm and resurrect our dreams.

Later on that evening, our family knelt in prayer. One of our children prayed a simple prayer: "God, I pray that this property would be used for Your glory." At that moment, my faith found a heartbeat. I sensed in my spirit that God was going to give us that property. I believed it would belong to us because I knew that it belonged to God. So for three months we circled that property in prayer. I marched around that block like the Israelites marched around Jericho. I knelt on the property. I laid hands on the old glass company that had occupied the lot since 1963. I even removed my shoes, just like Joshua did before the battle of Jericho, because I believed it was holy ground.

Out of Luck

At the end of the sixty-day feasibility period, the real estate developer who held the primary contract on the property asked for ten additional days to secure financing. That seemed like our window of opportunity so we offered a nonrefundable deposit, and the owner told us he would give us the contract. We thought God had answered our prayers, but we weren't done circling. Twenty-four hours later, the owner changed his mind, and we lost the contract a second time.

Finally, at the end of the ten-day extension, I anxiously awaited word from our realtor. I was hoping that the third time would be a charm — not three strikes and you're out. I got the text on a Friday night while our family was at the theater watching *The Karate Kid*. I was enjoying the remake of the original movie, but his text message ruined it for me. He double-thumbed the bad news: "We're out of luck." Then this Spirit-inspired thought fired across my synapses: We may be out of luck, but we're not out of prayer.

Despite losing the contract a third time, I somehow still believed that God was going to defy the odds and give us our Promised Land. Sometimes faith seems like a denial of reality, but that's because we're holding on to a reality that is more real than the reality we can perceive with our five senses. We didn't have a physical contract on that property, but we had a spiritual contract on it via prayer. And a spiritual contract is more binding than a written contract.

A few days after our third strike, I flew to Peru to hike the Inca Trail to Machu Picchu with my son, Parker. For four days we were out of communication with civilization. When we arrived at Aguas Calientes, a small town at the foot of the Andes Mountain range, I called Lora from a public telephone booth. I'm sure onlookers wondered why a large American was jumping up and down inside a small telephone booth, but I was overwhelmed by the news Lora shared with me: *We got the contract!* I couldn't believe it, but I could believe it. We prayed through, and God came through.

I couldn't help but chuckle at the circumstances. It's almost like God said, *Let's get Mark out of the way so we can get this deal done.* In retrospect, I think God wanted me out of the country and out of communication so there was no mistaking it for what it was: a Jericho miracle.

Praise Through

Now let me backtrack. Let me reverse-engineer this miracle. Let me retrace the prayer circle.

During the feasibility period, when the real estate developer had the primary contract on the property, I was rereading the story of the Jericho miracle, and I noticed something I had never seen before. During devotions one day, one phrase jumped off the page and into my spirit:

> *Now the gates of Jericho were securely barred because of the Israelites. No one went out and no one came in. Then the LORD said to Joshua, "See, I have delivered Jericho into your hands."*

Did you catch the verb tense? God speaks in the *past tense*, not the *future tense*. He doesn't say, "I will deliver." God says, "I have delivered." The significance is this: The battle was won before the battle even began. God had already given them the city. All they had to do was circle it.

As I read this story, I felt as though the Spirit of God said to my spirit, "Stop praying for it and start praising me for it." True faith doesn't just celebrate *ex post facto*, after the miracle has already happened; true faith celebrates before the miracle happens, as if the miracle has already happened, because you know that you know that God is going to deliver on His promise.

This is going to sound sacrilegious, but sometimes you need to quit praying. After you pray through, you need to *praise through*. You need to quit asking God to do something and start praising Him for what He had already done. Prayer and praise are both expressions of faith, but praise is a higher dimension of faith. Prayer is asking God to do something, future tense; praise is believing that God has already done it, past tense.

Before you write this off as some "name it, claim it" scheme, let me remind you that God cannot be bribed or blackmailed. God doesn't do miracles to satisfy our selfish whims. God does miracles for one reason and one reason alone: to spell His glory. We just happen to be the beneficiaries.

Keep Circling Jericho

Not long after making this devotional discovery, I shared this past-tense principle with our church. We literally stopped praying that God would give us the property. We started praising Him for it because we felt like God had promised it. The following week, I received an e-mail from a couple who had the same revelation. For many years, they had prayed to get pregnant. Then they stopped praying and started praising because they felt in their spirit that God had promised them children. And when God gives you a promise, you need to praise Him for it.

> That's exactly what God led us to do: stop praying and start praising Him for what He was about to do. We were infertile for five years, but God had already told me I would one day be a mother. In year three of being infertile, I started praising Him for the children he was going to give us instead of pleading for children. Today we have eight precious children that God has blessed us with through both birth and adoption. I have no doubt it is because I started praising Him. It was a true sign to Him that I believed He would give us children — and He did.

There are moments in life when you need to stop pleading and start praising. If God has put a promise in your heart, praise Him for it. You need to celebrate as if it has already happened. You need to stop asking, because God has already answered. And for the record, even if God doesn't answer the way you want, you still need to praise through. That is when it's most difficult to praise God, but that is also when our praise is most pure and most pleasing to God.

Right after God gave me this revelation, I went over to the property we were praying for, got down on my knees, and started praising God for the promise He had put in my heart. We lost that contract three separate times, but we kept praising God. The deal died three times, but resurrection is the central tenet of the Christian faith. And it isn't something we just celebrate on Easter. Resurrection is something we celebrate every day in every way. Prayer has the power to resurrect dead dreams and give them new life — eternal life.

I'm not sure what promise God has put in your heart. I don't know what dream you're holding on to or what miracle you're holding out for, but I offer this exhortation: Keep circling Jericho.

And don't just pray through; praise through.

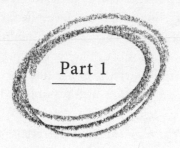

Part 1

The First Circle — Dream Big

Until the day he died, Honi the circle maker was mesmerized by one phrase in one verse of Scripture — Psalm 126:1. "When the Lord restored the fortunes of Zion, we were like those who dreamed." That phrase, "we were like those who dreamed," provoked a question that Honi grappled with his entire life:

Is it possible for a man to dream continuously for seventy years?

Neuroimaging has shown that as we age, the center of cognitive gravity tends to shift from the imaginative right brain to the logical left brain. And this neurological tendency presents a grave spiritual danger. At some point, most of us stop living out of imagination and start living out of memory. Instead of creating the future, we start repeating the past. Instead of living by faith, we live by logic. Instead of going after our dreams, we stop circling Jericho.

But it doesn't have to be that way.

Harriet Doerr dreamed of going to college in a day and age when university populations were mostly male. Money, and then children, kept her from going, but the dream never died. Half a century later, Harriet earned her bachelor's degree from Stanford University at the age of sixty-seven. While most of her contemporaries were retiring, Harriet was just getting started. She also dreamed of writing a book. Her first novel, *Stones for Ibarra*, was published when Harriet was seventy-four years young.

Is it possible to dream continuously for seventy years?

In the words of Harriet Doerr, "One of the best things about aging is being able to watch imagination overtake memory."

So who's right? The neurologists? Or Harriet? The answer is both.

As we age, either imagination overtakes memory or memory overtakes imagination. Imagination is the road less taken, but it is the pathway of prayer. Prayer and imagination are directly proportional: the more you pray the bigger your imagination becomes because the Holy Spirit supersizes it with God-sized dreams. One litmus test of spiritual maturity is whether your dreams are getting bigger or smaller. The older you get, the more faith you should have because you've experienced more of God's faithfulness. And it is God's faithfulness that increases our faith and enlarges our dreams.

There is certainly nothing wrong with an occasional stroll down memory lane, but God wants you to keep dreaming until the day you die. You're never too old to go after the dreams God has put in your heart. And for the record, you're never too young either. Age is never a valid excuse.

Is it possible for a man to dream continuously for seventy years?

Ironically, Honi answered his own question with his own life. He never stopped dreaming because he never stopped praying. And how could he, after God answered his impossible prayer for rain? Once you've experienced a miracle like that, you believe God for even bigger and better miracles.

If you keep praying, you'll keep dreaming, and conversely, if you keep dreaming, you'll keep praying. Dreaming is a form of praying, and praying is a form of dreaming. The more you pray the bigger your dreams will become. And the bigger your dreams become the more you will have to pray. In that process of drawing ever-enlarging prayer circles, the sphere of God's glory is expanded.

Our date of death is not the date etched on our tombstone. The day we stop dreaming is the day we start dying. When imagination is sacrificed on the altar of logic, God is robbed of the glory that rightfully belongs to Him. In fact, the death of a dream is often a subtle form of idolatry. We lose faith in the God who gave us the big dream and settle for a small dream that we can accomplish without His help. We go after dreams that don't require divine intervention. We go after dreams that don't require prayer. And the God who is able to do immeasurably more than all our right brain can imagine is supplanted by a god — lowercase *g* — who fits within the logical constraints of our left brain.

Nothing honors God more than a big dream that is way beyond our ability to accomplish. Why? Because there is no way we can take credit for it. And nothing is better for our spiritual development than a big dream because it keeps us on our knees in raw dependence on God. Drawing prayer circles around our dreams isn't just a mechanism whereby we accomplish great things for God; it's a mechanism whereby God accomplishes great things in us.

Is it possible for a man to dream continuously for seventy years?

If you keep drawing prayer circles, the answer is yes.

May you keep dreaming until the day you die. May imagination overtake memory. May you die young at a ripe old age.

Chapter 5

Cloudy with a Chance
of Quail

Before the first raindrop fell, Honi had to have felt a little foolish. Standing inside a circle and demanding rain is a risky proposition. Vowing that you won't leave the circle until it rains is even riskier. Honi didn't draw a semicircle; he drew a complete circle. There was no escape clause, no expiration date. Honi backed himself into a circle, and the only way out was a miracle.

Drawing prayer circles often looks like an exercise in foolishness. But that's faith. Faith is the willingness to look foolish. Noah looked foolish building a boat in the middle of a desert. The Israelite army looked foolish marching around Jericho blowing trumpets. A shepherd boy named David looked foolish charging a giant with a slingshot. The Magi looked foolish tracking a star to Timbuktu. Peter looked foolish getting out of a boat in the middle of the Sea of Galilee. And Jesus looked foolish wearing a crown of thorns. But the results speak for themselves. Noah was saved from the flood; the walls came tumbling down; David defeated Goliath; the Magi discovered the Messiah; Peter walked on water; and Jesus was crowned King of kings.

Foolishness is a feeling that Moses was very familiar with. He had to feel foolish going before Pharaoh and demanding that he let God's people go. He felt foolish raising his staff over the Red Sea. And he most certainly felt foolish promising meat to eat for the entire nation of Israel in the middle of the wilderness. But his willingness to look foolish resulted in epic miracles — the exodus of Israel out of Egypt, the parting of the Red Sea, and the quail miracle.

Drawing prayer circles often feels foolish. And the bigger the circle you draw the more foolish you'll feel. But if you aren't willing to step out of the boat, you'll never walk on water. If you aren't willing to circle the city, the wall will never fall. And if you aren't willing to follow the star, you'll miss out on the greatest adventure of your life.

In order to experience a miracle, you have to take a risk. And one of the most difficult types of risk to take is risking your reputation. Honi already had a reputation as a rainmaker, but he was willing to risk his reputation by praying for rain one more time. Honi took the risk — and the rest is history.

The greatest chapters in history always begin with risk, and the same is true with the chapters of your life. If you're unwilling to risk your reputation, you'll never build the boat like Noah or get out of the boat like Peter. You cannot build God's reputation if you aren't willing to risk yours. There comes a moment when you need to make the call or make the move. Circle makers are risk takers.

Moses had learned this lesson well: If you don't take the risk, you forfeit the miracle.

Food Miracles

I love miracles, and I love food, so I *really* love food miracles. And while there are multiple food miracles in Scripture, the day God provided quail meat in the middle of nowhere may rank as the most amazing. When the Israelites exited Egypt, a quailstorm was definitely *not* in the forecast.

The people of Israel also began to complain, "Oh, for some meat!" they exclaimed. "We remember the fish we used to eat for free in Egypt. And we had all the cucumbers, melons, leeks, onions, and garlic we wanted. But now our appetites are gone. All we ever see is this manna!"

The Israelites were complaining. I know, shocking! Instead of manna, they want meat to eat. And as a hardcore carnivore, I understand that. If you haven't eaten at an all-you-can-eat Brazilian steakhouse, you aren't ready to die yet. But talk about selective memory!

The Israelites longingly remember the free fish they ate in Egypt, and forget the little fact that the food was free because they weren't. The Israelites weren't just slaves; they had been the victims of genocide. Yet they missed the meat on the menu? And isn't it just a little ironic that the Israelites were complaining about one miracle while asking for another one? Their capacity for complaining was simply astounding, and we scoff at the Israelites for grumbling about a meal of manna that was miraculously delivered to their doorsteps every day, but don't we do the same thing?

There are miracles all around us all the time, yet it's so easy to find something to complain about in the midst of those miracles. The simple act of reading involves millions of impulses firing across billions of synapses. While you're reading, your heart goes about its business circulating five quarts of blood through a hundred thousand miles of veins, arteries, and capillaries. And it's amazing you can even concentrate, given the fact that you're on a planet that is traveling 67,000 miles per hour through space while spinning around its axis at a speed of 1,000 miles per hour. But we take those manna miracles, the miracles that happen day in, day out, for granted.

Pulling an Adam Taylor

Despite the Israelites' incessant complaining, God patiently responds to their food tantrum with one of the most unfathomable promises in Scripture. He doesn't just promise a one-course meal of meat; God promises meat for a month. And Moses can hardly believe it. Literally.

"Here I am among six hundred thousand men on foot, and you say, 'I will give them meat to eat for a whole month!' Would they have enough if flocks and herds were slaughtered for them? Would they have enough if all the fish in the sea were caught for them?"

Moses is doing the math in his mind, and it doesn't add up. Not even close! He is trying to think of any conceivable way that God could fulfill this promise, and he can't think of a single scenario. He doesn't see how God can fulfill His impossible promise for a day, let alone a month.

Have you ever been there?

You know God wants you to take the job that pays less, but it doesn't add up. You know God wants you to go on the mission trip, but it doesn't add up. You know God wants you to get married, go to grad school, or adopt, but it doesn't add up.

A couple years ago, Adam Taylor went on one of our annual mission trips to Ethiopia. While he was there, he knew God was calling him to invest more than one week of his life. God was calling him to go all in. The defining moment was when a fifteen-year-old boy named Lilly popped out of a sewer manhole cover. He didn't have any shoes on, so Adam spontaneously gave him his. Lilly took Adam on a tour of the sewer where he found an entire community of orphans living under the streets. In that moment, Adam knew that Ethiopia was his Jericho.

The prospect of leaving a six-digit salary didn't add up, but Adam didn't care. He moved to Addis Ababa, Ethiopia, trusting that God would provide, and he started a ministry called Change Boys, which rescues street kids and gives them a home to live in. In fact, twenty-two kids live with Adam in a house that God miraculously provided. Adam signed the lease on the house, not knowing how God would provide. Meanwhile, we released our annual Christmas catalog that raises money for a variety of mission projects. Adam didn't know it, but Change Boys was one of those projects. How appropriate that Adam's spiritual family, National Community Church, would cover an entire year's lease. When Adam heard the news, he cried. Then we cried.

Adam's story has inspired others within our church to step out in faith too. In fact, his name has been turned into a verb. "Pulling an Adam Taylor" has become synonymous with taking a step of faith that doesn't add up.

Impossible Promises

Meat for a month seems like an impossible promise. And Moses has to decide whether or not he is going to circle it. Logic is screaming no; faith is whispering yes. And Moses has to choose between the two.

This predicament reminds me of another food miracle that happened in the Judean wilderness about fifteen hundred years later. A crowd of five thousand is listening to Jesus speak. He doesn't want to send them away hungry, but there aren't any eating establishments anywhere. Then a nameless boy offers his brown-bag lunch of five loaves and two fish to Jesus. It's a nice gesture, but Andrew verbalizes what all the other disciples must have been thinking: "How far will they go among so many?" Like Moses, Andrew starts doing the math in his head and it doesn't add up.

In terms of addition, $5 + 2 = 7$. But if you add God into the equation, $5 + 2 \neq 7$. When you give what you have to God, He multiplies it so that $5 + 2 = 5,000$. Not only does God multiply the meal so that it feeds five thousand; the disciples actually end up with more leftovers than they had food to begin with. Only in God's economy! The twelve baskets of remainders means the most accurate equation is this: $5 + 2 = 5,000 \text{ R12}$.

If you put what little you have in your hand into the hand of God, it won't just add up; God will make it multiply.

One footnote.

Do you recall what Jesus did right before the miracle? It says Jesus "gave thanks." He didn't wait until *after* the miracle; He thanked God for the miracle *before* the miracle happened. Jesus put the Jericho principle into practice by praising God before the miracle happened as if it had already happened because He knew His Father would keep His promise. He didn't just pray through; He praised through.

This Is Crazy

You are only one defining decision away from a totally different life. One defining decision can change your trajectory and put you on a new path toward the Promised Land. One defining decision can totally change the forecast of your life. And it's those defining decisions that become the defining moments of our lives.

The quail promise was one of those defining moments for Moses. He had a defining decision to make: to circle or not to circle.

What do you do when the will of God doesn't add up? What do you do when a dream doesn't fit within the logical constraints of your left brain? What do you do with a promise that seems impossible? What do you do when faith seems foolish?

So Moses went out and told the people what the LORD *had said.*

Moses risked his reputation and circled the promise. He pushed all of his credibility chips to the middle of the table and told the Israelites that God was going to give them meat to eat. This had to be one of the toughest decisions he ever made, one of the scariest sermons he ever preached, one of the craziest visions he ever cast. It doesn't add up, but the will of God never does add up by human calculation. Moses had no earthly idea how God was going to keep His promise, but that isn't our business anyway. That is God's business. Too often we let *how* get in the way of *what* God wants us to do. We can't figure out how to do what God has called us to do, so we don't do it at all.

This is what I have come to call a "this is crazy" moment. If we had the transcript of Moses' thoughts, I wonder if it would read, *This is crazy, this is crazy, this is crazy.*

I had one of those "this is crazy" moments last summer while traveling in Peru. After hiking the Inca Trail to Machu Picchu, Parker and I had an opportunity to check a goal off our life goal list by paragliding over the Sacred Valley. Paragliding is one of those experiences that sounds amazing when your feet are firmly planted on terra firma, but the closer you get to the cliff the more you question whether you should be running off it. I have a minor fear of heights, and that fear was not alleviated by the sixty-second orientation given in broken English by my Peruvian tandem partner, who was half my height. His instructions? *Run as fast as you can toward the cliff.* That's it.

As I sprinted toward the ten-thousand-foot drop-off, one thought kept repeating itself like a broken record: *This is crazy, this is crazy, this is crazy!* But it was quickly followed by, *This is awesome, this is awesome, this is awesome!*

We ran off the cliff and caught an updraft in our parachute. The next thing I knew we were sailing over the Sacred Valley at 14,000 feet. Despite the fact that I lost my lunch seven times in twenty minutes, paragliding ranks as one of the most exhilarating experiences of my life. I learned that if you aren't willing to put yourself in "this is crazy" situations, you'll never experience "this is awesome" moments. If you aren't willing to run off the cliff, you'll never fly. I also learned that paragliding is amazing for your prayer life. You can't *not* pray when you are running off a cliff. The same is true when we take a flying leap of faith.

The Law of Measures

While it's not recorded in Scripture, I promise you that Moses prayed. Isn't that what we do when we cannot figure things out ourselves? When we find ourselves in situations that are beyond our control or beyond our comprehension, we pray. Moses must have felt like he was running off a cliff, but that is how the parachute of God's promises opens up. It often seems like circling the promises of God is risky, but it's not nearly as risky as *not* circling the promises of God. The greatest risk is failing to circle the promises of God because we forfeit the miracles God wants to perform.

One of the defining moments in the history of National Community Church was the day we made a defining decision to start giving to missions. We weren't even a self-supporting church at the time, but I felt like God was prompting us to start giving. To be honest, that prompting prompted a little argument. Have you ever felt like God has called you to do something, but after a quick calculation, you assume the Omniscient One miscalculated? I tried reasoning with Him. *How can we give what we don't have?* But here is what I learned about arguments with God: If you win the argument you actually lose, and if you lose the argument, you actually win.

I lost the argument, and God won the day. We wrote a $50 check to missions and what happened next doesn't add up. The next month, our monthly giving tripled from $2,000 to $6,000 and we never looked back. My only explanation is that Luke 6:38 is true. And when we circled this promise by writing that check, God multiplied His provision.

"Give, and it will be given to you. A good measure, pressed down, shaken together and running over, will be poured into your lap. For with the measure you use, it will be measured to you."

I believe in the law of measures. If you give big, God will bless big. That certainly doesn't mean that you can play God like a slot machine, but if you give for the right reasons, I'm convinced of this: *You'll never outgive God.* It's not possible because God has promised that in the grand scheme of eternity, He will always give back more than you gave up.

This year we're projecting a mission budget of more than a million dollars, but that $50 check still ranks as the hardest and largest gift we've ever given to missions. It didn't add up, but God made it multiply. And He'll do the same for you. If you respond to His promptings, "this is crazy" will turn into "this is awesome." When you live in obedience, you position yourself for blessing. And you never know how or when or where God is going to show up. He might just send winds out of the west at fifty miles per hour with a 100 percent chance of quail.

Quailmageddon

Now a wind went out from the LORD and drove quail in from the sea. It scattered them up to two cubits deep all around the camp, as far as a day's walk in any direction. All that day and night and all the next day the people went out and gathered quail. No one gathered less than ten homers.

The Israelites were parked in the Desert of Paran, a region about fifty miles inland from the Mediterranean Sea and fifty miles southwest of the Dead Sea. The significance is this: Quail tend to live by the water, and they don't fly long distances. If it hadn't been for a supernatural west wind, they would have never made it this far inland. So this is a meteorological miracle. And it's not just a miraculous west wind. The clouds burst and rained quail from the sky.

When quail get tired, they dive-bomb. We're not talking about a perfectly angled duck that makes a smooth landing on a watery runway; quail were falling from the sky like huge pieces of hail. There had to be more than one bruised noggin on *the day* it rained quail. They were popping Advil in Israel that day. Scripture also says that some of the quail flew into the camp about three feet off the ground, so there may have been some below-the-belt bruises as well.

Based on the Hebrew system of measurement, "a day's walk" was approximately fifteen miles in any direction. So if you square the radius and multiply by *pi*, we're talking about an area that was almost 700 square miles. To put that into perspective, Washington, DC, is 68.3 square miles. Not only was this an area ten times larger than the nation's capital, but the quail were piled three feet deep as well.

Can you imagine seeing that many birds fly into the camp? It was like a bird blizzard. Quailmageddon. The cloud of birds was so massive that it seemed like a solar eclipse. For the rest of their lives, when the eyewitnesses who were there that day closed their eyes at night, they counted quail.

Once the quail stopped falling, the Israelites started gathering. Each Israelite gathered no less than ten homers. Ten homers multiplied by 600,000 men equals 6 million homers at a minimum. A homer equated to roughly 200 liters, and assuming that the quail were of an average size, it rained somewhere in the neighborhood of 105 million quail. You read that right: *105 million quail.* God doesn't just provide in dramatic fashion; God provides in dramatic proportion.

One of the reasons I love this miracle is because it is a miracle pun. This miracle is recorded in the book of Numbers, and the Greek name for Numbers is *arithmoi.* That's where we get our word *arithmetic.* Recorded in the book of arithmetic is a miracle that doesn't even begin to add up.

Moses could have never anticipated this answer to prayer. It was unpredictable and unprecedented, but Moses had the guts to circle the promise anyway! And when you circle the promise, you never know how God will provide, but it's always cloudy with a chance of quail.

Do you think that perhaps you need to quit doing arithmetic and start doing geometry? Your job is not to crunch numbers and make sure the will of God adds up. After all, the will of God is not a zero-sum game. When God enters the equation, His output always exceeds your input. Your only job is to draw circles in the sand. And if you do the geometry, God will multiply the miracles in your life.

Multiplication Tables

I was recently helping our youngest son, Josiah, with his multiplication tables. We pulled out the flash cards, and I quizzed him on his fives. Once he gets his fives down, we'll move on to sixes. And once he get his sixes down, we'll move on to sevens. That's the way it works in the world of multiplication. You learn to multiply bigger and bigger numbers. That's also the way it should work spiritually, but many of us never graduate beyond addition and subtraction.

Jesus taught multiplication. He promised that He would multiply His blessings if we work like it depends on us and pray like it depends on God. And he used one hundred, sixty, and thirty as multipliers.

"Still other seed fell on good soil, where it produced a crop — a hundred, sixty or thirty times what was sown."

A few years ago, Lora and I circled this promise contained within the parable of the sower by making the largest faith promise of our lives. A faith promise is an amount of money pledged to missions above and beyond the tithe. It's not based on a budget; it's based on faith. Honestly, we had no idea how we'd be able to give the amount of money we pledged, but God had specifically spelled out the number we knew we were to give. We knew it would take some supernatural provision, but we believed that God was going to honor our pledge because our pledge honored God.

On the day we made the pledge, July 31, 2005, I blogged what I believed: "I have a holy anticipation that I can't even put into words. I can't wait to see how God provides what we promised." Two months later, on October 4, 2005, I landed my first book contract. The advance on that four-book deal was thirty times greater than the pledge we had made. Coincidence? I think not. It was like quail that came out of nowhere! I was thrilled about getting the book contract, but I was even more thrilled about writing the largest check we had ever written for a kingdom cause. I believe that contract was a direct result of having circled this promise.

In December 2010, I signed another book contract with my new publisher, and Lora and I felt led to give a significant percentage of the advance to National Community Church. It wasn't until tax time the next year that it dawned on me that this gift was exactly thirty times larger than the original faith promise we had made five years before. Coincidence? I think not.

I have no idea what your financial situation is, but I do know this. If you give beyond your ability, God will bless you beyond your ability. God wants to bless you thirty-, sixty-, hundredfold. And if you are willing to subtract what you are spending on yourself and add it to what you are investing in the kingdom, God will do the multiplication. If you believe that, you'll circle the promises of God and reap the reward. If you don't, you won't.

If you're still living in the world of addition and subtraction, the tithe is difficult to give because it feels like you're subtracting 10 percent from your income. But once you graduate to multiplication, you realize that God can do more with 90 percent than you can do with 100 percent. Why? Because when you add God into the equation of your finances, it changes the game. If you give generously and sacrificially, the day may come when you're giving more than you're currently making. If you believe that, that promise might be worth circling!

Multiplication Anointing

God isn't offended by big dreams; He's offended by anything less. Your dreams may start out small, and God will honor those humble dreams, but as your faith grows so do your dreams until you dare to dream thirty-, sixty-, hundredfold dreams. And when you draw those God-sized circles, it gives the Omnipresent One room to work.

In the fall of 2006, I was speaking at a men's conference in Baltimore, Maryland. It was the week before my first book, *In a Pit with a Lion on a Snowy Day*, was set to release. I spoke in a morning session to about twelve hundred men and then I sat back and listened to a circle maker named Tommy Barnett. Tommy shared the footnotes to the story of how he and his son, Matthew Barnett, started the L.A. Dream Center more than a decade ago. They circled the fifteen-story Queen of Angels Hospital, and God gave it to them for $60,000. Only in God's economy!

After sharing the story of God's miraculous provision, Tommy invited anyone who wanted a multiplication anointing to come to the altar. I wasn't sure if the idea of a multiplication anointing was even in the Bible at the time, but if Tommy was offering it, I was taking it. It felt a little awkward going to the altar, and it always does, but I was desperate for God's blessing on my first book. I was painfully aware of the fact that 95 percent of books don't sell five thousand copies, but I prayed a circle around the book and asked God to put a multiplication anointing on it. I mustered as much faith as I could and asked God to help it sell twenty-five thousand copies. Of course, I threw in the obligatory "if it be Your will" at the end. That tagline may sound spiritual, but it was less a submission to God's will and more a profession of doubt. If you aren't careful, the will of God can become a cop-out if things don't turn out the way you want. The truth is that my whisper number was one hundred thousand copies. In the deep recesses of my heart, that was my big dream. I just didn't have enough faith to verbalize that number. I felt foolish enough verbalizing twenty-five thousand.

In typical God fashion, He exceeded my highest expectations. He has a way of making our wildest dreams seem tame, our biggest dreams seem small. I believe that God's blessing on *In a Pit with a Lion on a Snowy Day* traces back to the prayer circle that I drew around it. I don't just write books; I circle them in prayer. To me, writing is praying with a keyboard. I also recruited a team of circle makers to pray for me while I wrote the book. Then we prayed circles around the people who would buy the book. We specifically prayed that God would get the book into the right hands at the right time. On one level, I'm surprised by the way God has used paragraphs within the book to save marriages and prompt decisions and birth visions. On another level, I'm not surprised at all. It's no coincidence when people tell me that God brought the book into their lives at the perfect time. It's providence. To me, a book sold is not a book sold; it's a prayer answered.

I was a frustrated writer for thirteen years. I dreamed of writing a book, but I could never seem to finish a manuscript. The turning point was when I drew a circle around the dream during forty days of prayer and fasting. I fasted from all forms of entertainment to stay focused on my goal. Then I stepped into a writing circle with a Honi-like determination that I wasn't coming out until I had a manuscript in my hand. Forty days later, the dream became a reality. I didn't write that book; I prayed that book.

As an author, I've learned to pray circles around my books. As a pastor, I've learned to pray circles around our church. As a parent, I've learned to pray circles around our children. It doesn't matter what you do, you need to circle it in prayer. If you're a teacher, pray circles around your class by laying hands on the desks and asking God to bless the students who sit there. If you're a doctor, pray circles around your patients and ask God to give you X-ray insight. If you're a politician, pray circles around the constituents you serve and the legislation you draft. If you're an entrepreneur, pray circles around your product.

If you do the geometry and draw prayer circles around your Jericho, God will take care of the multiplication. And the bigger the prayer circle the more God can multiply. If you claim the promise, who knows: God might just send 105 million quail into your camp.

Chapter 6

You Can't Never Always Sometimes Tell

I almost said no to a miracle.

A couple who had just started attending National Community Church requested a meeting, and I almost denied the request because they said they wanted to talk about church government. I *love* talking about the mission and vision of the church. Church government? Not as much! Plus, I was fighting a book deadline, so I didn't have much margin in my schedule. So I almost said no, and if I had, I would have missed out on a miracle.

As we sat in my office above Ebenezer's Coffeehouse, they peppered me with questions about bylaws, financial checks and balances, and decision-making protocols. And while I felt a little defensive at the time, I realize now that they were simply doing their due diligence. Like investors who research a company before purchasing stock, they wanted to make sure it would be a good return on investment. After answering nearly ninety minutes worth of questions, they ended by asking me about our vision. I had so much pent-up passion after talking about policies and protocols that I just let it rip. I shared our vision of starting a Dream Center in Ward 8, the poorest part of our city and the primary reason the nation's capital is always in the running for murder capital of the country. I talked about turning our coffeehouse on Capitol Hill into a chain of coffeehouses, with all the net profits reinvested in missions. I talked about launching our first international campus in Berlin, Germany. And I shared our vision of launching multisite campuses in movie theaters at metro stops throughout the greater Washington area. Then the meeting came to a rather abrupt and awkward ending. They said they wanted to invest in National Community Church, but they didn't say how or how much. They left, and I was left scratching my head.

I wasn't sure anything would come of that meeting, but a few weeks later, they asked my assistant for a phone appointment. On an otherwise uneventful Wednesday afternoon, right around 3:00 p.m. EST, I received one of the most unforgettable phone calls of my life.

"Pastor Mark, we wanted to follow up on our meeting and let you know that we want to give a gift to National Community Church."

My mind immediately started racing.

Our congregation is amazingly generous, but our median age is twenty-eight and nearly two-thirds of our congregation are single, which means that most of our attendees are nowhere near their peak earning potential. They are faithfully tithing on their income as Hill staffers or inner-city schoolteachers or coffeehouse baristas, but they don't have the income or savings to give large financial gifts. They are focused on paying off school loans or saving for a wedding.

The largest single gift we had ever received up to that point was a $42,000 tithe on the sale of a home, but I couldn't help but wonder if this gift might exceed that gift. After all, you don't announce a gift if it isn't a gift worth announcing, right?

"We want to give a gift, and there are no strings attached. But before I tell you how much we're going to give, I want you to know why we're giving it. We're giving this gift because you have vision beyond your resources."

I'll never forget that phrase: "vision beyond your resources."

The rationale behind the gift was just as meaningful as the gift itself. And that rationale has inspired us to keep dreaming irrational dreams. Those four words, *vision beyond your resources*, have become a mantra for the ministry of National Community Church. We refuse to let our budget determine our vision. That left-brained approach is a wrong-brained approach because it's based on our limited resources rather than on God's unlimited provision. Faith is allowing your God-given vision to determine your budget. That certainly does *not* mean you practice poor financial stewardship, spend beyond your means, and accumulate a huge debt load. It does mean that you take a step of faith when God gives you a vision because you trust that the One who gave you the vision is going to make provision. And for the record, if the vision is from God, it will most definitely be beyond your means.

Having vision beyond your resources is synonymous with dreaming big. And it may feel like you're setting yourself up for failure, but you're actually setting God up for a miracle. How God performs the miracle is His job. Your job is drawing a circle around the God-given dream. And if you do your job, you might just find yourself standing waist-deep in three feet of quail.

"We want to give the church $3 million dollars."

I was speechless. And I'm a preacher.

It was one of those holy moments when time stands still. I heard it, but I could hardly believe it. I was blindsided by the blessing. Like the wind that brought 105 million quail into the camp, God's provision came out of nowhere. We weren't even in a capital campaign!

It's not our man-made plans that move the Almighty; the Almighty is moved by big dreams and bold prayers. In the awkward silence of my speechlessness, I heard the still small voice of the Spirit. The Holy Spirit hit the rewind button and reminded me of a prayer circle that I had drawn four years before.

Let me retrace the circle.

Prayer Promise

On March 15, 2006, we opened the doors to our coffeehouse on Capitol Hill. The total cost of building Ebenezer's Coffeehouse was over $3 million, and our mortgage was $2 million. One day, I was praying for God's provision when I felt a prompting to pray for a $2 million miracle. The first thing I had to do was decipher whether this prompting was just my own desire to be debt free or whether it was the Holy Spirit who dropped that promise into my heart. It's tough to discern between natural desires and holy desires, but I was about 90 percent sure it was the Holy Spirit who put that promise in my heart. I had no idea how God would do it, but I knew I needed to circle that promise in prayer.

I mentioned the $2 million miracle to a few circle makers, who started praying with me for God's provision. There were certainly weeks and months when I failed to even think or pray about the promise, but we circled that $2 million promise off and on for four years.

About a year after God gave me that prayer promise, I got what I thought was a $2 million idea for an online company called GodiPod. com. Lora and I invested the capital to get the business off the ground, but that $2 million idea turned out to be a $15,000 personal loss. In retrospect, I think I was trying to manufacture the miracle for God. This is what we often try to do, isn't it? When God doesn't answer our prayer right away, we try to answer it for Him. Like the day Moses took matters into his own hands and killed an Egyptian taskmaster, we get ahead of God. But when we try to do God's job for Him, it always backfires. Trying to get ahead of God cost Moses forty years. Of course, even then, God redeemed the forty years Moses spent as a fugitive tending sheep by prepping him to tend His sheep, the people of Israel. If we repent, God always recycles our mistakes.

The one upside to our failed business is that I did learn some valuable lessons about unanswered prayers that are worth far more than the $15,000 hit we took on GodiPod.com. First of all, I came to the humble conclusion that our prayers are often misguided simply because we're not omniscient. I'll be the first to admit that I've drawn some prayer circles around the wrong things for the wrong reasons, and God didn't answer those prayers the way I wanted Him to! If we were absolutely honest, we would have to admit that most of our prayers have as their main objective personal comfort rather than God's glory. If God answered those selfish prayers, they would actually short-circuit the purposes of God in our lives. We would fail to learn the lessons God is trying to teach us or cultivate the character God is trying to shape in us.

A second lesson learned is that no doesn't always mean no; sometimes no means not yet. We're too quick to give up on God when He doesn't answer our prayers when we want or how we want. Maybe your deadline doesn't fit God's timeline. Maybe no simply means not yet. Maybe it's a divine delay.

Finally, I learned that we shouldn't seek answers as much as we should seek God. We get overanxious. We try to microwave our own answers instead of trusting God's timing. But here's an important reminder: If you seek answers you won't find them, but if you seek God, the answers will find you. There comes a point after you have prayed through that you need to let go and let God. How? By resisting the temptation to manufacture your own answer to your own prayer.

It would have been easy to cash out on the $2 million promise after GodiPod.com failed, but I keep circling that promise. I still believed God was going to answer that prayer somehow, someway, sometime. I would have never guessed that the payoff would happen in a meeting about church government, but I stopped trying to manufacture my own answer and simply trusted that God would give an answer when I was ready for it. Then one afternoon, right around three o'clock, God came out of nowhere and delivered on His promise with a holy surprise.

The Element of Surprise

Our family has a handful of sayings that have been passed down from generation to generation. They are part of our family folklore. I'm not sure where this one originated, but I remember my grandma repeating it more than once: *You can't never always sometimes tell.* That tongue twister is a mind-bender, so you might need to read it twice. Here's a translation: "Anything could happen."

Let me redeem that saying and give it a prayer twist. When you circle a promise in prayer, *you can't never always sometimes tell.* Anything could happen! You never know when or how or where God will answer it. Prayer adds an element of surprise to your life that is more fun than a surprise party or surprise gift or surprise romance. In fact, prayer turns life into a party, a gift, a romance.

God has surprised me so many times that I'm no longer surprised by His surprises. That doesn't mean I love them any less. I'm in awe of the strange and mysterious ways in which God works, but I have come to expect the unexpected because God is predictably unpredictable.

God always has a holy surprise up His sovereign sleeve! The only thing I can predict with absolute certainty is this: the more you pray the more holy surprises will happen.

A few months ago, God surprised me with the opportunity to speak at an NFL chapel. I've done a few of them, but this one was unique because it was for the team I have cheered for since I was a kid. Not only that, my all-time favorite player whose jersey I wear on game days was there. I'll be honest, I was a little nervous. There is something about speaking to very large men who paint their faces, put on helmets, and inflict pain that is a little intimidating, and the team sack leader was in the front row.

I preached my heart out that night because, quite frankly, I wanted them to win the next day! But I also knew it was a divine appointment, and I felt a unique anointing. There was a reason that God would choose a die-hard fan to speak to the team. Afterward I shook hands with the guys, and I thought that was that, but *you can't never always sometimes tell*. After the season was over, I had dinner with the guy I had cheered for during his entire career. After dinner we were standing in the parking lot of the restaurant, and I couldn't help but chuckle. I told him that I had prayed for him a thousand times, but every prayer was focused on football. That night I prayed for *him*. Not the football player. The person. That's just like God, isn't it? When you draw a prayer circle, even if that circle is limited by your ignorance, you never know how or when or where God will answer it. One prayer leads to another, which leads to another, and where they will take you no one knows except the One who knows all.

Over the past year, I've been repeating one prayer with great frequency: "Lord, do something unpredictable and uncontrollable."

That is a scary prayer, especially for a control freak like me, but it doesn't scare me nearly as much as a life void of holy surprises. And you can't have it both ways. If you want God to surprise you, you have to give up control. You will lose a measure of predictability, but you will begin to see God move in uncontrollable ways!

Anything could happen. Anyplace. Anytime.

One Afternoon

I believe that every word of Scripture is inspired by God, right down to the jot and tittle. And while chapters like Psalm 23 or verses like John 3:16 top the memorization charts, there are also moments when the same Holy Spirit who inspired the writers of Scripture will inspire the readers of Scripture with an unlikely jot or tittle. Some word or phrase will jump off the page and get into your spirit. One of those unlikely inspirations happened as I was reading Acts 10:3 right before our $3 million quail call.

One day at about three in the afternoon he had a vision.

Here's the context. There was a Roman captain named Cornelius who gave generously to the poor and "prayed to God regularly." That prayer habit kept him dialed into God's frequency and set the stage for this vision. At this point, Christianity was a sect of Judaism, but this vision changes the course of Christianity because the gospel is opened up to the Gentiles. Christianity crosses the Rubicon, and whosoever will may come!

The timing of the vision almost seems coincidental, doesn't it? "One day at about three in the afternoon." But that's what I love about it. When you pray regularly, you never know when God will show up or speak up. Today could be the day. When you live in prayer mode, you live with holy anticipation. You know that coincidences are providences. Any moment can turn into a holy moment. God can invade the reality of your life at three o'clock one afternoon and change everything.

The moment I heard *$3 million* I knew that God had answered our four-year prayer for a $2 million miracle. The only catch is that it was $3 million instead of $2 million. I was a little confused by the fact that it wasn't exactly $2 million. Of course, I wasn't about to complain. That's when the Holy Spirit in His still small voice said to my spirit, *Mark, I just wanted to show you that I can do one better.* And by one better, He meant one million better!

God didn't just do us one better one time. Less than a year later, we received a $4 million gift that was one better than the $3 million gift.

It was like God said, *I can do one better one more time.* With that $7 million-dollar provision that came out of nowhere, we purchased "the last piece of property on Capitol Hill" debt free.

Only God.

Perplex Me

One of the biggest surprises in Scripture happened on the day of Pentecost. No one could have scripted that miracle. When Peter got up that morning, he had no idea that God would pour out His Spirit like flames of fire or that the believers would spontaneously speak in the languages they had never learned or that they would baptize three thousand people before the day was done. It was unpredictable and uncontrollable. Yet how appropriate that this holy surprise happens on the birthday of the church. God threw a surprise party!

A few years ago, I had a revelation while reading the description of what happened on the day of Pentecost. It says the people were "amazed and perplexed." All of us want to be amazed by God, right? It's easy to pray, "Amaze me!" But I don't know anyone who prays, "Perplex me!" But it's a package deal. If you aren't willing to be perplexed, you'll never be amazed.

Cornelius had a vision one day at three in the afternoon. The next afternoon, around noon, Peter had a perplexing vision while praying on the rooftop of Simon the tanner's house. He saw a large sheet filled with animals, reptiles, and birds, and the Lord said to Peter, "Kill and eat." You've got to love Peter's response: "Surely not, Lord!" Peter rebukes Jesus. But before you criticize Peter, realize that we often do the same thing when God gives us a dream that is beyond our ability to comprehend.

Peter had a hard time processing this perplexing vision. He wasn't just perplexed; Scripture says he was "very perplexed." Why? Because the vision was in direct violation of everything he had ever known. Jewish dietary laws forbade eating unclean animals. Peter says, "I have never eaten anything impure or unclean." So God in His endless patience repeats the vision three times. That must have been Peter's magic number. And the third time was the charm.

It's at this place where God wants to do something unprecedented that many of us get stuck spiritually. Instead of operating by faith, we switch back to our default setting of logic. Instead of embracing the new move of God, we fall back into the rut of our old routines.

Peter was perplexed by this vision, but he took a step of faith. He risked his reputation by breaking every law in the Jewish books and stepping foot into Cornelius's house. It was unprecedented because it was considered unclean, but that one small step proved to be a giant leap. That doorframe was a wormhole. The nanosecond that Peter crossed that threshold, all Gentiles were given complete access to the gospel. If you are not Jewish, your spiritual genealogy traces back to this moment. Peter had the faith to cross the chasm because he circled a perplexing vision in prayer. Every Gentile who comes to faith in Jesus Christ is an answer to the prayer circle that Peter drew one afternoon on the rooftop of Simon the tanner's house.

Are you willing to be perplexed? Are you open to holy surprises? Do you have the courage for God to move in unpredictable and uncontrollable ways?

If you are not open to the unprecedented, you will repeat history. If you *are* open to the unprecedented, you will change history. The difference is prayer.

The Brown Grocery-Paper Vision

Hattie was born into the most distinguished family of clergymen in America. Her father, Lyman Beecher, was considered the greatest orator in America. That mantle was passed down to her brother, Henry Ward Beecher. But it was Hattie who would change the course of American history.

One Sunday morning in 1851, during a Communion service, Harriet fell into a trance not unlike the trance that Peter had on the rooftop of Simon the tanner's house. In her trance, Hattie saw an old slave being beaten to death. The vision left her so shaken that she could hardly keep from weeping. She walked her children home from church and skipped lunch. She immediately started writing down the vision God had given her as words poured from her pen. When she ran out of paper, she found brown grocery paper and continued to write. When she finally stopped, and read what she wrote, she could hardly believe she had written it. It was nothing short of divine inspiration. Hattie said that God wrote the book; she just put the words on paper.

In January 1852, a year after Harriet Beecher Stowe's vision, the forty-five-chapter manuscript of *Uncle Tom's Cabin* was ready for publication. The publisher, John P. Jewett, didn't think the book would sell many copies, but three thousand copies were sold the first day. The entire first printing was sold out by the end of the second day. The third and fourth printings were sold out before the book was even reviewed. The book that Jewett didn't think would sell many copies ended up in almost every house in America, including the White House. No novel has had a greater effect on the conscience of a country than Harriet Beecher Stowe's vision, *Uncle Tom's Cabin*. In fact, when Hattie met President Lincoln, he is purported to have said: "So you're the little woman who started this Great War!"

Never underestimate the power of a single prayer. God can do anything through anyone who circles their big dreams with bold prayers. With God, there is no precedent, because all things are possible. Providing meat for a month in the middle of nowhere is no problem when you own the cattle on the thousand hills. God can use the bold prayer of an eccentric sage to end a drought or the bold pen of a young mother to end slavery. If you have the courage to circle the dream in prayer, *you can't never always sometimes tell.*

Praystorm

I believe in planning. In fact, failing to plan is planning to fail. But I also believe this: One bold prayer can accomplish more than a thousand well-laid plans. So go ahead and plan, but make sure you circle your plans in prayer. If your plans aren't birthed in prayer and bathed in prayer, they won't succeed. This I know from personal experience. Prior to our church plant in Chicago, I developed a twenty-five-year plan. That well-laid plan was a project for one of my seminary classes, and I actually got an A on it. In reality, I should have gotten an F because it failed. I still have that twenty-five-year plan in my files. It keeps me humble. It also reminds me that "unless the LORD builds the house, the builders labor in vain."

Few things are more painful than a failed plan, but I've always drawn a little bit of levity and humility from the old adage "If you want to make God laugh, tell him your plans." While we're busy planning, sometimes God is chuckling. And if our plans are way off, that contagious chuckle probably makes its way through angelic ranks like a laugh track. It's not a vindictive chuckle, as if God relishes our failure. I just think God is sometimes amazed at how small our plans are. He allows our small plans to fail so that His big dream for us can prevail. So keep planning like it depends on you, but make sure you pray like it depends on God. Prayer is the alpha and omega of planning. Don't just brainstorm; praystorm.

When God gave me a second chance to plant a church, I did every bit as much planning, but I also did a lot more praying. It started with a prayer circle around Capitol Hill, but it was a perplexing vision while in prayer mode that changed the trajectory of our church.

I was walking home from Union Station one morning when God gave me a vision of our future at the corner of 5th and F Street NE. There weren't any angel choirs singing. No graffiti on the sidewalk. But in my mind's eye, I saw a map of the metro system in Washington, DC, and I envisioned us meeting in movie theaters at metro stops throughout the DC area. One reason the vision was perplexing is that the term "multisite church" didn't exist in the ecclesiological dictionary yet. It was unprecedented. A decade later, National Community Church meets in six theaters, and with thirty-nine theaters in the metro DC area, we've got plenty of room to grow! Our 2020 vision is twenty locations. Translation: We're coming soon to a theater near you! In faith, I dream of the day when there is a church in every theater in America. Why not?

Doing church in marketplace environments like movie theaters has become part of our DNA. We love the comfortable seats and large screens. We also love the smell of popcorn. It's our incense. Whenever I catch a whiff of buttered popcorn, my Pavlovian reaction is to raise my hands in worship.

Are you willing to be perplexed? If you are, then God can and will amaze you!

You can't never always sometimes tell.

Chapter 7

The Solution to
Ten Thousand Problems

Before the quailstorm appeared on Doppler radar, God asks Moses a question. It's more than *a* question; it's *the* question. Your answer to this question, *the question*, will determine the size of your prayer circles.

"Is there a limit to my power?"

The obvious answer to that question is no. God is omnipotent, which means by definition, there is nothing God cannot do. Yet many of us pray as if our problems are bigger than God. So let me remind you of this high-octane truth that should fuel your faith: God is infinitely bigger than your biggest problem or biggest dream. And while we're on the topic, His grace is infinitely bigger than your biggest sin.

The modern mystic, A. W. Tozer, believed that a low view of God is the cause of a hundred lesser evils, but a high view of God is the solution to ten thousand temporal problems. If that's true, and I believe it is, then your biggest problem isn't an impending divorce or failing business or doctor's diagnosis. Please understand, I'm not making light of your relational or financial or health issues. I certainly don't want to minimize the overwhelming challenges you may be facing. But in order to regain a godly perspective on your problems, you have to answer this question: Are your problems bigger than God, or is God bigger than your problems? Our biggest problem is our small view of God. That is the cause of all lesser evils. And it's a high view of God that is the solution to all other problems.

Is there a limit to my power?

Have you answered *the question*? There are only two options: yes or no. Until you come to the conviction that God's grace and power know no limits, you will draw small prayer circles. Once you embrace the omnipotence of God, you'll draw ever-enlarging circles around your God-given, God-sized dreams.

How big is your God? Is He big enough to heal your marriage or heal your child? Is He bigger than a positive MRI or a negative evaluation? Is He bigger than your secret sin or secret dream?

Sizing Up God

Moses was perplexed by the promise God had given him. How could God possibly provide meat for a month? It didn't add up! But at that critical juncture, when Moses had to decide whether or not to circle the promise, God posed *the question*.

Is there a limit to my power?

When God prompted me to pray for a $2 million miracle, I had to answer *the question*. It seemed like an impossible promise to me, but to the God who can provide 105 million quail out of nowhere, what's $2 million?

The size of prayers depends on the size of our God. And if God knows no limits, then neither should our prayers. God exists outside of the four space-time dimensions He created. We should pray that way!

It reminds me of the man who was sizing up God by asking, "God, how long is a million years to you?" God said, "A million years is like a second." Then the man asked, "How much is a million dollars to you?" God said, "A million dollars is like a penny." The man smiled and said, "Could you spare a penny?" God smiled back and said, "Sure, just wait a second."

With God, there is no big or small, easy or difficult, possible or impossible. This is difficult to comprehend because all we've ever known are the four dimensions we were born into, but God is not subject to the natural laws He instituted. He has no beginning and no end. To the infinite, all finites are equal. Even our hardest prayers are easy for the Omnipotent One to answer because there is no degree of difficulty.

If you're like me, you tend to use bigger words for bigger requests. You pull out your best vocabulary words for your biggest prayers, as if God's answer depends on the correct combination of words. Trust me, it doesn't matter how long or how loud you pray; it comes down to your answer to *the question*.

Is there a limit to my power?

With God, it's never an issue of "Can He?" It's only a question of "Will He?" And while you don't always know if He *will*, you know He *can*. And because you know He can, you can pray with holy confidence.

Warts

I answered *the question* when I was thirteen years old, or maybe I should say, *the question* was answered for me. Our family visited a new church one Sunday, and a prayer team from that church showed up unannounced at our front door on Monday. The doorbell caught us a little off guard. So did their faith. After introducing themselves, they simply asked if we needed prayer for anything. At that point in my life, I struggled with severe asthma. I was hospitalized half a dozen times during my preteen years. So we asked them to ask God to heal me. That prayer team formed a prayer circle around me and laid their hands on my head. It made me feel a little uncomfortable, but I had never heard anyone pray with that much intensity. They prayed as if they believed. Then they left.

Sometime between falling asleep that night and waking up the next morning, God did a miracle, but it wasn't the miracle I expected. God answered that prayer, but it wasn't the answer I anticipated. I still had asthma the next morning, but every wart on my feet was gone. No kidding. At first I wondered if God misinterpreted the prayer. Or maybe this was some kind of prayer joke? I couldn't help but wonder if prayer was like the game of telephone where a message gets passed from person to person until it finally gets to God. Maybe somewhere between here and heaven, asthma got translated into warts. Or maybe there was someone with warts who was breathing great that day because they got my answer while I got theirs.

That's when I heard the still small voice of the Holy Spirit for the first time in my life. Please understand that Spirit-whispers are few and far between, but those whispers echo forever. The Spirit said to my spirit, *Mark, I just want you to know that I'm able.*

Like the day after *the day* that God sent rain in answer to Honi's prayer, it was hard *not* to believe the next day. Once you experience a miracle, there is no turning back. It is difficult to doubt God. I wonder if that was how Moses was able to circle the impossible promise of meat to eat. God had already sent manna. God had already parted the Red Sea. God had already performed ten miraculous signs and delivered Israel out of Egypt.

How can you *not* believe when God has proven Himself over and over again?

One footnote.

This question — Is there a limit to my power? — is translated differently in different versions of the Bible. One version reads, "Is the LORD's arm too short?" Another translation reads, "Is the LORD's hand waxed short?" In both instances, the hand or arm of the Lord is referenced as a metaphor for God's power.

With this as a backdrop, reconsider the ten miracles God performed to deliver Israel out of Egypt. These miracles are not attributed to the hand of God or arm of God.

"This is the finger of God."

While we don't know which finger it was, those ten miracles were attributed to one digit. My guess? His pinky! And if one finger is capable of ten miracles, then what can the hand of God or arm of God accomplish?

When it comes to the will of God, I'm hit-and-miss. And my prayer batting average is no better than anyone else when it comes to hitting God's curveballs. I often second-guess the will of God, but I don't doubt the power of God. God is able. I don't always know if He will, but I always know that He can.

15.5 Billion Light-Years

While God's power is technically measureless, the prophet Isaiah gives us a glimpse of God's omnipotence and omniscience by comparing them to the size of the universe. The distance between His wisdom and ours, His power and ours, is likened to the distance from one side of the universe to the other.

As the heavens are higher than the earth,
so are my ways higher than your ways
and my thoughts than your thoughts.

The universe is so large that it requires an awfully long tape measure. The basic unit of measurement is a light-year. Light travels at 186,000 miles per second, which is so fast that in the time it takes to snap your fingers, light circumnavigates the globe half a dozen times.

To put the speed of light and size of the universe into perspective, the sun is 94.4 million miles away from the earth at its farthest distance from us. If you could drive to the sun traveling 65 miles per hour, 24 hours a day, 365 days a year, it would take you more than 163 years to get there. The light that warms your face on a sunny day, on the other hand, left the surface of the sun only 8 minutes ago. So while 94.4 million miles may seem like a long distance by earthly standards, it's our next-door neighbor by celestial measurements. The sun is the nearest star in our tiny little galaxy known as the Milky Way. There are more than 80 billion galaxies in the universe, which, for the record, equates to more than 10 galaxies per person! I don't think you have to worry about running out of things to do when you get to heaven. It's an awfully big sandbox.

In one minute, light travels 11 million miles. In one day, light travels 160 billion miles. In one year, light travels an unfathomable 5 trillion, 865 billion, 696 million miles. But that's just one light-year. The outer edge of the universe, according to astrophysicists, is 15.5 billion light-years away! If that seems incomprehensible, it's because it's virtually unimaginable. Yet God says that this is the distance between His thoughts and our thoughts. So here's my thought: Your best thought on your best day falls 15.5 billion light-years short of how great and how good God really is. Even the most brilliant among us underestimate God by 15.5 billion light-years. God is able to do 15.5 billion light-years beyond what you can ask or imagine.

By definition, a big dream is a dream that is bigger than you. In other words, it's beyond your human ability to accomplish. And this means there will be moments when you doubt yourself. That's normal. But that's when you need to remind yourself that your dream isn't bigger than God; God is 15.5 billion light-years bigger than your dream.

If you've never had a God-sized dream that scared you half to death, then you haven't really come to life. If you've never been overwhelmed by the impossibility of your plans, then your God is too small. If your vision isn't perplexingly impossible, then you need to expand the radiuses of your prayer circles.

Qualified Versus Called

A big dream is simultaneously the best feeling and worst feeling in the world. It's exhilarating because it's beyond your ability; it's frightening for the same exact reason. So if you are going to dream big, you have to manage the emotional tension. Facing your fears is the beginning of the battle. Then you have to circle them over and over again.

Have you ever felt like your dream was too big for you?

Moses felt that way more than once. When God called him to lead the Israelites out of Egypt, Moses felt like it was too big. He felt like he wasn't qualified, so he asked God to send someone else to do it. That is par for the course. In my experience, you'll never feel qualified. But God doesn't call the qualified; God qualifies the called.

I wasn't qualified to pastor National Community Church. The only thing I had on my résumé was a nine-week summer internship. We had no business going into the coffeehouse business. No one on our team had ever worked in a coffeehouse when we started pursuing that dream. But it doesn't matter if you qualify for the loan, qualify for the job, or qualify for the program. If God has called you, you're qualified.

The issue is never, "Are you qualified?" The issue is always, "Are you called?"

I make this distinction between *qualified* and *called* with aspiring writers all the time. Too many authors worry about whether or not their book will get published. That isn't the question. The question is this: Are you called to write? That's the only question you need to answer. And if the answer is yes, then you need to write the book as an act of obedience. It doesn't matter whether anyone reads it or not.

I remember the day I walked into Union Station to inquire about renting the movie theaters for our Sunday services. I felt intimidated by the opportunity. It seemed too good. It seemed too big. We were a church of only fifty people at that point, and Union Station was the most visited destination in Washington, DC. How could fifty people hold services in a place where twenty-five million people pass through every year? We barely filled a large living room. How could we fill what was once the largest room under a single roof in the world? The dream was too big for me, but it's never too big for God. And what seemed too big then eventually became too small to contain what God was doing in us and through us.

If you want to keep growing spiritually, you need to keep stretching. How? By going after dreams that are bigger than you are. When NCC was a church of fifty people, we took a huge step of faith by hosting a Convoy of Hope outreach that fed five thousand people. We knew it required four hundred volunteers. We knew we only had fifty people. But we felt that God was calling us to go for it.

A few years ago, we hosted another Convoy of Hope at RFK Stadium. This time we fed ten thousand guests. As we were recuperating from the huge expenditure of time, energy, and resources, we felt God challenging us: *Why don't you do this every day?* To be honest, we were pretty satisfied doing it once a year, but God upped the ante. Now our dream is a Dream Center in southeast DC that serves as a need-meeting machine 24/7. It's beyond our ability, but that is why we believe God will bless it.

Moses Complex

Bill Grove had a big dream. He also had a self-described Moses complex. His big dream was to be the general manager of the TPC

Scottsdale, the PGA's flagship golf course of the West. But that dream seemed too big for the former golf pro. Like Moses, Bill had a hard time believing he was qualified to manage what *Golfweek* magazine called "one of the America's best courses."

Bill doubted himself, but he didn't doubt God. He circled that dream for more than a decade. The defining moment was the Wednesday evening, after a prayer service at their church, when Bill and his wife, Debbie, and their eight-year-old daughter, Kacey, drove to the TPC Scottsdale and pulled into the parking lot. They joined hands and circled the clubhouse like it was Jericho. Seven times they circled it. The diners in the clubhouse restaurant gave them a few strange looks, but Bill and Debbie and Kacey kept circling. They prayed for God's favor. They prayed for God's glory. They prayed for God's will.

With each circle, it was like God got bigger and bigger. With each circle, self-doubt shrunk and a holy confidence grew. With each circle, a prayer battle was won.

Not long after drawing that prayer circle, Bill got his dream job as general manager of the TPC Scottsdale, and God has been answering Bill's prayer for the seventeen years he has been in that capacity. TPC Scottsdale now plays host to the largest PGA tournament in the country, and it has been named one of the top fifty golf resort destinations in the world by *Condé Nast Traveler*, one of the premier traveling magazines. And while you would have to discover it on your own because Bill is too humble to mention it, Bill has been recognized for his achievements by the Southwest Section PGA with one of its highest honors: Golf Professional of the Year.

Bill is the first to give God all of the glory for his personal and professional achievements. They aren't a testament to Bill Grove; they are a testament to what God can achieve through a humble servant who dares to dream big dreams and pray bold prayers.

A Letter to God

Now let me retrace this circle a little farther back.

Sometimes when you hear answers to prayer that others have experienced, it can be discouraging instead of encouraging because you wonder why God has answered their prayers but not yours. But let me remind you that these answers have rarely happened as quickly or easily as they sound. There is usually a backstory. So we are quick to celebrate the answer to prayer, but the answer probably didn't come quickly. I've never met a person who didn't experience some big disappointments on the way to his or her big dream.

Bill would never have gotten his dream job if he hadn't lost his job of eleven years as the head professional at a private golf club in 1985. It was a devastating blow to his ego, even though he lost the job for righteous reasons. When Bill would not agree to an unfair business deal, his plan went out the window, along with his job. Bill was so afraid and so desperate that he fell on his knees in the shower one night and cried out for mercy. He prayed the only promise he could remember: "Casting all your care upon him; for he careth for you." Bill said, "I went from walking into a shower feeling like I was carrying five hundred pounds to leaving that shower feeling as though I had the strength to lift five hundred pounds."

Sometimes the power of prayer is the power to carry on. It doesn't always change your circumstances, but it gives you the strength to walk through them. When you pray through, the burden is taken off of your shoulders and put on the shoulders of Him who carried the cross to Calvary.

After Bill had worked odd jobs as a golf pro for six years, he and Debbie threw up their arms and got back on their knees because they weren't any closer to their dream than they had been a decade before. That's when they decided to write a letter to God. They posted that letter on their refrigerator, and every time they walked by the refrigerator, they praised God, Jericho style, for the job that He was going to provide.

Over the next decade, one job led to another until Bill landed his dream job as general manager at TPC Scottsdale. It didn't happen overnight, but it did happen. Every time they needed to sell an old house or get a new job, Bill and Debbie wrote a letter to God and posted it on their refrigerator. It was their unique way of circling their situation in prayer. They didn't always get what they wanted, when they wanted it. Sometimes it felt like God was taking His time, and

He was. But God never misses His postmark. After a decade of divine delays and detours, Bill got the dream job he had circled in prayer for more than a decade.

Is your dream too big for you?

It better be because that will force you to pray circles around it. If you keep circling it in prayer, God will get bigger and bigger until you see your impossible prayer for what it really is: an easy answer for an almighty God.

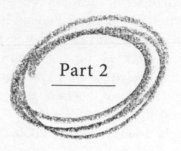

Part 2

The Second Circle — Pray Hard

One day Jesus told his disciples a story to show that they should always pray and never give up. "There was a judge in a certain city," he said, "who neither feared God nor cared about people. A widow of that city came to him repeatedly, saying, 'Give me justice in this dispute with my enemy.' The judge ignored her for a while, but finally he said to himself, 'I don't fear God or care about people, but this woman is driving me crazy. I'm going to see that she gets justice, because she is wearing me out with her constant requests!'"

The parable of the persistent widow is one of the most pixilated pictures of prayer in Scripture. It shows us what praying hard looks like: knocking until your knuckles are raw, crying out until your voice is lost, pleading until your tears run dry. Praying hard is *praying through*. And if you pray through, God will come through. But it will be God's will, God's way.

The phrase used to describe the widow's persistence, "she is wearing me out," is boxing terminology. Praying hard is going twelve rounds with God. A heavyweight prayer bout with God Almighty can be excruciating and exhausting, but that is how the greatest prayer victories are won. Praying hard is more than words; it's blood, sweat, and tears. Praying hard is two-dimensional: praying like it depends on God, and working like it depends on you. It's praying until God answers, no matter how long it takes. It's doing whatever it takes to show God you're serious.

Desperate times call for desperate measures, and there is no more desperate act than praying hard. There comes a moment when you need to throw caution to the wind and draw a circle in the sand. There comes a moment when you need to defy protocol, drop to your knees, and pray for the impossible. There comes a moment when you need to muster every ounce of faith you have and call down rain from heaven. For the persistent widow, this was that moment.

While we don't know what injustice took place, we do know that the persistent widow wouldn't take no for an answer. That's what made her a circle maker. Maybe her son was falsely imprisoned for a crime he didn't commit. Maybe the man who molested her daughter was still on the streets. Whatever it was, the judge knew she would never give up. The judge knew she would circle his house until the day she died if she didn't get justice. The judge knew there was no quit in the persistent widow.

Does *The Judge* know that about you?

How desperate are you for the miracle? Desperate enough to pray through the night? How many times are you willing to circle the promise? Until the day you die? How long and loud will you knock on the door of opportunity? Until you knock the door down?

If you aren't desperate, you won't take desperate measures. And if you don't pray like it depends on God, the biggest miracles and best promises will remain out of your prayer reach. But if you learn how to pray hard, like the persistent widow, God will honor your bold prayers because your bold prayers honor God.

Like Honi the circle maker, the persistent widow's methodology was unorthodox. She could have, and technically should have, waited for her court date. Going to the personal residence of the judge crossed a professional line. I'm almost surprised the judge didn't get a restraining order against her. But this reveals something about the nature of God. God couldn't care less about protocol. If He did, Jesus would have chosen the Pharisees as His disciples. But that isn't who Jesus honored. Jesus honored the prostitute who crashed a party at a Pharisee's home to anoint His feet. Jesus honored the tax collector who climbed a tree in his three-piece suit just to get a glimpse of Jesus. Jesus honored the four friends who cut in line and cut a hole in someone's ceiling to help their friend. And in this parable, Jesus honored the woman who drove a judge crazy because she wouldn't stop knocking.

The common denominator in each of these stories is holy desperation. People took desperate measures to get to God, and God honored them for it. Nothing has changed. God is still honoring spiritual desperadoes who crash parties and climb trees. God is still honoring those who defy protocol with their bold prayers. God is still honoring those who pray with audacity and tenacity. And the persistent widow is selected as the gold standard when it comes to praying hard. Her unrelenting persistence was the only difference between justice and injustice.

The viability of our prayers is not contingent on scrabbling the twenty-six letters of the English alphabet into the right combinations like abracadabra. God already knows the last punctuation mark before we pronounce the first syllable. The viability of our prayers has more to do with intensity than vocabulary. That is modeled by the Holy Spirit Himself, who has been intensely and unceasingly interceding for you your entire life.

Psalm 32:7 is a must-circle promise. I like the King James Version: "Thou shalt compass me about with songs of deliverance."

Long before you woke up this morning and long after you go to sleep tonight, the Spirit of God was circling you with songs of deliverance. He has been circling you since the day you were conceived, and He'll circle you until the day you die. He is praying hard for you with ultrasonic groans that cannot be formulated into words, and those unutterable intercessions should fill you with an unspeakable confidence. God isn't just for you in some passive sense; God is for you in the most active sense imaginable. The Holy Spirit is praying hard for you. And supernatural synchronicities begin to happen when we tag-team with God and do the same.

Chapter 8

Persistence Quotient

In standardized math tests, Japanese children consistently score higher than their American counterparts. While some assume that a natural proclivity toward mathematics is the primary difference, researchers have discovered that it may have more to do with effort than ability. In one study involving first graders, students were given a difficult puzzle to solve. The researchers weren't interested in whether or not the children could solve the puzzle; they simply wanted to see how long they would try before giving up. The American children lasted, on average, 9.47 minutes. The Japanese children lasted 13.93 minutes. In other words, the Japanese children tried about 40 percent longer. Is it any wonder that they score higher on math exams? Researchers concluded that the difference in math scores might have less to do with intelligence quotient and more to do with persistence quotient. The Japanese first graders simply tried harder.

That study not only explains the difference in standardized math scores; the implications are true no matter where you turn. It doesn't matter whether it's athletics or academics, music or math. There are no shortcuts. There are no substitutes. Success is a derivative of persistence.

More than a decade ago, Anders Ericsson and his colleagues at Berlin's elite Academy of Music did a study with musicians. With the help of professors, they divided violinists into three groups: world-class soloists, good violinists, and those who were unlikely to play professionally. All of them started playing at roughly the same age and practiced about the same amount of time until the age of eight. That is when their practice habits diverged. The researchers found that by the age of twenty, the average players had logged about four thousand hours of practice time; the good violinists totaled about eight thousand hours; the elite performers set the standard with ten thousand hours. While there is no denying that innate ability dictates some of your upside potential, your potential is only tapped via persistent effort. Persistence is the magic bullet, and the magic number seems to be ten thousand.

Neurologist Daniel Levitin notes:

> The emerging picture from such studies is that ten thousand hours of practice is required to achieve the level of mastery associated with being a world-class expert — in anything. In study after study, of composers, basketball players, fiction writers, ice skaters, concert pianists, chess players, master criminals, and what have you, this number comes up again and again … No one has yet found a case in which true world-class expertise was accomplished in less time. It seems that it takes the brain this long to assimilate all that it needs to know to achieve true mastery.

Is prayer any different?

It is a habit to be cultivated. It is a discipline to be developed. It is a skill to be practiced. And while I don't want to reduce praying hard to time logged, if you want to achieve mastery, it might take ten thousand hours. This I know for sure: the bigger the dream the harder you will have to pray.

A Small Cloud

Several centuries before the drought that threatened to destroy Honi's generation, there was another drought in Israel. For three long years, there was no puddle jumping in Israel. Then the Lord promised Elijah that He would send rain, but like every promise, Elijah still had to circle it via persistent prayer. So Elijah climbed to the top of Mount Carmel, fell on his face, and prayed for rain. Six times he told his servant to look toward the sea, but there was no sign of rain. And this is when most of us give up. We stop praying because we can't see any tangible difference with our natural eyes. We allow our circumstances to get between God and us instead of putting God between us and our circumstances.

Like Honi who said, "I will not move from here," Elijah held his holy ground. He stood on the promise God had given him. I think Elijah would have prayed ten thousand times if that is what it took, but between the sixth and seventh prayer, there was a subtle shift in atmospheric pressure. After the seventh circle, Elijah's nearsighted servant strained his eyes and saw a small cloud the size of a man's hand rising from the sea.

I can't help but ask the counterfactual question: What if Elijah had quit praying after the sixth circle? The obvious answer is that he would have defaulted on the promise and forfeited the miracle. But Elijah prayed through, and God came through. The sky turned black; heavy winds blew across the barren landscape; raindrops fell for the first time in three years. And it wasn't a light drizzle; it was a terrific rainstorm.

It's easy to give up on dreams, give up on miracles, give up on promises. We lose heart, lose patience, lose faith. And like a slow leak, it often happens without us even knowing it until our prayer life gets a flat.

I recently realized that I had stopped circling one of the seven miracles I had written on my prayer stone during the ten-day Pentecost fast I did years ago. I once believed that God would heal my asthma, but I got tired of asking. It felt like God had put me on hold, so I just hung up. Then a conversation with a friend reactivated my faith, and I've started circling that miracle again.

Is there some dream that God wants to resurrect? Is there some promise you need to reclaim? Is there some miracle you need to start believing for again?

The reason many of us give up too soon is that we feel like we have failed if God doesn't answer our prayer. That isn't failure. The only way you can fail is if you stop praying.

Prayer is a no-lose proposition.

Live Unoffended

John and Heidi have experienced amazing answers to prayer. They are part of the prayer circle that prays for me while I'm in a writing season. They were also part of the prayer circle that prayed for the $2 million miracle. God has given them amazing answers to their prayers for others, but many of their own prayers for their own challenges have gone unanswered. A step of faith into the world of filmmaking resulted in the loss of their life savings because financial backing didn't materialize as promised. Their family had to move out of their home because of a fire. They lost three of four parents in four years. And a rare genetic condition has taken a toll physically, emotionally, and financially. It almost seems like God answers every prayer they pray, except for the prayers they pray for themselves.

There have been moments when they've been tempted to throw in the prayer towel, but one promise has sustained them through the toughest times: "Blessed is the one who is not offended by me."

Here's the context of that promise.

Jesus is doing miracles right and left. He is healing diseases, driving out demons, and restoring sight to the blind, but John the Baptist misses the miracle train. It seems like Jesus is rescuing everybody except His most faithful follower, who is in prison. And John is His cousin, nonetheless. It seems like Jesus could have, and maybe should have, organized a rescue operation and busted him out before he was beheaded. Instead He sends a message via John's disciples. He tells them to tell John about all the miracles He is doing, and then He asks them to relay this promise: "Blessed is the one who is not offended by me."

Have you ever felt like God was doing miracles for everyone and their brother, but you seem to be the odd man out? It seems like God is keeping His promises to everyone but you?

I wonder if that's how John the Baptist felt.

What do you do when you feel like God is answering everyone's prayers but yours?

In the words of my friends who have experienced their fair share of unanswered prayers, "We try to live our lives unoffended by God.

Jesus promises that we will be blessed if we aren't offended. Obviously we aren't in prison about to be beheaded, but we have seen many answers to our prayers for other people when we have prayed for their finances, their health, and their kids. Yet in our own lives, well ..."

That's where most of us live most of the time — in the triple-dot punctuation known as an *ellipsis*. The ellipsis indicates a pause in speech or an unfinished thought. When we're waiting for God to answer a prayer, it's a period of ellipsis.

You can give up or hang on. You can let go or pray through. You can get frustrated with God or choose to live unoffended.

My friends have chosen to live unoffended: "Jesus promises blessing if we are not offended when He does things for others. And if He does it for them, He might do it for us. We don't know why God does what He does. We do know that 100 percent of the prayers we don't pray won't get answered."

I love that approach to prayer, that approach to life. It's the circle maker's mantra: 100 percent of the prayers I don't pray won't get answered.

God's Grammar

It's hard to hold on to hope during a period of ellipsis, but whenever I'm tempted to give up, I'm reminded of an old preacher's sermon titled "God's Grammar." I've forgotten most of the sermons I've ever heard, and that's a little depressing as a preacher, but this one statement was unforgettable: "Never put a comma where God puts a period, and never put a period where God puts a comma."

Sometimes what we perceive as a period is really just a comma. We think that God's silence is the end of the sentence, but it's just a providential pause. Praying through is the conjunction that allows God to not just finish the sentence but to make a statement.

"Lord, ... if you had been here, my brother would not have died. But I know that even now God will give you whatever you ask."

Did you catch the conjunction? This is one of the most amazing statements of faith in all of Scripture because of the little conjunction, *but*, right in the middle of the sentence. It seems like the sentence should end after Martha says, "Lord, if you had been here, my brother would not have died." Why? Because her brother, Lazarus, has been dead for four days! But Martha doesn't put a period there. She puts a comma. Even though her brother is dead and buried, she is still holding out hope.

The little phrase "even now" is underlined and circled in my Bible. Even when it seems like God is four days late, it's too soon to give up. Even when it seems like your dream is dead and buried, it's too soon to put a period there. After all, *you can't never always sometimes tell.*

There are two degrees of faith in the two statements that Martha makes. The first statement is first-degree faith: "Lord, if you had been here, my brother would not have died." First-degree faith is preventative faith. Like the prayer of Martha, who believed that Jesus could have kept her brother from dying, first-degree prayers take preventative measures. We ask God to keep bad things from happening. So we pray for safety as we travel, or we pray a hedge of protection around our children. And there is nothing wrong with that, but there is another dimension of faith that believes that God can undo what has already been done. Second-degree faith is resurrection faith. It's a faith that refuses to put periods at the end of disappointments. It's a faith that believes that God can reverse the irreversible. It's a faith that believes it's not over until God says it's over. And it's epitomized by Martha's "even now" profession of faith: "But I know that even now God will give you whatever you ask."

Have you ever felt like God was a day late or a dollar short?

That's how Bill felt after applying for the same job twelve years in a row! His dream job was working at the State Department, but that dream was denied eleven years in a row. He could have put a period after the second or third or seventh denial, and some of his friends and family thought he should. But when a dream is from God, it has more than nine lives. It was Bill's second-degree faith that enabled him to pray through the setbacks. He never put a period where God put a comma. Finally, after his twelfth trip around Jericho, Bill beat out twelve hundred other applicants and got the job.

So how do you go from first-degree faith to second-degree faith?

Well, there is no easy answer. It's hard times that teach us to pray hard. Even when the application is denied or the adoption falls through or the business goes bankrupt, you put a comma there. *Even then* you believe *even now*. And during those periods of ellipsis, your persistence quotient will increase exponentially.

Hyperlink

Even after three years of drought, even after a severe bout with depression, Elijah believed that God could send rain *even now*.

I can't help but wonder if Honi the circle maker was inspired by the story of Elijah praying for rain seven times. I wonder if Israel's original rainmaker was Honi's childhood hero. And I wonder if Honi's persistence in prayer was hyperlinked to this miracle? *If God did it for Elijah, He can do it for me.* By the same token, I can't help but wonder if Elijah's persistence in prayer was hyperlinked to the miracle of raining quail? *If God can send a quailstorm, He can certainly send a thunderstorm.*

One thing is certain: Our most powerful prayers are hyperlinked to the promises of God. When you know you are praying the promises of God, you can pray with holy confidence. It's the difference between praying on thin ice and praying on solid ground. It's the difference between praying tentatively and praying tenaciously. You don't have to second-guess yourself because you know that God wants you to double-click on His promises.

One of the challenges John and Heidi have faced as they try to live unoffended by God involves their son. He was a normally developing toddler until the day he suddenly and mysteriously lost all communication. They wondered if he would ever talk again. The fear of a wide variety of diagnoses, including high-functioning autism, dropped them to their knees.

During those desperate days, they went to visit their pastor for counsel and encouragement. While praying for them, the pastor received a promise from God. He jotted Isaiah 59:21 on a sticky note and handed it to them.

"As for me, this is my covenant with them," says the LORD. "My Spirit, who is on you, will not depart from you, and my words that I have put in your mouth will always be on your lips, on the lips of your children and on the lips of their descendants — from this time on and forever," says the LORD.

The pastor shut his Bible and said, "I guess that settles it. Your child will talk."

For the past ten years, their prayers have been hyperlinked to that promise. In that moment, John and Heidi said "a wall came crashing down" and "a promise came rushing in." It was the most naturally supernatural moment of their lives. Has it been clear sailing since then? No. Have they experienced disappointments? Yes. But that promise is circled in their Bible. "God gave us a promise, and no matter how many times we have to keep circling, it's settled."

You've heard the adage: "God said it, I believe it, and that settles it." Here's a fresh take on that old truth: God said it, I've circled it, and that settles it.

It was settled on the cross when Jesus said, "It is finished." It wasn't just the final installment on our sin debt; it was the down payment on all of His promises. "No matter how many promises God has made, they are 'Yes' in Christ."

Remember the promise in Joshua 1:3 that I circled when I did my prayer walk around Capitol Hill? God promised Joshua that He would give him every place where he set his foot, but there is a little addendum at the end of the promise: "as I promised Moses." The promise was originally given to Moses. Then it was transferred to Joshua. In much the same way, all of God's promises have been transferred to us via Jesus Christ. While these promises must be interpreted intelligently and applied accurately, there are moments when the Spirit of God will quicken your spirit to claim a promise that was originally intended for someone else. So while we have to be careful not to blindly claim promises that don't belong to us, our greatest challenge is that we don't circle the promises we could or should circle.

By the most conservative estimates, there are more than three thousand promises in Scripture. By virtue of what Jesus Christ accomplished on the cross, every one of them belongs to you. Every one of them has your name on it. The question is: How many of them have you circled?

Tree Island

Because this principle of hyperlinking our prayers to the promises of God is so important, let me paint another picture. The promises of God are the high ground, the holy ground, on which we stand. Circling those promises is the way we take our stand.

I have a friend who owns a log cabin on Lake Anna in central Virginia, and he has been gracious enough to let us vacation there a few times. During our first stay, Summer and I were six weeks out from the Escape from Alcatraz swim in San Francisco, so we put on wetsuits and did a training swim. There was a tree in the middle of the lake that piqued our curiosity. I'd never seen anything quite like it, so we decided to swim out to it. Sure enough, it was literally a solitary tree that was growing on an island in the middle of the lake that wasn't more than five feet in diameter. I have no idea how it got there, but you can actually see it on Google maps.

While we swam, Lora pulled Josiah on an inner tube behind the pontoon boat. As we approached the tree island, I told him to jump off the inner tube and swim to me, but Josiah was afraid because we were in the middle of the lake. Like most eight-year-old kids, Josiah felt much more comfortable in the shallow end of a pool where he could see the bottom. What he didn't know is that the lake had gotten shallow as we approached the tree island. I could feel it under my feet, but everybody else still thought it was deep because we were in the middle of the lake. Then, in one dramatic gesture, I literally stood up in the middle of the lake, and it looked like I was standing on water! When Josiah realized it wasn't as deep as he had thought, he jumped off the inner tube and swam to the island. Then *he* stood on water! That moment is more than a fun family memory; it's the mental image that comes to mind every time I think about standing on the promises of God.

The promises of God are like that tree island in the middle of the lake. They are the difference between sinking and swimming because they give you a place to stand. When John and Heidi felt like they were going to drown, Isaiah 59:21 was a tree island. It gave them a place to stand, a place to rest. And when God keeps His promises, you won't just stand on the water; you will waltz into the Promised Land through the waters God has parted.

Start Circling

What I'm about to share has the power to revolutionize the way you pray and the way you read the Bible. We often view prayer and Scripture reading as two distinct spiritual disciplines without much overlap, but what if they were meant to be hyperlinked? What if reading became a form of praying and praying became a form of reading?

One of the primary reasons we don't pray through is because we run out of things to say. Our lack of persistence is really a lack of conversation pieces. Like an awkward conversation, we don't know what to say. Or like a conversation on its last leg, we run out of things to talk about. That's when our prayers turn into a bunch of overused and misapplied clichés. So instead of praying hard about a big dream, we're left with small talk. Our prayers are as meaningless as a conversation about the weather.

The solution? Pray through the Bible.

Prayer was never meant to be a monologue; it was meant to be a dialogue. Think of Scripture as God's part of the script; prayer is our part. Scripture is God's way of initiating a conversation; prayer is our response. The paradigm shift happens when you realize that the Bible wasn't meant to be *read through*; the Bible was meant to be *prayed through*. And if you pray through it, you'll never run out of things to talk about.

The Bible is a promise book and a prayer book. And while reading is reactive, prayer is proactive. Reading is the way you get through the Bible; prayer is the way you get the Bible through you. As you pray, the Holy Spirit will quicken certain promises to your spirit. It's very difficult to predict what and when and where and how, but over time, the promises of God will become *your* promises. Then you need to circle those promises, both figuratively and literally. I never read without a pen so that I can underline, asterisk, and circle. I literally circle the promises in my Bible. Then I do it figuratively by circling them in prayer.

One of my treasured possessions is my grandfather's Bible. I sometimes do devotions in his Bible because I want to see the verses he underlined. I love reading his notes in the margins. And I love seeing what promises he circled. The thing that I love most about his Bible is that it literally had to be taped together because it was falling apart. It wasn't just well read. It was well prayed.

Chapter 9

The Favor of Him Who Dwells in the Burning Bush

The first time I saw the old crack house I was surprised that an eyesore like that could exist just five blocks from the Capitol building. Cinder blocks filled the cavities where doors and windows once were. The brick walls were painted a hideous green color that must have come into and gone out of style very quickly many decades before. And the graffiti on the walls seemed like the appropriate finishing touch on this nuisance property.

I had walked by it hundreds of times. In fact, I walked right by the corner of 2nd and F Street NE when I prayed a circle around Capitol Hill fifteen years ago. But as I walked by it this particular time, it was like a dream was conceived in my spirit by the Holy Spirit: *This crack house would make a great coffeehouse.*

It seemed like a crazy idea for lots of reasons. First of all, no one on our staff had ever worked at a coffeehouse. Besides that, churches build churches, *not* coffeehouses. We had no business going into the coffeehouse business, but the more I thought about it the more it made sense in a counterintuitive sort of way. After all, Jesus didn't just hang out at the synagogue. He hung out at wells, and wells were the natural gathering places in ancient culture. One day it dawned on me that coffeehouses are postmodern wells. The only difference is that we draw shots of espresso instead of drawing water out of a well.

So the dream of creating a postmodern well where our church and community could cross paths was born, and that dream is fulfilled hundreds of times every day with each customer who walks through our doors. Ebenezer's Coffeehouse has been voted the #1 coffeehouse in the metro DC area. The performance space doubles as one of our seven church campuses. And to top it off, every penny of our six-digit net profit goes to local community projects and our humanitarian efforts in other countries. It's more than a miracle; it's a miracle squared.

Now let me retrace the circle.

Casing a Crack House

One reason the coffeehouse seemed like a crazy idea was that National Community Church was just getting off the ground when the dream was conceived. We barely had any people or any money, but that's a great prescription for prayer. And we prayed hard for nearly eight years. We laid hands on the walls and prayed. We knelt on the property and prayed. We fasted and prayed. And I lost count of how many circles we prayed around that old crack house.

Inspired by the story of the Jericho miracle, I would often pray around that property seven times at a pop. It was usually around the fourth or fifth lap that I would get strange looks from the security guards at the Federal Judiciary Building across the street. *Is this guy casing a crack house?* Many of those guards are now regular customers at our coffeehouse. And while I no longer circle the property in prayer, my favorite place to pray is the rooftop of Ebenezer's Coffeehouse. I climb the ladder, pop the hatch, and pray on the rooftop — so I'm still getting strange looks from the high-rise offices across the street. We've gotten more than one inquiry asking why someone is pacing back and forth on the rooftop.

Do you have a favorite place to pray? A place where you get better reception? A place where your mind is more focused? A place where you have more faith?

I love praying on top of the coffeehouse because I feel like I'm praying on top of a miracle. It's hard *not* to pray with faith when you're praying in a place where God has already done a miracle.

I wonder if that is how Elijah felt praying for rain on top of Mount Carmel. God had just answered an impossible prayer right there.

Elijah challenged the 450 prophets to a prayer duel on Mount Carmel as each side asked God to consume their sacrifice with fire. Elijah won that sudden-death showdown in dramatic fashion as God grilled his sacrifice. The God who sent fire can certainly send rain, right? God's answer to Elijah gave him the faith he needed to pray hard. And that is one of the by-products of answered prayer. It gives us the faith to believe God for bigger and better miracles. With each answered prayer, we draw bigger prayer circles. With each act of faithfulness, our faith increases. With each promise kept, our persistence quotient grows.

In retrospect, I'm glad the coffeehouse took eight years of hard prayer because it stretched our faith in the process. When you have to pray that long, you aren't even tempted to take it for granted. This may sound commonsensical, but if it hadn't taken a miracle, it wouldn't be a miracle.

Binding Contract

Originally, the two lawyers who owned 201 F Street NE wanted $1 million dollars for the crack house because of its location, location, location. It's just one block from Union Station and kitty-corner to the largest office building in DC, which is home to the Securities and Exchange Commission. The corner of 2nd and F Street NE also forms the NW corner of the Capitol Hill historic district.

We couldn't touch $1 million, so we prayed, and the harder we prayed the more the price dropped. We ultimately purchased the property for $325,000, but that was less of a miracle than the fact that four people offered more money for the property than we did. And two of them were real estate developers!

So how did we get it?

My only explanation is that we circled Matthew 18:18. Our prayers were hyperlinked to that promise, and we double-clicked it by praying hard.

"Whatever you bind on earth will be bound in heaven."

The word *bind* means "to place a contract on something." This is precisely what happens when you pray. When you pray for something in the earthly realm, God puts a contract on it in the heavenly realm if you are praying in accordance with the will of God. So while February 7, 2002, is the date we signed the physical contract, the spiritual contract predates it by several years. The deal dates back to the first prayer circle we drew around it.

It's interesting to note that after cooler heads prevailed, and Honi was honored for his prayer that saved a generation, the Sanhedrin sent him a missive citing Job 22:28: "Thou shalt also decree a thing, and it shall be established unto thee." They recognized the binding power of Honi's prayer: "You have decreed [on earth] below and the Holy One ... fulfills your word [in heaven] above." This language is very similar to the promise Jesus made in Matthew 18:18. There is a strong likelihood that Jesus was familiar with the legend of the circle maker because of its historical proximity. Who knows, maybe He had Honi in mind when He made this promise.

Watching and Waiting

The Bible tells us that the Lord is watching over His word to perform it.

There is nothing God loves more than keeping His promises. He is actively watching and waiting for us to simply take Him at His word. He is watching over Matthew 18:18. He is watching over Isaiah 59:21. He is watching over Luke 7:23. He is watching over each and every promise, and if that doesn't fill you with holy confidence, nothing will.

Praying hard is standing on the promises of God. And when we stand *on* His word, God stands *by* His word. His word is His bond.

We sometimes pray as if God doesn't want to keep His promises. You have no idea how badly God wants to keep His promise! That's why He made the promise in the first place. We sometimes pray as if our bold prayers that circle the promises of God might offend the God who made them. Are you kidding me? God is offended by anything less! There is nothing God wants to do more than prove His power by keeping His promises. But we doubt God because we doubt ourselves. We don't ask God to extend His hand because we don't know His heart.

Psalm 84:11 captures the heart of the heavenly Father:

> *No good thing does he withhold*
> *from those who walk uprightly.*

God is not holding out or holding back. It's not in His nature to withhold any good thing from us. He most certainly won't bless disobedience, but He most certainly will bless obedience. If you take God at His word, you'll make the joyful discovery that God wants to bless you far more than you want to be blessed. And His capacity to give is far greater than your capacity to receive.

I think I got the joy of gift giving from my mom. I also picked up a little idiosyncrasy. Typically, children beg their parents to open gifts before the designated date, whether it is a birthday or Christmas. Not in my family. My mom used to beg me to open my gifts before the designated day because she could hardly wait to give them. And now I do with our kids what she did with me. Parents begging their children to open their gifts early may seem a little dysfunctional, but this is the heart of our heavenly Father. He can hardly wait to keep His promises. He can hardly wait to perform His word. He can hardly wait to answer our prayers. And when we simply take Him at His word, He can hardly contain His joy.

My favorite sentence in the twenty-third psalm is this: "Surely goodness and mercy shall follow me all the days of my life." The word *follow* isn't a strong enough translation. It's a hunting term in Hebrew. It's like God is hunting you down — but not to harm you; God is hunting you down to bless you. He wants to show you His goodness and His mercy, but too often we run away from it. Why? Because we doubt His good intentions. We can't believe that God is for us. This is why God reminds us so many different times in many different ways and with many different words.

Circling Our Children

If you asked me what I pray for more than anything else, the answer is the favor of God. While it's tough to describe or define, I think the favor of God is what God does for you that you cannot do for yourself. I pray the favor of God around National Community Church. I pray the favor of God around my books. I pray the favor of God around my children.

When Parker was a baby, I circled Luke 2:52 and turned it into a prayer blessing. I have prayed that blessing around each of my children thousands of times. Almost every night, I circle my kids with this simple prayer: "Lord, let them grow in wisdom and stature, and in favor with God and man." I realize that Luke 2:52 isn't technically a promise, but I think I'm on sound theological ground. Luke 2:52 is a time-lapse description of Jesus' development as a child, and we're called to be just like Jesus, so why wouldn't I circle it? Why shouldn't I turn it into a blessing and pray it around my children?

I believe that God is watching over my children just like He is watching over His word. He has one eye on Luke 2:52 and one eye on my kids. And He has no problem watching over both of them. He is watching and waiting for opportunities to favor His children.

One of my responsibilities as a father is not only circling my children in prayer but also teaching them to circle the promises of God. Parents are prophets to their children. And part of our prophetic role is knowing the Scriptures and knowing our children well enough to know what promises they need to circle. Josiah has been fighting some fears lately, so we've been circling Philippians 4:4 – 8. I've been praying that the peace of God, which transcends all understanding, would guard Josiah's heart and mind in Christ Jesus. My bedtime prayers have been hyperlinked to this promise. So we circle Scripture by praying it. Then Scripture encircles us.

A few years ago, our friends Dennis and Donna, who pastor a neighboring church on Capitol Hill, told us about something God had impressed upon them to do for their children. They identified words that were descriptive and prescriptive of their kids; then they had them framed to hang on the walls in their rooms. They often wondered whether those words meant anything, but their oldest daughter, who is now grown up and out of their house, recently told them that on some nights when she couldn't fall asleep, she would look at those words on the wall, and they would speak to her. Those framed words started to frame her. She started to see herself in light of her God-ordained identity and destiny.

Lora and I loved that idea, so we adapted it for our daughter, Summer. Prior to Summer's most recent birthday, Lora recruited two of Summer's aunts to help come up with a list of prophetic words to speak into Summer's life. Each of them took three words and talked about them over a special birthday dinner. Then we had a graphic designer turn those nine words into a poster. Each word is in a different font, and these different fonts represent nine different dimensions of her destiny. That poster hangs in Summer's room as a reminder of her true identity in Christ.

Not unlike the day I defined success at a Starbucks on the Third Street Promenade in Santa Monica, these nine words define the character of Christ that we see in Summer. These nine words are nine prophecies that we will pray around Summer for the rest of our lives. Putting them on a poster was a way of circling them.

The Favor of Him Who Dwelt In the Burning Bush

The longer I live the more I crave the favor of God. The greatest moments in life are the moments when God intervenes on our behalf and blesses us way beyond what we expect or deserve. It's a humble reminder of His sovereignty. And these favor moments become our favor-ite memories.

I'll never forget August 12, 2001.

National Community was a fledgling church for five years. Like plowing rock-hard soil, there was nothing easy about planting a church in Washington, DC. It took us five years to grow from our core group of 19 to 250 people. Then it was almost like the Lord declared, "Now is the time of God's favor."

A religion reporter from *The Washington Post* asked for an interview because she was intrigued by our church demographics. She proceeded to write an article about how we were reaching emerging generations and told me it would appear in the religion section. I picked up a two-inch-thick Sunday edition on my way into Union Station that morning and quickly flipped to the religion section. I was disappointed when I didn't find the article. I figured it didn't make the editorial cut, so I put the newspaper back on the stand because I wasn't going to buy it if we weren't in it. That's when I discovered that the article was on the front page!

That was the day God put National Community Church on the map. It had taken five years to grow to 250 people, but we doubled in size over the next year. It was as though God had opened the flood-gates of favor, and hundreds of readers visited National Community Church as a result of that one article. And the beautiful thing about it is that we couldn't take credit for it. It was nothing more, or maybe I should say nothing less, than the favor of God. It was God's time. It was God's favor. It was God's word. And God was watching over it.

Every verse on favor is circled in my Bible, but my personal favorite is one of the blessings that Moses pronounced over Joseph:

> *May the LORD bless his land*
> *with the precious dew from heaven above*
> *and with the deep waters that lie below;*
> *with the best the sun brings forth*
> *and the finest the moon can yield;*
> *with the choicest gifts of the ancient mountains*
> *and the fruitfulness of the everlasting hills;*
> *with the best gifts of the earth and its fullness*
> *and the favor of him who dwelt in the burning bush.*

Did you catch "the favor" in the last phrase? God's favor is multi-dimensional, but this may rank as my favorite kind: "the favor of him who dwelt in the burning bush." And I love the fact that this blessing is pronounced by Moses himself. He knew whereof he spoke because he is the one who heard the Voice in the bush.

The hard thing about praying hard is letting God do the heavy lifting. You have to trust the favor of God to do for you what you cannot do for yourself. You have to trust God to change hearts, even the heart of Pharaoh.

Full Circle

Let me circle all the way back to the old crack house.

We prayed for that old crack house at 201 F Street NE for several years before I finally mustered up the courage to call the phone number listed on the For Sale sign. I felt foolish. What was I going to say? "Hi, I'm the pastor of a church with no people and no money. We'd like to buy your crack house and turn it into a coffeehouse." It sounded like a ridiculous idea to me, and I thought it would sound even more ridiculous to them. But, believe it or not, that is precisely what God told me to say.

I knew that the two lawyers who owned the property, both of whom were Jewish, might not understand or appreciate who we were or what we wanted to do as a church, but I felt like God wanted me to humbly yet boldly tell them who we were and what we wanted to do. So I didn't pull any punches. I prayed for favor. Then I shared our vision like I was casting it to our congregation. And guess what? They loved it. My only explanation for their reaction is the favor of Him who dwells in the burning bush.

The favor of Him who dwells in the burning bush is a unique dimension of God's favor that enables you to stand before those who would naturally stand in opposition to you, but they supernaturally step aside or stand behind you. That is how the favor of Him who dwells in the burning bush manifested itself when Moses stood before Pharaoh. It gave a slave, on whom there was a warrant out for his arrest, the boldness to declare the promise God had given him at the burning bush: "Let my people go."

Purchasing the property at 2nd and F Street was the first miracle in the process of building Ebenezer's Coffeehouse. I would not recommend this kind of risk unless you know it is Spirit prompted, but we purchased the property knowing that we would need to get a change in the zoning code in order to build the coffeehouse. If our rezoning efforts were unsuccessful, our dream would die. For eighteen long months, we met with everybody from Historic Preservation to the Office of Planning to the Capitol Hill Restoration Committee. Overall, we had tremendous community backing. After all, we were investing $3 million to turn a crack house into a coffeehouse. But during the rezoning process we discovered that some influential neighbors decided to oppose our rezoning efforts because of misinformation about what we planned to do. I followed a link to a website where they were slandering our motives. To be perfectly honest, I was ticked off. Their opposition had the potential to short-circuit our dream of building a coffeehouse, and I got angrier and angrier every time I thought about it. That's when I discovered the power of praying circles around the pharaohs in your life. Every time I got angry, I converted that anger into a prayer. Let's just say that I came as close as I had ever come to praying without ceasing!

I prayed for those neighbors for several months leading up to our hearing before the zoning commission. I'll never forget the feeling as we walked into the hearing room and sat down at our tables on either side of the aisle. I had absolutely no animosity toward the people who were opposing us. None whatsoever! I felt an unexplainable compassion for the people who opposed us and I wasn't worried at all about what they said or did because I had circled them in prayer. I had also circled the zoning commissioners. Not only did we win unanimous approval from the Zoning Commission, which is a testament to the favor of Him who dwells in the burning bush, but one of those people who opposed us is now a regular customer at Ebenezer's.

I'm not going to lie. The entire two-year ordeal of rezoning was emotionally and spiritually exhausting, but that is how you increase your persistence quotient. When it was all over, I thanked God for the opposition we encountered because it galvanized our resolve and unified our church. It also taught us how to pray like it depends on God and work like it depends on us. I learned that we don't have to be afraid of the enemy's attacks. They are counterproductive when we counteract them with prayer. The more opposition we experience, the harder we have to pray, and the harder we have to pray, the more miracles God does.

Chapter 10

The Cattle
on a Thousand Hills

Shortly after Dallas Theological Seminary opened its doors, their doors almost closed because of bankruptcy. Before their 1929 commencement day, the faculty gathered in the president's office to pray that God would provide. They formed a prayer circle, and when it was Harry Ironside's turn, he circled Psalm 50:10 with a simple Honi-like prayer: "Lord, we know you own the cattle on a thousand hills. Please sell some of them, and send us the money."

The time lapse between our requests and God's answers is often longer than we would like, but occasionally God answers immediately. While the faculty was praying, a $10,000 answer was delivered. One version of the story attributes the gift to a Texas cattle rancher who had sold two carloads of cattle. Another version attributes it to a banker from Illinois. But one way or another, it was God who prompted the gift and answered the prayer.

In a moment that is reminiscent of the day Peter knocked on the door of the house where his friends were praying for a miraculous jailbreak, the president's secretary interrupted the prayer meeting by knocking on the president's door. Dr. Lewis Sperry Chafer, founder and president of DTS, answered the door, and she handed him the answer to prayer. Turning to his friend and colleague, Dr. Harry Ironside, President Chafer said, "Harry, God sold the cattle!"

One of my oldest and fondest memories is driving from Minneapolis to Red Wing, Minnesota, to go apple picking with my grandparents. I can still hear my Grandpa Johnson singing the old chorus "God owns the cattle on a thousand hills."

I don't just believe that promise of provision. I hear my grandfather singing it every time I read Psalm 50:10. While I've certainly gone through tough financial times, I've also experienced enough miracles to know that when God gives a vision, He makes provision.

Back On Our Knees

I'll never forget the day we signed the contract to purchase 201 F Street NE. Part of what made it so memorable is that the deal went down the day after Josiah was born. Our realtor had to come to the hospital so I could sign the papers.

We celebrated that miracle for a few minutes, but then we got right back on our knees because we needed another one. We got the contract knowing that we didn't have the cash for the down payment. We had thirty days to come up with a 10 percent down payment or the contract would be null and void.

After twenty-nine days of exhausting all options, we had scraped together $25,000, leaving us $7,500 short. We didn't know where else to turn, so we turned to Him who owns the cattle on a thousand hills. We knew the dream of building a coffeehouse on Capitol Hill was from God, and we kept circling the promise in Psalm 50:10.

The very next day, the day before our deadline, we received two checks in the mail from former NCCers. Both couples had recently moved away from the DC area, but they hadn't found a church home yet, so they continued to tithe to NCC. I later found out that one of the checks was larger than their normal tithe because it was the tithe on a signing bonus with a new law firm. Neither couple had any clue that we had twenty-four hours to come up with $7,500, but God knew. Neither couple knew that their obedience was our miracle, but God knew. He always knows. And if we pray in alignment with the will of God, He always provides. The total of the two checks combined? Exactly $7,500.

The Game of Chicken

God must love the game of chicken because He plays it with us all the time. He has this habit of waiting until the very last moment to answer our prayer to see if we will *chicken out* or *pray through*. If we chicken out, we miss out on the miracle; if we pray through, God will come through, but it may well be at the last moment possible. And, of course, if you chicken out of the game of chicken, God will always give you another chance to get back in the game.

This pattern of last-second provision is repeated throughout Scripture, and I think it reveals God's playful personality. Sometimes we are so focused on the character of God that we forget that God has a personality too. He loves hiding around corners and surprising us. You can't convince me that Jesus didn't have fun sneaking up on the disciples in the middle of the night in the middle of the lake by walking on water. You can't convince me that God didn't enjoy the befuddled look on Moses' face when he heard the talking bush. As I read Scripture, I can come to no other conclusion than this: God loves showing up in unexpected ways at unexpected times.

I love this part of God's personality. While it sometimes adds stress, it also adds drama. In big and small ways, it is prayer that adds the unexpected twists and turns in our personal plotlines that make life worth living. It is prayer that precipitates and culminates in the climatic moments when God shows up in dramatic fashion. It is prayer that can turn any story, your story, into an epic drama.

I have scribbled the initials *JEJIT* in the margins of my Bible at various places where God provides *just enough just in time*. He did it with the widow who is down to her last jar of olive oil. He did it when the Israelites are trapped between the Egyptian army and Red Sea. He did it when the boat is about to capsize on the Sea of Galilee because of hurricane-force winds. And He did it with us when we had twenty-four hours to come up with $7,500.

Maybe you're in a desperate situation right now. It feels like you're down to your last jar of olive oil, or the Egyptian army is closing in on you, or your boat is about to capsize. It may seem like God is nowhere to be seen, but maybe God is setting the stage for a miracle. This I know for sure: God is always stage right. He's ready to make His grand entrance. All He is waiting for is your prayer cue.

The Manna Miracle

When God provided the miraculous manna for the Israelites as they wandered in the wilderness, it says He provided "enough for that day." *Just enough*. The language describing God's provision is extremely precise. Those who gathered a lot had nothing left over, and those who gathered a little had enough. God provided just enough. Then He gave them a curious command: "Do not keep any of it until morning."

So why does God provide just enough? Why would God forbid leftovers? What's wrong with taking a little initiative and gathering enough manna for two days or two weeks?

Here's my take on the manna miracle: The manna was a daily reminder of their daily dependence on God. God wanted to cultivate their daily dependence by providing for their needs on a daily basis. Nothing has changed. Isn't that the point of the Lord's Prayer? "Give us today our daily bread."

We want a one-week or one-month or one-year supply of God's provision, but God wants us to drop to our knees every day in raw dependence on Him. And God knows that if He provided too much too soon, we'd lose our spiritual hunger. He knows we'd stop trusting in our Provider and start trusting in the provision.

One of our fundamental misunderstandings of spiritual maturity is thinking that it should result in self-sufficiency. It's the exact opposite. The goal isn't independence; the goal is codependence on God. Our desire for self-sufficiency is a subtle expression of our sinful nature. It's a desire to get to a place where we don't need God, don't need faith, and don't need to pray. We want God to provide more so we need Him less.

Holy Complications

One reason many people get frustrated spiritually is that they feel like it should get easier to do the will of God. I don't know if this will be encouraging or discouraging, but the will of God doesn't get easier. The will of God gets harder. Here's why: the harder it gets, the harder you have to pray.

God will keep putting you in situations that stretch your faith, and as your faith stretches, so do your dreams. If you pass the test, you graduate to bigger and bigger dreams. And it won't get easier; it'll get harder. It won't get less complicated; it'll get more complicated. But complications are evidence of God's blessing. And if it's from God, then it's a holy complication.

You need to come to terms with this two-sided truth: The blessings of God won't just bless you; they will also complicate your life. Sin will complicate your life in negative ways. The blessings of God will complicate your life in positive ways. When I married Lora, it complicated my life, and it *really* complicated her life! Praise God for complications. We have three complications named Parker, Summer, and Josiah. I can't imagine my life without those complications. With every promotion, there are complications. As you earn more income, your taxes will become more complicated. My point? Blessings will complicate your life, but they will complicate your life in ways God wants it complicated.

A few years ago, I prayed a prayer that changed my life. I believe it can change your life as well, but it takes tremendous courage to pray it like you mean it. And you have to count the cost.

Lord, complicate my life.

Afflict the Comfortable

My portfolio as a pastor is twofold: (1) comfort the afflicted and (2) afflict the comfortable. It's the second half of the job description that is more difficult. Let's be honest: many, if not most, of our prayers are selfish in nature. We pray as if God's chief objective is our personal comfort. It's not. God's chief objective is His glory. And sometimes His gain involves a little pain.

Sometimes we pray without considering the implications or ramifications. When I pray that God will bless National Community

Church, I am praying that God will make my life more complicated and less comfortable. It was much more comfortable when the church had twenty-five people. It was much less complicated when we had one service at one location. As God has blessed National Community Church, I've had to count the cost. On a very practical level, the answer to my prayers meant giving up more of my weekend to God. When we launched a Saturday night and Sunday night service, the cost was two more time slots every weekend that I gave back to God. Here's the bottom line: Praying hard is asking God to make your life harder. The harder you pray, the harder you will have to work. And that is a blessing from God.

Praying hard is hard because you can't just pray like it depends on God; you also have to work like it depends on you. You can't just be willing to pray about it; you also have to be willing to do something about it. And this is where many of us get stuck spiritually. We're willing to pray right up to the point of discomfort, but no further. We're willing to pray right up to the point of inconvenience, but no further. Praying hard is uncomfortable and inconvenient, but that is when you know you're getting close to a miracle!

The reason God doesn't answer our prayers isn't that we aren't praying hard enough; the reason, more often than not, is that we aren't willing to work hard enough. Praying hard is synonymous with working hard. Think of praying hard and working hard as concentric circles. It's the way we double-circle our dreams and His promises. There comes a moment, after you have prayed through, when you have to start doing something about it. You have to take a step of faith, and that first step is always the hardest.

Woolly Socks

I recently spoke at Church of the Highlands in Birmingham, Alabama, for my friend Chris Hodges. I toured their Dream Center in downtown Birmingham because we want to do something similar in Washington, DC. They have an amazing outreach to pimps and prostitutes. They mentor kids. They feed the hungry. You name the need, and they are trying to meet it.

One of the women working there is a former journalist named Lisa. She had a good job with a good salary, but she quit because she knew God wanted her to work at the Dream Center. Lisa is one of those people who exude joy, life, energy.

During our tour, Lisa talked about their daily dependence on God to meet the overwhelming needs in their community. It takes hard work and hard prayer. Then she told me about one of the miracles she had experienced. One day, as she was circling the Dream Center in prayer, she felt the Holy Spirit prompting her to take her woolly socks with her to work. She thought she was losing her mind. It was one of the strangest promptings she'd ever had, but she couldn't shake the impression. So she grabbed her woolly socks, put them in her purse, and headed downtown. When she got there, a prostitute was literally passed out on the doorstep. Lisa opened the door, carried her inside, and cradled her in her arms until she regained consciousness a few minutes later. She was so cold that she was shaking. That's when Lisa asked her, "If you could have anything, what would it be?" Without hesitation, she said, "Woolly socks." Lisa about lost it. As she told me the story, she started tearing up. Then I started tearing up. Lisa then told her, "Look what I have." She pulled out the woolly socks, and the woman said, "They even match my outfit."

God is great not just because nothing is too big for Him; God is great because nothing is too small for Him. A sparrow doesn't fall without His noticing and caring, so it shouldn't surprise us that He cares about a woman who wants woolly socks. God loves showing His all-encompassing compassion in little ways, and if we would learn to obey His promptings, as Lisa did, we would find ourselves in the middle of miracles a lot more often.

The reason many of us miss the miracles is that we aren't looking and listening. The easy part of prayer is talking. It's much harder listening to the still small voice of the Holy Spirit. It's much harder looking for the answers. But two-thirds of praying hard is listening and looking.

Look toward the Sea

Do you remember what Elijah did while he prayed for rain? He sent his servant to look toward the sea. Why? Because he expected an answer. He didn't just pray; he acted on his sanctified expectations by looking toward the sea.

Elijah is set up in the New Testament (James 5:17) as the standard of praying hard. It was his prayer for no rain that crippled Israel's agricultural economy and brought the nation to its knees. And it was his Honi-like prayer for rain that ended a three-and-a-half-year drought.

Elijah was as human as we are, and yet when he prayed earnestly that no rain would fall, none fell for three and a half years! Then, when he prayed again, the sky sent down rain and the earth began to yield its crops.

Praying earnestly literally means "praying with a prayer." It's more than words. It means acting on your prayers because you expect an answer. Elijah didn't just pray against the prophets of Baal; he challenged them to a sacrifice showdown. He didn't tell the widow of Zarephath to pray; he told her to bake a loaf of bread with her last batch of dough. And in a remake miracle, Elijah didn't pray for God to part the Jordan River; he struck it with his rolled-up cloak.

Each miracle was precipitated by a concrete step of faith: setting up a sacrifice on Mount Carmel, baking a loaf of bread, and striking the Jordan River. And God honored those steps of faith by sending fire to consume Elijah's sacrifice, multiplying that last loaf of bread so it lasted until the drought ended, and parting the Jordan River so that Elijah and Elisha walked through on dry ground.

One reason many of us never get an answer to our prayers is that all we do is pray. You can't just pray like Elijah; you have to act like Elijah. You can't just get on your knees; you also have to look toward the sea.

I learned this lesson during our first year of church planting. We desperately needed a drummer because I was leading worship and I have no rhythm. We must have asked God for a drummer two hundred times. We just kept repeating the same request over and over again like a two-year-old toddler: *Give us a drummer, give us a drum-*

mer, give us a drummer. Then one day, it was like God finally got tired of the broken record and said, *If you want a drummer, why don't you go get a drum set?* We had never thought about actually taking a step of faith *as if* God was going to answer our prayer. Why? Because we want the answer before we exercise our faith! But if you want God to move, sometimes *you* have to make a move.

Those were the pre-Google days, so I searched the classifieds and found a used drum set for sale in Silver Spring, Maryland. By faith, I decided to buy it, but it took all the faith I had because it took all the money we had. Our monthly income was $2,000, and $1,600 was taken off the top to rent the DC Public School where we held services. That left $400 for our salary and all other expenses. The cost of the drum set? $400. God has a way of pushing us to our absolute limits, doesn't He?

There was part of me that felt foolish. *Why am I spending all of our cash on a drum set for a drummer who doesn't even exist?* But it was our "field of dreams" moment: "If you buy it, they will come." I knew God was prompting me to take a step of faith, and I believed He would honor it. I bought that drum set on a Thursday, and our first drummer showed up that Sunday. And God sent us the best. When he wasn't playing for us on Sundays, he was playing for political and military dignitaries as a member of the United States Marine Drum and Bugle Corps.

Wet Feet

When the Israelites were on the verge of entering the Promised Land, God commanded the priests to not just look toward the sea but to step into the river. It's one of the most counterintuitive commands in Scripture.

> *"When you reach the banks of the Jordan River, take a few steps into the river."*

I don't know about you, but I don't particularly like getting my feet wet. I'd much rather have God part the river, and *then* I'll step into the miracle. We want God to go first. That way we don't get our feet wet. But it's often our unwillingness to take a step of faith and get our feet wet that keeps us from experiencing a miracle. Some people spend their entire lives on the eastern shore of the Jordan waiting for God to part the river while God waits for them to get their feet wet.

After you have prayed hard, you need to swallow hard and take a flying leap of faith. That's how you circle the miracle.

A few years before we purchased the old crack house on Capitol Hill, Lora and I went to a live auction at our children's school. One of the items up for auction was a three-inch-thick binder donated by the Capitol Hill Restoration Society. It contained all of the zoning codes and guidelines for new construction on Capitol Hill. I knew we'd need to know those zoning codes if we were going to build our coffeehouse on Capitol Hill, but we didn't own the property yet. *Shouldn't I wait until we get a contract?* But I felt the Holy Spirit's elbow give me a little nudge, and I took an $85 step of faith. It was my way of getting my feet wet and stepping into the Jordan. After all, if you aren't willing to risk $85 on your dream, then you're probably not ready for a $2 million miracle. Not only did that binder help us during the zoning and design phases of our project; it still sits in a special place in my office as a reminder to step into the river, to step into the miracle.

At flood tide, the Jordan River was about a mile wide. That was all that separated the Israelites from their four-hundred-year-old promise. Their dream was a stone's throw away. But what if the priests hadn't stepped into the river? What if they had waited for God to part the Jordan River? They may well have spent the rest of their lives on the eastern banks of the Jordan River. And that's where many of us spend our lives. We're so close to the dream, so close to the promise, so close to the miracle. But we aren't willing to get our feet wet.

Many people never see God part the Jordan River in their lives because their feet are firmly planted on dry ground. We're waiting for God to make a move while God is waiting for us to make a move. We say to God, "Why don't you part this river?" And God says to us, "Why don't you get your feet wet?" But if you make a move, you'll see God move. And He can move heaven and earth.

Prayer Promptings

Peter is the patron saint of wet feet. He may have failed the persistence test by falling asleep in Gethsemane, but he passed the wet-feet test by getting out of a boat in the middle of the Sea of Galilee when Jesus uttered one of the craziest commands in Scripture: "Come." Peter risked far more than wet feet. The Sea of Galilee was a 91-square-mile dunk tank, and he was in the middle of it in the middle of the night.

The key to getting out of the boat is hearing the voice of God. If you're going to get out of the boat in the middle of a lake in the middle of the night, you better make sure that Jesus said, "Come." But if Jesus says, "Come," you better not stay in the boat.

Have you ever had a moment, as Lisa did, when the Holy Spirit prompted you during prayer to do something that seemed border-line crazy? Have you ever had a moment, as Peter did, when God called you to do something that seemed unsafe? Your response to those promptings will make you or break you. It may seem unsafe or insane, but if you stay in the boat, you'll never walk on water.

A few years ago, a friend of mine shared one of his prayer prompt-ings with me because it involved me. I was on a speaking trip, away from my family, when God woke Rick up in the middle of the night. He felt the Lord prompting him to pray for my family, and the prompt-ing was so intense that he woke up his roommates. For the record, you better make sure the prompting is from God if you're going to wake up your roommates! After praying, he felt like they needed to drive over to our house. So at four in the morning they drove across the Hill and parked in front of our home and prayed for my family. He said to me afterward, "This has never happened to me before. I don't know why God got me up at four in the morning, but we knew we needed to pray for you."

I honestly have no idea why God prompted him to pray that way, but some of God's greatest answers to prayer won't be revealed on this side of the space-time continuum because they are invisible answers. When God makes something happen, we can thank Him because we can see it. When God keeps something from happening, we don't know how to thank Him because we don't know what He did. But someday God will reveal the invisible answers, and we'll praise Him for them.

Praying hard starts with listening to the still small voice of the Holy Spirit. And if you are faithful in the small things and obey those little promptings, then God can use you to do big things.

Go Fish

Let me paint one more picture. It only seems appropriate, since praying is a lot like fishing. More than anything else, it takes a high persistence quotient.

> *After Jesus and his disciples arrived in Capernaum, the collectors of the two-drachma temple tax came to Peter and asked, "Doesn't your teacher pay the temple tax?"*
>
> *"Yes, he does," he replied.*
>
> *When Peter came into the house, Jesus was the first to speak. "What do you think, Simon?" he asked. "From whom do the kings of the earth collect duty and taxes — from their own children or from others?"*
>
> *"From others," Peter answered.*
>
> *"Then the children are exempt," Jesus said to him. "But so that we may not cause offense, go to the lake and throw out your line. Take the first fish you catch; open its mouth and you will find a four-drachma coin. Take it and give it to them for my tax and yours."*

This has to rank as one of the craziest commands in Scripture. Part of me wonders if Peter thought Jesus was joking. He was a little off balance because I'm sure Jesus had pulled more than one prank on Peter.

So why does Jesus do it this way? He could have provided the four-drachma coin in a more conventional manner, but He tells Peter to go fish for it. I think there are a few reasons. First of all, God loves doing different miracles in different ways because it reveals different dimensions of His power and personality. But I wonder if the biggest reason is that Jesus wanted to see if Peter would trust Him in the realm where Peter had the greatest professional proficiency and self-sufficiency. As a professional fisherman, fishing was the one area where Peter would have been most tempted to think he didn't need Jesus. He thought he knew every trick of the fishing trade, but Jesus wanted to show him a new trick. We'll call it "the coin in the mouth of the fish" trick.

We know how the story ends. Peter catches a fish and cashes in a smelly coin. But if you've caught hundreds of thousands of fish, none of which has ever had a coin in its mouth, how do you have the faith to believe that the next one will have a four-drachma coin? It seems impossible, doesn't it? But there is only one way to find out if God will keep His promise: Obey the crazy prompting.

Now let me ask you a question: Where do you feel like you need God least? Where are you most proficient, most sufficient? Maybe that is precisely where God wants you to trust Him to do something beyond your ability. It's just when you think you have God all figured out that He pulls the coin out of the fish's mouth. And it is God's strange and mysterious ways that renew our awe, our trust, and our dependence.

Let me spell it out: If you want to see crazy miracles, obey the crazy promptings of the Holy Spirit. Grab your pole, head to the lake, row the boat, cast the line, set the hook, and reel it in. As you obey the promptings by casting your line, you never know what kind of miracle you'll catch on the other side.

Go fish.

Chapter 11

No Answer

For much of my life, basketball was my life. When I graduated from high school, I went to the University of Chicago on a full-ride scholarship and earned a starting position on the basketball team by the end of my freshman year. Then I transferred to Central Bible College, where I earned first-team all-American honors my senior season. Of course, it was the NCCAA, not the NCAA; the extra C stands for Christian. I was our leading scorer, averaging 21.3 points per game, and we were favorites to win the national championship, the NCCAA championship.

I was having my best season ever, and I wasn't just playing well; I was playing for God. I wanted to win a national championship because I thought it would be a great way to glorify God, but that dream died with one cut to the basket when my right knee buckled. Two weeks before the national tournament, my basketball career came to a painful end with a torn anterior cruciate ligament.

To be honest, the spiritual pain was worse than the physical pain. At first, I was angry. *God, I was playing for you. How could you let this happen?* Eventually, my anger turned to mourning, and then my mourning turned to begging. I remember weeping in prayer and begging God to heal my knee. I knew He could do it, but for reasons unknown to me, He chose not to. I was relegated to cheering for my teammates as we lost in the semifinals. In the grand scheme of things, I realize that a game is a game, but it was a bitter disappointment. And I still don't know why.

Some of the hardest moments in life are when you've prayed hard but the answer is no and you don't know why. And you may never know why. But that is the litmus test of trust. Do you trust that God is for you even when He doesn't give you what you asked for? Do you trust that He has reasons beyond your reason? Do you trust that His plan is better than yours?

I have a Deuteronomy 29:29 file that is filled with unanswered questions. It simply states that there are some mysteries that won't be revealed until we cross into eternity. I don't understand why God wouldn't heal my knee. I don't understand why my father-in-law passed away in the prime of life. I don't understand why loved ones have lost babies. I have a lot of unanswered questions, and many of them derive from unanswered prayers.

The hardest thing about praying hard is enduring unanswered prayers. If you don't guard your heart, unresolved anger toward God can undermine faith. Sometimes your only option is trust because it is the last card in your hand, but it's the wild card. If you can trust God when the answer is no, you're likely to give Him praise when the answer is yes. You need to press in and press on. By definition, praying hard is praying when it's hard to pray. And it's the hard times that teach us to pray hard. But if you keep praying through, the peace that transcends understanding will guard your heart and your mind.

So sometimes the answer to our prayers is no and you'll never understand why. But here's some good news: What we perceive as unanswered prayers are often the greatest answers.

What's Going On, God?

During our first two years of church planting, our church office was in the spare bedroom in our home. It was an awfully convenient commute, but it eventually became a huge inconvenience when our daughter, Summer, was born. Our spare bedroom turned into her bedroom by night and my office by day. I would set up her porta-crib at night and tear it down in the morning. That got real old real fast, so we started looking for office space.

After a few months of searching, I finally found a row house in the 400 block of F Street NE that we could convert into offices. It was perfectly situated halfway between our home and Union Station, and it had the ideal floor plan. We prayed that God would give us that contract, but when we presented the offer the next morning, we discovered that someone beat us to the punch the night before. It felt like a sucker punch that knocks the wind out of you. I was sure that this row house was the answer we were looking for, so it was both confusing and frustrating.

It took a few days to recuperate from that disappointment, but we resumed our search. A few weeks later, we found a row home in the 600 block of 3rd Street NE, just two blocks from Union Station. It was even more perfect than the previous place, so we prayed even harder. Once again, when we presented the offer the next morning, we discovered that someone got in ahead of us the night before. It felt like a second sucker punch that knocked the faith out of us.

After two bitter disappointments, I threw my arms up in the air. It was one of those "What's going on, God?" moments. Not only was God not answering our prayers; it felt like He was opposing our efforts. It felt like God was actually getting in the way. And He was. And I'm glad He was.

The Greatest Answers

Two weeks later, after those two unanswered prayers, I was walking home from Union Station. As I passed by 205 F Street, the Holy Spirit jogged my memory, and a name surfaced out of the deep recesses of my long-term memory. I had met the owner a year before, but I'm not very good at remembering names. I honestly wondered if it really was *Robert Thomas*. But one way or another, I felt prompted to call him.

There was no For Sale sign on the property, but I knew I needed to obey that prayer prompting, so I looked up his name in the Yellow Pages and found several listings for Robert Thomas. I made an educated guess and dialed the number. When he answered, I said, "Hi, this is Mark Batterson. I don't know if you remember me, but — " He didn't even let me finish my sentence. He interrupted me. "I was just thinking about you. I'm thinking about selling 205 F Street, and I wanted to know if you want to buy it before I put it on the market."

Only God.

That row home became our first office, but even more significant than its function was its location. 205 F Street abuts 201 F Street. We started laying hands on those abutting walls and asking God to give us the old crack house next door. I refused to believe that it was coincidental. I chose to believe it was providential. And it was.

If God had answered our prayers for the row homes in the 400 Block of F or 600 Block of 3rd, He would have given us second or third best. I was frustrated and confused because they seemed like good options, but they weren't the *best* option. And God doesn't settle for what is good. In His providence, God knew that we needed 205 F Street if we were going to eventually get 201 F Street. Because of construction and zoning complications, it would have been impossible for us to build our coffeehouse at 201 F if we hadn't owned 205 F.

Thank God for unanswered prayers!

Our heavenly Father is far too wise and loves us far too much to give us everything we ask for. Someday we'll thank God for the prayers He didn't answer as much or more than the ones He did. Our frustration will turn to celebration if we patiently and persistently pray through. It may not make sense for a few years. In fact, it may never make sense on this side of eternity. But I've learned a valuable lesson about unanswered prayer: *Sometimes God gets in the way to show us the way.*

Talking Donkeys

One of the wackiest miracles in the Bible involves a talking donkey. A prophet named Balaam is headed to Moab because he has been offered an honorarium to curse the Israelites. On his way, an angel of the Lord gets in the way. Balaam doesn't see the angel, but his donkey does. Three times the donkey saves Balaam's life by stopping, but Balaam is infuriated at his dumb donkey. That's when God opens the donkey's mouth, and it says to Balaam, "What have I done to you to make you beat me these three times?" Balaam's response to this donkey that saved his life three times? "You have made a fool of me! If only I had a sword in my hand, I would kill you right now."

In all fairness, I don't think any one of us knows how we would respond if one of our pets started talking to us! But Balaam is so enraged that he is not thinking straight. Dude, if you have a talking donkey on your hands, the last thing you want to do is kill it! You don't even need that honorarium anymore. You're going to make a fortune. You can take your talking donkey show on the road. Do a gig in Vegas.

I love the donkey's rational response. And I can't help but wonder if he had a distinguished British accent to go along with his superior intellect. "Am I not your own donkey, which you have always ridden, to this day? Have I been in the habit of doing this to you?"

The most respected prophet in the ancient world has no comeback. His only response to his erudite donkey is, "No." And he probably mumbled it.

Then the Lord opened Balaam's eyes to see the angel of the Lord, who said this to Balaam:

> *"I have come here to oppose you because your path is a reckless one before me. The donkey saw me and turned away from me these three times. If it had not turned away, I would certainly have killed you by now, but I would have spared it."*

Sometimes we get as ticked off as Balaam when we can't get to where we want to go. We hate detours! They are frustrating. They are confusing. But the divine detours often get us where God wants us to go. The real miracle in this story isn't the talking donkey; the real miracle is a God who loves us enough to get in the way when we're going the wrong way. These are the miracles we don't want, but these are the miracles we need. And when I look back on my own life, I'm grateful for the moments God got in the way of my plans and rerouted me. What seems like an unanswered prayer means that God has a better answer.

When I was a senior in college, I was offered a staff position with one of my heroes in ministry. He was an incredibly charismatic leader and communicator. It felt like a dream job, but as I paced our chapel balcony praying about it, I felt a check in my spirit. It felt like God was getting in the way. I knew I needed to say no, but I didn't know why. I turned down the offer and went to graduate school instead. Less than a year later, this pastor had an affair, left his family and his church, and eventually committed suicide. I have no doubt that God could have protected me in that situation, but he kept me from it altogether. He rerouted me from Missouri to Illinois.

Then, while I was in seminary in the Chicago area, I tried to plant a church, but once again, it felt like God got in the way. It was the wrong time and the wrong place. That church plant imploded, and God rerouted us from Illinois to Washington, DC. And I'm so glad He did. I wouldn't want to be anyplace else doing anything else with anyone else. Our destiny was in DC, but God had to get in the way a few times to get us there. He had to leave a few prayers unanswered so that He could give a better answer.

I'm so grateful that God doesn't answer all of my prayers. Who knows where I would be? But part of praying hard is persisting in prayer even when we don't get the answer we want. It's choosing to believe that God has a better plan. And He always does!

The Key of David

"These are the words of him who is holy and true, who holds the key of David. What he opens no one can shut, and what he shuts no one can open. I know your deeds. See, I have placed before you an open door that no one can shut."

One of my most circled promises is Revelation 3:7 – 8. I've prayed this promise hundreds of times in hundreds of different ways. I've seen God open doors that I never imagined I would have access to. I've done things and gone places and met people that I had no business doing, going to, or meeting. I recently had lunch with a former president and thought to myself, *You can't never always sometimes tell.* That certainly isn't something I could have orchestrated, but when you follow in the footsteps of Jesus, you never know what door He may open.

The key of David is an allusion to Eliakim, the mayor of David's palace. The key wasn't just a means of access; it was a symbol of authority. There was nothing that Eliakim could not close or open, lock or unlock. The Son of David, Jesus Christ, now holds the key of David and gives us access to this promise and every other promise.

The picture that comes to mind when I think about this open door promise is the opening sequence of the television series *Get Smart*. I can even hear the theme music. Maxwell Smart walks through seven different types of doors that automatically open on his way into the high-security CONTROL headquarters. Prayer is like that. It has a way of opening the right doors at the right time, even if we're sometimes as clueless as Agent 86.

The first time I circled this open door promise was in 1996.

Let me retrace the circle.

The Red Carpet

We had just received notice that the DC public school where National Community Church met was being closed because of fire code violations. We were on the verge of becoming a homeless church, and we had nowhere to go. We looked into at least twenty-five options, but every door we knocked on was slammed in our face. That's when I dared to dream big and pray hard. And while I've already shared the story of approaching the manager of the movie theaters at Union Station, here's the rest of the story.

Before asking the manager if we could rent the movie theaters on Sunday mornings, I prayed seven circles around Union Station. It was no easy task weaving through commuters, taxicabs, and tourist buses. Actually, I prayed seven circles around Union Station on several occasions. The more courage I need the more circles I draw. Finally, after circling Union Station long enough to build up enough courage, I walked in the front doors, through the Great Hall, down the escalator, under the marquee, and into the theater.

When the doors to that DC public school closed, it felt like the church was going to fall apart. I should have known that God was setting us up. Three days before I walked into the theater, AMC Theatres rolled out a nationwide program recruiting businesses and nonprofits to use their theaters when the screens were dark. As far as I know, we were the first group to respond to that initiative, and we had no idea it was going on. But God did. And God didn't just open an amazing door of opportunity; He rolled out the red carpet.

On the way out of Union Station, after signing a lease with the theater, I picked up *A History of Washington's Grand Terminal*. I immediately opened it, and the first thing I saw was an italicized phrase on the first page: "and for other purposes."

That phrase was part of the Bill of Congress signed by Teddy Roosevelt on February 28, 1903. It stated simply, "A Bill of Congress to create a Union Station and for other purposes." It's that last phrase, *and for other purposes*, that jumped off the page and into my spirit. Nearly a hundred years after that bill passed, Union Station started serving *God's purposes* through the ministry of National Community Church. Roosevelt thought he was building a train station. He had no idea that he was building a church — a church with a mass transportation system, parking garage, and forty-restaurant food court, no less! And our capital campaign was funded by Congress!

As I look back, I laugh at the fact that we were so scared when the doors to Giddings School closed. If God hadn't closed those doors, we would have never looked for the open door at Union Station. And that's the way it works: God closes doors in order to open bigger and better doors.

In recent years, I've realized that I only circled half of the promise in Revelation 3:8. I prayed for open doors but not closed doors. Quite frankly, we love it when God opens doors for us! When God slams a door in our face? Not so much! But you can't half-circle the promise. It's a package deal. You can't pray for open doors if you aren't willing accept closed doors, because one leads to the other.

For what it's worth, that DC public school eventually reopened as Results Gym, where I have a membership. Every time I walk through those doors, I thank God that He closed them on us. It all worked out, literally.

Stand Still

Thirteen years after walking through the open doors at Union Station, those doors were slammed shut. On a Monday morning in October

2009, I got a phone call from the theater manager at Union Station informing me that Union Station management was shutting down the theaters. As if that wasn't a big enough blow, she told me that the next Sunday would be our last Sunday. We didn't even have time to mourn because we had six days to figure out how to share the news with our congregation and decipher what was next. My mind was on spin cycle.

Part of the reason the phone call was so devastating is that we had prayed hard that God would miraculously help us buy those movie theaters. Instead, we lost the lease. We knew in our hearts that God was the only one who could close the doors He had miraculously opened, but it still felt like an anti-miracle. We had no idea where to go or what to do, but that's when God has us right where He wants us.

That week, our entire team was scheduled to attend the Catalyst Conference in Atlanta, Georgia. I was tempted to cancel the trip to keep working on an emergency evacuation plan for Union Station. It seemed like terrible timing, but it was perfect timing. Sometimes you have to get out of your routine so God can speak to you in a non-routine way. I knew that I couldn't just preach a sermon that weekend; I needed a word from the Lord. And God gave me one. During one of the teaching sessions, God gave me a promise to stand on and I put every ounce of my weight on Exodus 14:13 – 14:

"Don't be afraid. Just stand still and watch the LORD rescue you today. The Egyptians you see today will never be seen again. The LORD himself will fight for you. Just stay calm."

What would be the hardest thing to do with the Egyptian army charging straight at you at full speed? The hardest thing to do is precisely what God told them to do: *stand still.* God doesn't just play chicken; He also plays flinch. When we find ourselves in this kind of situation, we want to do something, anything. We have a nervous energy that wants to solve the problem as quickly as possible. But God tells them to do nothing but pray. The closer the Egyptian army got, the more intense their prayers became. They clenched their jaws. They stood their holy ground. They prayed like they had never prayed before.

Just in Time

All of us love miracles. We just don't like being in a situation that necessitates one. We hate finding ourselves between an Egyptian army and a Red Sea, but this is how God reveals His glory. We want God to part the Red Sea when the Egyptian army is still in Egypt. We want God to provide for our need before we even need it. But sometimes God waits. And then He waits longer. At first, the Israelites can see a dust cloud in the distance. Then they can hear the hooves of their horses and the wheels of their chariots. Then they are so close that they can recognize the faces of their former taskmasters.

The Israelites are sitting ducks, and God is the one who led them to this place. It seems like a tactical error, doesn't it? I'm no general, but I've TPed enough houses to know that you always plan your escape route. Yet God sets up camp where there is no means of retreat. I think it reveals something about His mysterious maneuverings. Sometimes God leads us to a place where we have nowhere to turn but to Him; our only option is to trust Him.

So why does God wait until the very last second to make His move? Why does He let the Egyptian army get that close? Because you could make a movie about that someday! And we love those kinds of movies, don't we? Unless, of course, we're in the middle of them. Once again, the God who provides *just enough* parts the Red Sea *just in time*.

Praying hard is trusting that God will fight our battles for us. It's the way we take our hands off the challenges we face and put them into the hands of God Almighty. And He can handle them. The hard thing is keeping our hands off.

When Union Station closed, I wanted to solve the problem, but I couldn't. All I could do was stand still. I had never felt more helpless as a leader, but I had never felt more energized as well. I felt like Moses as I stood before our congregation that day and stood on this promise: "I don't know what we're going to do, but I do know what we're not going to do. We're not going to be afraid. We're going to stand still. And we're going to see the deliverance of the Lord."

And God delivered.

Less than a year after closing that door, God opened two sets of doors at the Gala Theatre in Columbia Heights and Potomac Yard in Crystal City, our fifth and sixth locations. That closed door prompted a search for property that led to us purchasing *the last piece of property on Capitol Hill*. And what I didn't know then is that those closed doors at Union Station would lead to the biggest miracle in the history of National Community Church. God opened a door that had a dead bolt on it.

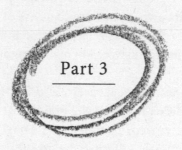

Part 3

The Third Circle — Think Long

Toward the end of his life, Honi the circle maker was walking down a dirt road when he saw a man planting a carob tree. Always the inquisitive sage, Honi questioned him. "How long will it take this tree to bear fruit?" The man replied, "Seventy years." Honi said, "Are you quite sure you will live another seventy years to eat its fruit?" The man replied, "Perhaps not. However, when I was born into this world, I found many carob trees planted by my father and grandfather. Just as they planted trees for me, I am planting trees for my children and grandchildren so they will be able to eat the fruit of these trees."

This incident led to an insight that changed the way Honi prayed. In a moment of revelation, the circle maker realized that praying is planting. Each prayer is like a seed that gets planted in the ground. It disappears for a season, but it eventually bears fruit that blesses future generations. In fact, our prayers bear fruit forever.

Even when we die, our prayers don't. Each prayer takes on a life, an eternal life, of its own. I know this because of the moments in my life when the Holy Spirit has reminded me that the prayers of my grandparents are being answered in my life right now. Their prayers outlived them.

Prayer is the inheritance we receive and the legacy we leave. Honi the circle maker didn't just pray the prayer that saved a generation; his perennial prayers were answered in the next generation too. His grandson, Abba Hilkiah, inherited the prayer legacy his grandfather left. During droughts, Israel came to his doorstep, and Hilkiah would go up on to his rooftop to pray for rain, just as his grandfather had done.

When we pray, our prayers exit our own reality of space and time. They have no time or space restrictions because the God who answers them exists outside of the space and time He created. You never know when His timeless answer will reenter the atmosphere of our lives, and that should fill us with holy anticipation. Never underestimate His ability to show up anytime, anyplace, anyhow. He has infinite answers to our finite prayers. He answers them more than once. He answers them forever. The problem, of course, is that we want immediate results. Forever is fine, but we want answers instantly.

When the Russian comedian Yakov Smirnoff immigrated to the United States, he said that the thing he loved most about America were the grocery stores. He said, "I'll never forget walking down one of the aisles and seeing powdered milk; just add water and you get milk. Right next to it was powdered orange juice; just add water and you get orange juice. Then I saw baby powder, and I thought to myself, *What a country!*"

We live in a quick-fix, real-time culture. Between the news ticker and Twitter, we're always in the know, always in the now. We don't just want to have our cake and eat it too; we want the *instant* brand. We want to reap the second after we sow, but this isn't the way it works with dreaming big and praying hard. We need the patience of the planter. We need the foresight of the farmer. We need the mind-set of the sower.

Because we are surrounded by technologies that make our lives faster and easier, we tend to think about spiritual realities in those terms. But almost all spiritual realities in Scripture are described in *longer* and *harder* agricultural terms. We want things to happen at the speed of light instead of the speed of a seed planted in the ground. We want our dreams to become reality overnight. We want our prayers answered immediately, if not sooner. But the key to dreaming big and praying hard is *thinking long*. Instead of thinking in terms of time, we must think in terms of eternity. Instead of thinking in terms of ourselves, we must think in terms of our children and grandchildren. Instead of thinking in seven-day cycles, we must think in terms of seventy-year timelines, as Honi the circle maker did.

On the Swedish island Visingsö, there is a mysterious forest of oak trees; mysterious because oak trees aren't indigenous to the island, and its origin was unknown for more than a century. Then in 1980, the Swedish Navy received a letter from the Forestry Department reporting that their requested ship lumber was ready. The Navy didn't even know it had ordered any lumber. After a little historical research, it was discovered that in 1829, the Swedish Parliament, recognizing that it takes oak trees 150 years to mature and anticipating a shortage of lumber at the turn of the twenty-first century, ordered that 20,000 oak trees be planted on Visingsö and protected for the Navy.

That is thinking long.

For the record, the lone objector was the Bishop of Strängnäs. He didn't doubt that there would still be wars to fight at the end of the twentieth century, but he was the only one who anticipated that ships might be built of other materials by then.

One dimension of thinking long is *thinking different*, and prayer is the key to both. Prayer doesn't just change circumstances; more important, it changes *us*. It doesn't just alter external realities; it alters internal realities so that we see with spiritual eyes. It gives us peripheral vision. It corrects our nearsightedness. It enables us to see beyond our circumstances, beyond ourselves, beyond time.

It's not enough to dream big and pray hard. You also have to think long. If you don't, you'll experience high degrees of discouragement. Why? Because we tend to overestimate what we can accomplish in a year. Of course, we also tend to underestimate what we can accomplish in a decade. The bigger the vision the harder you'll have to pray and the longer you'll have to think. But if you keep circling, it'll come to pass in God's time.

The 2020 vision of National Community Church is twenty locations by the year 2020. This isn't just dreaming big; it is thinking long. When I get discouraged, nine times out of ten it's because I've lost my carob-tree perspective. The solution? Think long. I have to remind myself of God's power, which knows no space-time limitations. I have to remind myself of God's faithfulness to answer my prayers, even after I am long gone.

Chapter 12

Long and Boring

I recently had the honor of giving the invocation at the annual benefit for the International Justice Mission at the Omni Shoreham in Washington, DC. My friend, the founder of IJM, Gary Haugen, shared the story of a thirteen-year-old girl who was miraculously rescued out of a brothel in the Philippines. It's hard to hear about the horrors she endured, especially when you have a thirteen-year-old daughter. Then Gary showed a picture of her smiling face.

Only God.

He is the God who heals hearts and restores smiles.

Like many girls enslaved in the utter darkness of sex trafficking, she wasn't allowed outside. Ever. Imagine not seeing the light of day or feeling the warmth of the sun for years on end. Then, through the legal efforts of IJM, she was rescued.

I'll never forget the way Gary described it. He played a Sara Groves remix of Peter Gabriel's song "The Book of Love" and pulled a line of lyrics from it. The melody is catchy, but the lyrics caught me. They've been echoing in my auditory cortex ever since. It may seem like a slam, but I think it's a celebration of "long love." The longer you've been in love the more it will make sense.

The book of love is long and boring ... It's full of charts and facts and figures ... But I love it when you read to me.

Gary then used the phrase from those lyrics — "long and boring" — to describe the process of rescuing the young girl out of that brothel. It took fifty long and boring trips to a courthouse twelve hours from the IJM office. It took 6,100 long and boring billable hours of filing and refiling paperwork, which of course, the young girl couldn't pay a penny of. And who knows how many long and boring prayer circles were drawn around that brothel and around that girl.

Praying through is long and boring, but it is the price you pay for miracles. And no matter how long and boring it is, you can't put a price on a girl rescued from darkness and brought into the light. There is nothing boring about that, but very few of us are willing to love that long or pray that hard.

IJM is the catalyst for hundreds of long and boring miracles every year, and I think I know why. I made the discovery when I sat in on one of their staff meetings. It should have been called a prayer meeting. It was simultaneously convicting and inspiring. It was convicting because they prayed with far more intensity and intentionality than we did, but it inspired me to make prayer our top priority. I'm not talking about the kind of prayer that is the first thing on the agenda; I'm talking about the kind of prayer that *is* the agenda. Since our staff meetings have turned into prayer meetings, I've come to the conviction that one prayer can accomplish more than a thousand plans. I can't help but wonder what would happen if more staff meetings turned into prayer meetings. I'm guessing those long and boring meetings would result in many more exciting miracles.

Like any good lawyer, the lawyers at IJM know how to work like it depends on them, but they also know how to pray like it depends on God. This is a lethal combination when it comes to fighting injustice. If you're willing to dream big *and* pray hard *and* think long, you might just brings kings to their knees and shut the mouths of lions.

Stop, Drop, and Pray

One of my favorite paintings at the National Gallery of Art is the larger-than-life portrait of Daniel in the Lions' Den by Flemish artist Sir Peter Paul Rubens. Daniel is ripped, to the point of steroid suspicion (and who knows, maybe it's an accurate depiction), but far greater than his external physique was his internal fortitude. His persistence quotient was unparalleled, as evidenced by his habit of getting on his knees three times a day and praying through an open window toward Jerusalem. Even when King Darius outlawed prayer, Daniel continued to stop, drop, and pray three times a day.

> *Now when Daniel learned that the decree had been published, he went home to his upstairs room where the windows opened toward Jerusalem. Three times a day he got down on his knees and prayed, giving thanks to his God, just as he had done before.*

Few people prayed with more consistency or intensity than Daniel, and what makes his persistence so remarkable is that he knew his dream of rebuilding Jerusalem wouldn't be fulfilled during his lifetime. He prayed toward the city that he knew he would never see with his physical eyes, yet he saw it with his spiritual eyes. Daniel prophesied that it would take "seventy years" for the desolation of Jerusalem to come to an end.

Is it possible for man to dream continuously for seventy years?

Daniel did just that. He never stopped dreaming big or praying hard, because he was thinking long. That is what prophets do. He wasn't just looking beyond the Babylonian captivity to the restoration of Jerusalem; he was looking even further into the future to the first and second coming of Jesus Christ. Daniel was thinking in terms of millennia. His prayers and prophecies were the seeds of our salvation, and we reap these blessings until Christ returns.

The thing that impresses me about Daniel is that he knew his prayers wouldn't be answered for seventy years, yet he prayed with a sense of urgency. As a procrastinator, I would have been tempted to wait until the last week of the sixty-ninth year to even *start* praying. Not Daniel. He had the ability to pray with urgency about things that weren't urgent. That is an important dimension of thinking long.

Drawing prayer circles often feels like a long and boring process, and it can be frustrating when you feel like you've been circling forever. You start to wonder if God really hears, if God really cares. Sometimes His silence is deafening. We circle the cancer. We circle our children. We circle the dream. But it doesn't seem to be making a difference. What do you do? My advice: Stop, drop, and pray. Keep circling. Circle for seventy years if you have to! What else are you going to do? Where else are you going to turn? What other options do you have? Pray through.

We live in a culture that overvalues fifteen minutes of fame and undervalues lifelong faithfulness. Maybe we have it backward. Just as our greatest successes often come on the heels of our greatest failures, our greatest answers often come on the heels of our longest and most boring prayers. But if you pray long and boring prayers, your life will be anything but boring. Your life will turn into the spiritual adventure it was destined to be. It won't always get you where you want to go, but it will get you through.

Sleepless Nights

The night that Daniel spent in the lions' den had to be the longest night of his life. He didn't sleep a wink. Going into it, it seemed like the worst thing, and last thing, that would ever happen to him. Coming out of it, it proved to be the best thing that ever happened to him. His faith didn't just shut the mouths of lions; his faith brought a king and kingdom to its knees. Plus his picture wound up hanging in the National Gallery of Art.

We love a good night's sleep, but sleepless nights are what define our lives. If you're going to bring kings to their knees or shut the mouths of lions, sometimes you need to pull an all-nighter. I'm more and more convinced that the biggest difference between success and failure, both spiritually and occupationally, is your waking-up time on your alarm clock. If you snooze, you lose. But if you pray through, God will come through as surely as the sun will rise.

Some of the longest nights of my life were some of the sleepless nights when Parker was a baby. He had a bad case of colic that caused him to cry incessantly for no discernible reason. The joy of having our first child was quickly displaced by sleep deprivation. He cried harder than hard, making those nights longer than long. The only thing that would calm his crying was running the bathtub. I remember going into the bathroom, turning on the faucet, and holding him for hours on end. Our water bill was so uncharacteristically high that the water company actually thought there had been some kind of mistake. Nope. Just a crying baby!

When you're holding a baby who won't stop crying, you can't stop praying. It's all we knew to do. Parker must be one of the most prayed-for babies in his generation. That's the reason I'm grateful for his colic. That's the reason I believe God will use him in great ways. We wrapped our arms around him and prayed circles around him every time he cried. Those were some long and boring prayers, but now that we're seeing them answered in his life as a teenager, we wouldn't trade those sleepless nights for anything in the world.

How You Get There

Along with caring for a newborn baby, I was trying to pastor a newborn church. That caused some sleepless nights too. We had one member in particular who needed a lot of crisis counseling, and it was always in the wee hours of the morning. One time he called my home phone at four in the morning, genuinely concerned that he was Jesus. No kidding. I reassured him that I knew Jesus, and he wasn't him. I told him I'd be happy to give him a few good reasons after a few more hours of sleep. Of course, Parker started crying right after I hung up!

When I was starting out as a church planter, I didn't want it to be a long and boring job. I wanted to pastor a thousand people by the time I turned thirty. When I was starting out as an author, I didn't want it to be the slow climb of an unknown writer out of obscurity. I wanted to write a *New York Times* bestseller. I'm a typical Type-A personality. I want to get where I'm going as quickly as possible. But as I look back on my journey, I am genuinely grateful that National Community Church didn't grow as quickly as I wanted it to. I'm not sure I would have survived if the church had thrived too soon. I am genuinely grateful that it took a dozen years and a half dozen unfinished manuscripts to finally publish my first book, *In a Pit with a Lion on a Snowy Day*. If I had written it at twenty-five instead of thirty-five, it would have been all theory and no substance.

I love what God is doing at National Community Church right

now. Miracles are happening right and left. There is more momentum than we know what to do with. God is touching thousands of lives week in and week out. And I love every second of it. But I wouldn't trade the days when our monthly income was $2,000, when we would start services with six people in attendance, or when we met in a school cafeteria without air-conditioning. Those difficult days taught us to pray hard and forced us to think long.

Every once in a while, I need a no-agenda day with nothing to do, but those aren't the days we're going to celebrate at the end of our lives. We won't even remember those days. What we'll remember are the days when we had everything to do, and with God's help, we did it. We won't remember the things that came easy; we'll remember the things that came hard. We'll remember the miracles on the far side of "long and boring."

Hiking the Inca Trail is one of the hardest things I've ever done. It took four days to traverse a trail that was breathtaking because of its beauty and breathtaking because of its elevation. It was nearly dawn on the fourth day when we finally arrived at the Sun Gate and got our first glimpse of Machu Picchu. It has to be one of the most spectacular places on the planet to watch the sunrise.

We had already hiked close to thirty precipitous miles over three days. The last leg of the journey, from the Sun Gate to the mountain-top city of Machu Picchu, took about an hour. By the time we arrived, the city was already swarming with tourists who had taken a bus to the top. It was easy to smell who was who. We looked and smelled like we had just hiked four days to get there; the tourists looked like they had just eaten over-easy eggs washed down with a cup of coffee.

At first I felt sorry for myself — we had to hike four days to get here! Then I felt sorry for them. We saw it through "Inca eyes" because we got there the way they did. We walked their trail. Ancient ruins shouldn't be arrived at easily. Neither should ancient truths. That experience taught me something that is true in all of life: It's not just where you end up that's important; it's how you get there.

The harder the better.

It's true in life; it's true in prayer.

Deep Roots

My father-in-law, Bob Schmidgall, was a circle maker. He founded Calvary Church in Naperville, Illinois, and pastored there for more than thirty years. The church grew from one member to thousands of members and became one of the leading missions-giving churches in America. The greatest lesson I learned from him is this: If you plant yourself in one place and let your roots grow deep, there is no limit to what God can do. His example of longevity inspired one of my life goals: Pastor one church for forty-plus years. And his legacy of generosity inspired another: Lead National Community Church to give $25,000,000 to missions.

My father-in-law grew up on a farm in central Illinois, which meant he had a carob-tree perspective. It also meant he got up very early in the morning. He was one of the godliest men I've ever known, and I think it's because he got up at ungodly hours to pray. He spent an hour on his knees before the rest of the world even woke up. On a good day, he also read three newspapers and logged two miles on the treadmill. My mother-in-law once told me that she had to reinforce the knees on his pants because they were always the first thing to go. For thirty years, he planted himself in one place. For thirty years, he planted seeds. For thirty years, he let his roots grow deep.

One of the longest and hardest days of my life was the day of his funeral, a few days after his shocking death at the age of fifty-five. Thousands of people came to pay their respects, some of whom had never even met him but whose lives had been indirectly impacted by the sermons he preached or the prayers he prayed. We met people who put their faith in Christ while listening to one of his radio messages. We met people whose mom or dad, son or daughter, brother or sister started following Christ at Calvary. Even now, when I travel and speak at leadership conferences across the country, it's rare that I don't meet someone who was touched by his ministry, even though he died thirteen years ago. His perennial prayers are still bearing fruit.

After the funeral service, our family exited the side door of the sanctuary and got into a car right behind the hearse at the head of the funeral procession. As we drove down Route 59 from Calvary Church to Naperville Cemetery, I looked in the rearview mirror and saw the longest line of cars I had ever seen. According to the Naperville police, cars were still pulling out of the church parking lot as we pulled into the cemetery five miles away.

That's what dreaming big, praying hard, and thinking long looks like. His legacy is a long love. His legacy is the stop, drop, and pray. His legacy is a lot of early mornings and some sleepless nights.

On Call

Our family started attending Calvary Church when I was in the eighth grade. It was already a megachurch with thousands of members, but my father-in-law had an amazing memory for names and faces. If he met you once, he would remember your name forever. Despite the size of the church, he never lost his shepherd's heart. He had a hospitable spirit that gave him an air of accessibility. Maybe that's why my parents felt like they could call him at two in the morning after my doctor issued a code blue and half a dozen nurses came rushing into my hospital room in ICU. I thought I was taking my last breath.

My mom stayed by my side while my dad called information and got a home phone number for the Schmidgalls. In less than ten minutes, my future father-in-law was at my bedside in his black double-breasted superman suit that I would later swear he slept in.

My father-in-law was a large man with large hands. They looked more like meat hooks than hands. And when he prayed for people, his hands would envelop their head like a skullcap. When he laid his hands on my head, I remember thinking that there is no way God won't answer his prayer. He had a familiarity with God that was disarming. He had a faith in God that was reassuring.

He could have called a staff member to make the visit. He didn't. He could have waited until morning. He didn't. He settled for a short night's sleep on short notice to pray for a thirteen-year-old kid who was fighting for his life. Little did he know that this thirteen-year-old kid would one day marry his daughter. Little did he know that this thirteen-year-old kid would one day give him his first grandchild, a colicky baby boy named Parker. There is no way he could have ever known, but that is the glorious mystery of prayer.

You never know who you are praying for. You never know how or when God will answer your prayers. But if you pray long and boring prayers, God will give you some exciting answers. If you are willing to interrupt your sleep cycle, your dreams might just come true.

Praying through Writer's Block

Aspiring authors often ask me what it takes to write a book. I'm certainly no authority, but here's my short answer: sleep deprivation. When I'm in a writing season, I set my alarm several hours earlier than I'd like, drag myself out of bed, and pound on my keyboard for several hours before putting on my pastor hat.

Getting a book published is fun. Writing is anything but. It's a long and boring process that is painfully painstaking when you're a perfectionist. Do I love writing? Yes. But what I really love is having written. And I wish it got easier, but it doesn't. Writing this book was just as boring and long as the last one, and I'm sure the next one will be just as boring and long as this one. But that long and boring process will translate into someone else's miracle.

I had a bout with writer's block the other day — I've come to expect it as part of the process of writing. There are days that you need to pray through and write through, even when you don't feel any creative flow. But I had a bad case, and it was made worse by my looming deadline. I got so frustrated that I decided to get my third caffeinated drink of the day. That's the danger of having an office above a coffeehouse. Our baristas know to cut me off after three!

While waiting in line, I overheard one of our regular customers who works across the street talking about my last book, *Soulprint*. The barista pointed at me and said, "The author is right there." He told me that the book had helped him in his journey of recovery. It reminded him of step four in the long and boring twelve-step process called AA. He thought our encounter was a divine appointment for him. The truth is, it was a divine appointment for me. I sat down at my computer with a renewed sense of destiny that helped me pray through and break through my writer's block.

That encounter reminded me of why I write. My perennial prayer is that readers would circle one page, one paragraph, one sentence that may have helped to change their life. I've come to terms with the fact that those miracles only happen after the long and boring process of writing and rewriting. But if I pray through the writer's block, I believe there is a miracle waiting on the other side.

Chapter 13

The Greatest of Them All

1931 was a long and boring year. The stock market crash of 1929 plunged America into the depths of the Great Depression, and most businesses struggled to stay afloat. Among the struggling businessmen was a hotelier named Conrad Hilton. Americans weren't traveling, and hotels were suffering. Hilton was borrowing money from a bellhop so he could eat.

It was during those difficult days of the Depression that Hilton came across a photograph of the Waldorf Astoria in New York City. The Waldorf was the holy grail of hotels with six kitchens, two hundred chefs, five hundred waiters, and two thousand rooms. It even had its own private hospital and railroad. In retrospect, Hilton observed that 1931 was "an outrageous time to dream." But the economic crisis didn't keep him from dreaming big, praying hard, or thinking long. Hilton clipped the photograph of the Waldorf out of the magazine and wrote across it, "the greatest of them all." Then he placed the photograph under the glass top of his desk. Every time Hilton sat down at his desk, his dream was staring him in the face.

Nearly two decades came and went. America emerged from the Great Depression and entered the Second World War. The big band era gave way to bebop. And the baby boom began. All the while, Hilton kept circling the Waldorf. Every time he walked by the Waldorf, he tipped his hat in deference to his dream.

Hilton acquired an impressive portfolio of hotels, including the Roosevelt in New York City and the Mayflower in Washington, DC, but the Queen, as he called the Waldorf, eluded him. Several attempts to purchase the hotel failed, but Hilton kept circling. Finally, on October 12, 1949, eighteen years after drawing a circle around his dream, Hilton made his move. He purchased 249,024 shares of the Waldorf Corporation and crowned his collection of hotels with the Queen.

How did he do it?

Well, Hilton certainly possessed his fair share of business acumen and negotiating prowess. He was a hardworking visionary with a lot of charisma. But the true answer is revealed in his autobiography. It's the answer he learned from his mother who had prayed circles around her son. In Hilton's own words, "My mother had one answer for everything. Prayer!"

When Conrad was a young boy, his horse, Chiquita, died. He was devastated and demanded an answer. His mother's answer was the answer to everything: "Go and pray, Connie ... Take all your problems to Him. He has answers when we don't." That lesson was not lost on him as a young boy or as an old man. For eighteen long and boring years, Hilton worked like it depended on him and prayed like it depended on God. Then his persistence paid off.

The final section of Hilton's autobiography is titled "Pray Consistently and Confidently." Here Hilton provides a succinct summary of his approach to business — essentially his approach to everything in life: "In the circle of successful living, prayer is the hub that holds the wheel together. Without our contact with God we are nothing. With it, we are 'a little lower than the angels, crowned with glory and honor.'"

The next time you stay in a Hilton, remember that long before it was bricks and mortar, it was a bold prayer. It was a long shot, a long thought. But if you pray like it depends on God and work like it depends on you for eighteen years, anything is possible. I particularly love the fact that Hilton tipped his hat to the Waldorf whenever he walked by. It was a gesture of humility, of respect, of confidence. When you dream big, pray hard, and think long, you know your time will eventually come.

Hilton certainly celebrated the acquisition of his big dream, but he never viewed the Queen as his greatest investment or achievement. His greatest privilege and potential was kneeling before the King. That's what made the Queen possible. The Queen was always subject to the King.

To Their Knees

Daniel ranks as one of the most brilliant minds the ancient world has ever known. He was a Renaissance man two thousand years before the Renaissance, with an unusual aptitude for both philosophy and science. He could explain riddles and solve problems unlike anyone in his generation, and no one could dream or interpret dreams like Daniel. But the thing that set him apart wasn't his IQ; it was his PQ. Daniel prayed circles around the greatest superpower on earth, and because he got on his knees, he brought kings and kingdoms to their knees.

Daniel didn't just pray when he had a bad day; he prayed every day. He didn't just dial up 911 prayers when he was in a lions' den; prayer was part of the rhythm and routine of his life. Prayer was his life, and his life was a prayer.

I'm sure Daniel prayed with a greater degree of intensity right before he was thrown into the lions' den, but that intensity was the byproduct of consistency. He approached every situation, every opportunity, every challenge, and every person prayerfully. And it was this prayerful posture that led to one of the most unlikely rises to power in political history. How does a prisoner of war become prime minister of the country that took him captive in the first place?

Only God.

The ascendance of Daniel defies political science, but it defines the power of prayer circles. Prayer invites God into the equation, and when that happens, all bets are off. It doesn't matter whether it's the locker room, the boardroom, or the classroom. It doesn't matter whether you practice law or medicine or music. It doesn't matter who you are or what you do. If you stop, drop, and pray, then you never know where you'll go, what you'll do, or who you'll meet.

Prayer Postures

Physical posture is an important part of prayer. It's like a prayer within a prayer. Posture is to prayer as tone is to communication. If words are what you say, then posture is how you say it. There is a reason that Scripture prescribes a wide variety of postures such as kneeling, falling prostrate on one's face, the laying on of hands, and anointing someone's head with oil. Physical postures help posture our hearts and minds.

When I extend out my hands in worship, it symbolizes my surrender to God. Sometimes I'll raise a clenched fist to celebrate what Christ has accomplished for me on the cross and declare the victory He has won. We do it after a great play, so why not during a great song?

During the most recent Lenten season, Parker and I got up a half hour earlier than normal to allow a little extra time to read Scripture. We also decided we would get on our knees when we prayed. The physical posture of kneeling, coupled with a humble heart, is the most powerful position on earth. I'm not sure that the kneeling position betters my batting average in prayer, but it gets me in the right stance. All I know is this: Humility honors God, and God honors humility. Why not kneel? It certainly can't hurt.

One of my favorite prayer postures I learned from the Quakers. I lead our congregation in this prayer frequently. We begin with hands facing down, symbolizing the things we need to let go of. It involves a process of confessing our sins, rebuking our fears, and relinquishing control. Then we turn our hands over so they are facing up in a posture of receptivity. We actively receive what God wants to give — joy unspeakable, peace that transcends understanding, and unmerited grace. We receive the fruit and gifts of His Spirit with open hands and open hearts.

There is nothing magical about the laying on of hands or bowing the knee or anointing the head with oil, but there is something biblical about it. There is also something mystical about it. When we practice these prescribed postures, we are doing what has been done for thousands of years, and part of thinking long is appreciating the timeless traditions that connect us to our spiritual ancestors.

The church I pastor is absolutely orthodox in belief but somewhat unorthodox in practice. Meeting in movie theaters makes it difficult to have a lot of High Church traditions. The movie screens are our postmodern stained glass; the smell of popcorn is our incense. But just because we don't practice a lot of extrabiblical religious rituals doesn't mean we devalue biblical tradition. Just because we believe the church should be the most creative place on the planet doesn't mean we devalue tradition. We aren't religious about religion, the human constructs created over the generations to surround our faith with rituals. We do, however, hold religiously to the timeless traditions of Scripture.

I've learned that what goes around comes around. What is in vogue now will eventually be out of vogue, and what is out of vogue now will eventually be in vogue. Human tradition is like a swinging pendulum. Singing hymns may be old-school, but give it enough time, and singing hymns will be cutting-edge creative once again. One thing I know for sure: Biblical traditions never go out of style. They are as relevant now as they were in ancient times. And when we practice the prayer postures prescribed in Scripture, it helps us dream big, pray hard, and think long.

Tip the Hat

I love the detailed description of Daniel's prayer posture. The nuances are not insignificant. He prayed three times a day. He went upstairs. He got down on his knees. And he opened a window toward Jerusalem. It's the open window that intrigues me. Even when prayer was outlawed, Daniel didn't close the window to conceal his illegal actions. I bet he opened the window a little wider and prayed a little louder. The question, of course, is *why* he opened a window toward Jerusalem in the first place.

It wasn't like God couldn't hear him if the window was closed. It wasn't like God's answer depended on his principal direction. God can hear us, whether we're facing north, south, east, or west, but facing Jerusalem kept Daniel pointed in the direction of his dream. His physical posture mirrored his mental posture. It was his way of staying focused. It was his way of keeping the dream front and center. It was his way of circling the promise. Opening his window toward Jerusalem was Daniel's way of tipping his hat at the Waldorf.

There is something powerful about being in proximity to the person, place, or thing you are praying for. If there wasn't, my future father-in-law would have just prayed over the phone and gone back to bed. Sometimes physical contact creates a spiritual conduit. Proximity creates intimacy. Proximity proclaims authority. Drawing a prayer circle is one way of marking territory — God's territory.

I spent many a Saturday night praying on the plaza in front of Union Station when we held services there. Then on Sunday mornings, I walked the aisles, laying hands on every single theater seat. When we did our first bulk mailing as a church, we couldn't afford to get the envelopes labeled, so we did the work ourselves. We didn't just put labels on envelopes; we laid hands on every single name, every single address, every single mailer. One of the most unique and special proximity prayers involved the dedication of a Senate office to God. We went from office to office laying hands on everything from chairs to cabinets to candy jars.

After I introduced our congregation to Honi the circle maker, I've heard dozens of different applications. There are lots of offices and apartments in Washington, DC, that have been circled in prayer. In each instance, praying in proximity made these prayers more than perfunctory. Like the promise given to Joshua, "I will give you every place where you set your foot," it's a way of exercising the authority God has given us as His children.

For many years, we laid hands on the walls at 205 F Street, praying that God would give us 201 F Street. When God answered those prayers, we laid our hands on the other side of those walls. We climbed down twenty-foot ladders and held a prayer meeting in the concrete foundation of our coffeehouse. We didn't just lay hands on those walls; we circled the promises of God by writing them on the walls. Those walls are primed with prayers and prophecies. We have long since covered them with acoustic treatments in our performance space, but they are ever present.

Spiritual Priming

One of the summer jobs I had during college was painting, but it didn't last long because, quite frankly, I wasn't very good. I got fired in less than a week. I did learn one thing before I was deservedly downsized: priming is an important part of painting. If you don't have the right primer, you'll be painting forever. If you're painting the wall a light color, you need a light primer; if you're painting the wall a dark color, you need a dark primer. It may seem like the primer is unnecessary. It may seem like a primer takes more time and more work, but it actually increases quality while decreasing the quantity of work.

Hold that thought.

Over the last few decades, New York University psychologist John Bargh has conducted priming experiments on unsuspecting undergraduates. One of the experiments involved a scrambled-sentence test. The first test was sprinkled with rude words like *disturb*, *bother*, and *intrude*. The second test was sprinkled with polite words like *respect*, *considerate*, and *yield*. In both cases, the subjects thought they were taking tests measuring intelligence. None of the subjects picked up on the word trend consciously, but it primed them subconsciously.

After taking the five-minute test, students were asked to walk down the hall and talk to the person running the experiment about their next assignment. An actor was strategically engaged in conversation with the experimenter when the students would arrive. The goal was to see how long it would take students to interrupt.

Bargh wanted to know if the subjects who were primed with polite words would take longer to interrupt the conversation than those primed with rude words. He suspected that the subconscious priming would have a slight effect, but the effect was profound in quantitative terms. The group primed with rude words interrupted, on average, after five minutes, but 82 percent of those primed with polite words never interrupted at all. Who knows how long they would have patiently and politely waited if the researchers hadn't given the test a ten-minute time limit.

Our minds are subconsciously primed by everything that is happening all the time. It's a testament to the fact that our minds are "fearfully and wonderfully made." It also testifies to the fact that we had better be good stewards of the things we allow into our visual and auditory cortices. Everything we see and hear is priming us in a positive or negative way. That's one reason I believe in starting the day in God's Word. It doesn't just prime our minds; it also primes our hearts. It's doesn't just prime us spiritually; it also primes us emotionally and relationally. When we read the words that the Holy Spirit inspired, it tunes us to His voice and primes us for His promptings.

A few years ago, two Dutch researchers did a similar priming experiment with a group of students by asking them forty-two questions from the Trivial Pursuit board game. Half of the subjects were told to take five minutes to contemplate what it would mean to be a university professor and write down everything that came to mind. The other group was told to sit and think about soccer for five minutes.

The professor group got 55.6 percent of the questions right.

The soccer group got 42.6 percent of the questions right.

The people in the professor group weren't any smarter than the people who were in the soccer group. And if watching sports decreased intelligence, I'd be an idiot. Especially during football season! The professor group was simply in a smart frame of mind.

What does that have to do with prayer?

Prayer is priming. Prayer puts us in a spiritual frame of mind. Prayer helps us see and seize the God-ordained opportunities that are all around us all the time.

Larks and Owls

Daniel was so primed with prayer that it didn't just sanctify his subconscious; it gave him supernatural discernment to prime the subconscious mind of King Nebuchadnezzar. Daniel discerned the king's dream because he could read his mind. It's almost as though prayer gives us a sixth sense.

Somewhere near the intersection of science and spirituality is a paradigm-shifting principle best seen in the priming exercise practiced by King David:

> *In the morning, LORD, you hear my voice;*
> *in the morning I lay my requests before you*
> *and wait expectantly.*

One of the reasons that many people don't feel an intimacy with God is because they don't have a daily rhythm with God; they have a *weekly* rhythm. Would that work with your spouse or your kids? It doesn't work in God's family either. We need to establish a daily rhythm in order to have a daily relationship with God. The best way to do that is to begin the day in prayer.

The most important ten minutes of my day are the ten minutes I spend reading Scripture and praying with my kids at the beginning of the day. Nothing even comes in a close second. It sets the tone for the day. It opens the lines of communication. It gets us started on the right foot.

I realize that there are larks and owls. Owls are just getting started when the rest of the world is winding down; larks are way too happy way too early. But whether you're an owl or a lark, you still need to begin the day in prayer for the purposes of priming.

For what it's worth, one of the defining paragraphs in my own personal reading came out of a biography of D. L. Moody. Page 129 is dog-eared and underlined. Moody said he felt guilty if he heard blacksmiths hammering before he was praying. Somehow that imagery converted me from an owl into a lark. I felt like my destiny would be determined in the early daylight hours. Moody was an amazing preacher, but he was an even better pray-er. In his own words, "I would rather be able to pray like David than to preach with the eloquence of Gabriel."

I love the determination in David's voice: "In the morning, LORD, you hear my voice." That's what it takes, doesn't it? It's hard to get up early, but that is what makes praying hard so hard. It's the same determination that I see in Daniel.

Then David declares, "I lay my requests before you and wait expectantly." Most of us just wait; David waited expectantly. There is a big difference.

Our biggest shortcoming is low expectations. We underestimate how good and how great God is by 15.5 billion light-years. The solution to this problem is prayer. Prayer is the way we sanctify our expectations. Laying his requests before the Lord was David's way of circling the promises of God. I'm not sure whether they were written requests, but they created a category in David's reticular activating system. After laying his requests before the Lord, he was primed and ready.

One way I've put this principle into practice is praying through my calendar instead of just looking through it. It's amazing what a difference it makes when I pray circles around the people I'm meeting with. It turns appointments into divine appointments. When you go into a meeting with a prayerful posture, it creates a positively charged atmosphere.

Laying his requests before the Lord was David's way of tipping his hat to the Waldorf. It was his way of opening his window toward Jerusalem. It was his way of praying through the calendar.

We don't know what he did with his daily requests. Maybe he posted them on the royal refrigerator; maybe he stuck them to his throne with a sticky note. What we do know is that they sanctified his expectations.

Idiosyncrasies

Like everyone else, I have my fair share of idiosyncrasies. I don't know why, but I always set my alarm clock to an even number. An odd number would totally mess me up. I always start shaving on the right side of my face. I never drive off after pumping gas without checking my left-hand rearview mirror because the last time I did that, I pulled the gas hose that was still in my gas tank right off of the gas pump. And I always take my shoes off while I write.

Even Jesus had idiosyncrasies. He loved to pray early in the morning, even after a late night of ministry. And He must have felt a special closeness to his Father when He hiked mountains and walked beaches. He gravitated to those places because proximity is an important part of prayer, but it goes beyond geography; I think it also has to do with genealogy.

One of my idiosyncrasies is that I occasionally do devotions out of my grandfather's Bible. In fact, I started this year in the book of Daniel because I was doing a Daniel fast. Toward the end of his life, my grandfather suffered from a medical condition that caused his hands to tremble so that his writing was virtually indiscernible. But based on the number of underlinings, Daniel was one of his favorite books. I actually know it was because I've heard stories of him and his brothers and cousins sitting around the table for hours on end talking about prophecies in Daniel. They were long thinkers and long talkers.

Seeing the verses that my grandfather underlined is powerful and meaningful because it helps me get into his mind and his spirit. I hope that the promises I have circled in my Bible will help my grandchildren do the same thing.

One important dimension of prayer is finding your own ritual, your own routines. Just like Daniel, you need to find your open window toward Jerusalem.

I'm sure Honi the circle maker prayed in a lot of different ways at a lot of different times. He had a wide variety of prayer postures. But when he needed to pray through, he drew a circle and dropped to his knees. His inspiration for the prayer circle was Habakkuk. He simply did what the prophet Habakkuk had done:

"I will stand upon my watch, and station me within a circle."

Where do you dream big? When do you pray hard? What helps you think long?

You need to identify the times, places, and practices that help you dream big, pray hard, and think long. When I want to dream big, I hang out at the National Gallery of Art. When I want to pray hard, I climb the ladder to the rooftop of Ebenezer's Coffeehouse. When I need to think long, I take the elevator up to the sixth-floor observation gallery at the National Cathedral.

It takes time to discover the rhythms and routines that work for you. What works for others might not work for you, and what works for you might not work for others. I've always subscribed to a sentiment shared by Oswald Chambers: "Let God be as original with other people as He is with you."

One of the great dangers in writing *The Circle Maker* is the application of these prayer principles without any thought. It's not a formula;

it's faith. It's not a methodology; it's theology. It honestly doesn't matter whether it's a circle, an oval, or a trapezoid. Drawing prayer circles is nothing more than laying our requests before God and waiting expectantly. If walking in circles helps you pray with more consistency and intensity, then make yourself dizzy; if not, then find something, find anything, that helps you pray through.

Prayer Experiment

We have a core value at National Community Church: everything is an experiment. And because we value experimentation, our congregation feels empowered to practice ancient spiritual disciplines in new ways.

Several years ago, I officiated at the wedding of David and Selina. During premarital counseling, Selina told me the backstory to their love story. It was a prayer experiment that led to wedding bells. Selina had a friend who used to organize prayer circles by recruiting ten people to pray for one thing for one person every day for thirty or forty or sixty days. The net results were amazing. That prayer experiment planted a seed in her spirit, and a few weeks later, she adapted the idea and came up with her own prayer experiment.

Selina recruited nine friends, and together they formed a prayer circle. They covenanted to pray for each other every day, and they decided to focus their prayers on their greatest struggles — the men in their lives. Not everybody in the prayer circle knew each other. In fact, not all of them liked each other. But as they started praying for each other each day, God began to bond them. They would often call each other if they felt prompted to share what the Lord was impressing on them during prayer, and it was amazing how often their prayers were perfectly targeted or timed.

At the end of forty days, the group decided to renew their prayer experiment for another forty days. The first forty days were full of spiritual attacks, but they were encouraged by that because it was evidence that they were doing something right. During the second forty-day period, the group saw tremendous victories in big things and little things. It was during those forty days that Selina met David, but it was the focused prayers of nine friends that prepared her to meet him. She identified some of the lies she had believed and mistakes she had made. Then she circled them in prayer while her prayer circle double-circled them.

I love this particular prayer experiment not just because I had the privilege of marrying David and Selina; I love it because it's the perfect marriage of praying hard and thinking long. Praying hard + thinking long = staying focused.

What would happen if you focused your prayers on one thing for one person for one month or one year? There's only one way to find out: do your own prayer experiment.

Game with Minutes

On January 30, 1930, Frank Laubach began a prayer experiment he called "the game with minutes." He was dissatisfied with his intimacy with God and decided to do something about it. Like Honi, who wrestled with a singular question his entire life, Laubach grappled with a question that framed his prayer experiment: "Can we have contact with God all the time?" He chose to make the rest of his life an experiment in answering this question.

Laubach sought to deconstruct the false constructs he had been taught. Then he rebuilt his prayer life from the ground up. We must do the same. Prayer isn't something we do with our eyes closed; we pray with our eyes wide-open. Prayer isn't a sentence that begins with "Dear Jesus" and ends with "Amen." In fact, the best prayer doesn't even involve words at all; the best prayer is a life well lived. All of life is meant to be a prayer, just as all of life is meant to be an act of worship.

Laubach described "the game with minutes" in these terms:

> We try to call Him to mind at least one second of each minute. We do not need to forget other things nor stop our work, but we invite Him to share everything we do or say or think. Hundreds of us have experimented until we have found ways to let Him share every minute of our waking hours.

One of the ways that Frank Laubach played "the game with minutes" was shooting people with prayer. Some people would walk by without any reaction, but some people would do a sudden about-face and smile. Sometimes a person's entire demeanor would change.

Six months into his experiment, Laubach wrote these words in his prayer journal:

> Last Monday was the most completely successful day of my life to date, so far as giving my day in complete and continuous surrender to God is concerned ... I remember how as I looked at people with a love God gave, they looked back and acted as though they wanted to go with me. I felt then that for a day I saw a little of that marvelous pull that Jesus had as He walked along the road day after day "God-intoxicated" and radiant with the endless communion of His soul with God.

A prayer experiment like this can turn a commute or walk or workout or meeting into a meaningful spiritual discipline. Though I advise against the actual shooting motion, it's a great way to pull the trigger on 1 Timothy 2:1: "I urge, then, first of all, that petitions, prayers, intercession and thanksgiving be made for all people."

What if we stopped reading the news and started praying it? What if lunch meetings turned into prayer meetings? What if we converted every problem, every opportunity, into a prayer?

Maybe we'd come a lot closer to our goal: praying without ceasing.

Chapter 14

The Speed of Prayer

In the world of aviation, the sound barrier was once considered the unbreakable barrier. Many engineers believed that Mach 1 represented an impenetrable wall of air, and the dozens of pilots who died trying to break the barrier solidified that belief. At low speeds, shock waves are a non-factor, but as an aircraft reaches higher speeds, new aerodynamics are introduced. When a plane approaches the speed of sound, shock waves increase and cause pilots to lose control. The buildup of air pressure in front of the aircraft causes a wave drag. And because the air on top of the wing is traveling faster than air on the bottom, due to Bernoulli's principle it typically results in a catastrophic nosedive. The British, among others, put on hold their attempt to break the sound barrier when their prototype, the Swallow, self-destructed at Mach .94. But that didn't keep a young American pilot named Chuck Yeager from attempting the impossible.

On October 14, 1947, a four-engine B-29 took off from Muroc Field high up in the California desert. Attached to the belly of the bomber was the Bell X-1 experimental plane. At 25,000 feet, the X-1 dropped from the fuselage, its rocket engine fired into life, and then it ascended to 42,000 feet. As the plane approached Mach 1, it began to shake violently. The challenge of controlling the plane was compounded by the fact that Yeager had broken two ribs while horseback riding two days before. He didn't tell his colleagues because he didn't want to delay history and his chance to make it. As his plane hit Mach .965, the speed indicator went haywire. At Mach .995, the g-force blurred his vision and turned his stomach. Then, just as it seemed as if the plane would disintegrate, there was a loud sonic boom followed by an almost instantaneous and eerie silence. As the plane crossed the sound barrier, 761 miles per hour, the air pressure shifted from the front of the plane to the back. The shock waves that had buffeted the cockpit turned into a sea of glass. Yeager reached Mach 1.07 before cutting his engines and coming back down to earth. The unbreakable barrier had been broken.

I had the privilege of hearing Chuck Yeager recount his experiences at the Smithsonian National Air and Space Museum with Parker's Cub Scout troop. Right outside the IMAX Theater where Yeager gave the speech, the Bell X-1 is symbolically suspended in midair, along with other historic aircraft and spacecraft. Each one represents a breakthrough. Each one is a symbol of the impossible becoming possible. Each one is a testament to the ingenuity and irrepressibility of the human spirit, which of course, is a gift of the Holy Spirit.

Just like the sound barrier, there is a faith barrier. And breaking the faith barrier in the spiritual realm is much like breaking the sound barrier in the physical realm. If you want to experience a supernatural breakthrough, you have to pray through. But as you get closer to the breakthrough, it often feels like you're about to lose control, about to fall apart. That is when you need to press in and pray through. If you allow them to, your disappointments will create drag. If you allow them to, your doubts will nosedive your dreams. But if you pray through, God will come through and you'll experience a supernatural breakthrough.

Sonic Boom

Almost like a sonic boom in your spirit, there comes a moment in prayer when you know that God has answered your prayer. In that moment, your frustration and confusion give way to quiet confidence. Your spirit becomes like a sea of glass because you know it's out of your hands and in the almighty hands of God. The natural resistance that was thwarting you turns into supernatural momentum that is propelling you.

I remember the moment when I knew in my spirit that God was going to give us the last piece of property on Capitol Hill that we had been circling in prayer. I didn't find out we got the contract until my trip to Peru, but I knew we were going to get it, even after we lost it. We were having a relatively routine staff meeting that turned into a prayer meeting. We got down on our knees, but I felt like that wasn't low enough. I felt so dependent and so desperate that I ended up flat on my face. The next thing I knew, I was crying uncontrollably. My body was actually heaving as I cried out to God for an answer.

Those moments of absolute brokenness before God are too few and far between. Usually self-consciousness gets in the way, but not that day. I lost it. And to be perfectly honest, it was embarrassing, but if you are embarrassed for righteousness reasons, then it's holy embarrassment. And when you get to the point where you care more about what God thinks and less about what people think, you're getting close to the breakthrough.

I think our staff was taken a little off guard, but they prayed with me as I prayed through. They formed a prayer circle around me. And when you agree in prayer, it's like a double circle. At some point, when I felt like I was falling apart, there was a sonic boom in my spirit. It was like the shifting of tectonic plates deep within my soul. Doubt gave way to faith. I knew that I could quit praying because I had prayed through. It was a done deal.

Daniel Fast

At critical junctures in my life I've done a Daniel fast. It's called a Daniel fast because it's inspired by and patterned after the fasts that Daniel did at critical junctures in his life. It's different from an absolute fast because the diet generally consists of fruits, vegetables, and water. And it is typically done with a specific goal and defined timeline in mind. It was a ten-day fast that kick-started Daniel's precipitous climb to political power; it was a twenty-one-day fast that ended with an angelic encounter.

When you fast and pray in tandem, it's almost like a moving sidewalk that gets you to your desired destination in half the time. Fasting has a way of fast-tracking our prayers. Because fasting is harder than praying, fasting is a form of praying hard. In my experience, it is the shortest distance to a breakthrough.

Listen in to these words spoken to Daniel:

"Do not be afraid, Daniel. Since the first day that you set your mind to gain understanding and to humble yourself before your God, your words were heard, and I have come in response to them. But the prince of the Persian kingdom resisted me twenty-one days. Then Michael, one of the chief princes, came to help me, because I was detained there with the king of Persia. Now I have come to explain to you what will happen to your people in the future, for the vision concerns a time yet to come."

Can you imagine having a conversation with your guardian angel? It'll be one of our most revealing conversations when we get to heaven, but Daniel got to have a short conversation on this side of the space-time continuum. For some of us, it'll be an awfully long conversation because we kept our angel awfully busy. This is certainly true of Daniel. I can't help but wonder if they had a little side conversation about the lions' den.

Like all angelic greetings, it begins with "do not be afraid." I guess that's angelic protocol. Then the angel reveals the realities of the spiritual realm in a way seen nowhere else in Scripture. We know that our struggle is not against flesh and blood, but this encounter fleshes it out. The angel reveals the importance of praying through. The angel reveals the spiritual warfare being waged beyond the curtain of our consciousness. The angel reveals the way prayers are processed.

Daniel's prayer was heard before the words even passed through his vocal chords, but it wasn't until the twenty-first day that he experienced a breakthrough because of spiritual oppression. An evil spirit known as the prince of the Persian kingdom resisted the call for angelic backup until the twenty-first day.

I can't help but ask a counterfactual question: What if Daniel had quit praying through on day twenty? The answer is simple: Daniel would have forfeited the miracle the day before *the day*. I don't know where you are on the timeline between praying through and breaking through. Maybe you're at day one; maybe you're at day twenty. Either way, you can pray with a holy confidence, knowing that with each prayer circle you are one prayer closer. Don't give up. Like Daniel, the answer is on the way!

Empty Stomach

There is more than one way to draw a prayer circle. In fact, sometimes it involves more than prayer. I believe that fasting is a form of circling. In fact, an empty stomach may be the most powerful prayer posture in Scripture.

Even Jesus said that some miracles are not possible via prayer. Some miracles are only accessible via prayer and fasting. It takes the combination of prayer and fasting to unlock some double dead bolts.

When I have a big decision to make, I circle it with a fast. It doesn't just purge my body; it also purges my mind and spirit. When I need a breakthrough, I circle it with a fast. It doesn't just break down the challenges I'm facing; it also breaks down the calluses in my heart.

Maybe there is something you've been praying for that you need to start fasting for. You need to take it to the next level. You need to draw a double circle by fasting for your children or for a friend or for your business.

I've tried to make fasting a regular routine by doing a Daniel fast at the beginning of the calendar year. During this year's Daniel fast, I felt led to pray for seven miracles. I know what you're thinking: *Is that all he ever does?* You're probably wondering if I have a fixation with the number *seven* too. I promise you, I don't. And the truth is that I've only done this twice in my life. I don't even come close to believing for the quantity and quality of miracles that I could or should.

It had been several years since writing seven miracles on a rock, and I believed that God wanted to stretch my faith again. Instead of writing them on a rock, I downloaded the Evernote App and double-thumbed these prayer requests into my iPhone.

I was two for seven the last time. I'm five for seven this time. And these seven miracles are bigger than the last seven miracles.

One of the seven miracles I prayed for was a $1 million payoff of our mortgage on Ebenezer's Coffeehouse. During the fast, we paid off that million-dollar debt. In fact, we paid off all of our debt. And so in the past twelve months we've acquired more than $10 million dollars in property *and* we're debt free for the first time in ten years! Only God.

But the biggest miracles aren't financial. The biggest miracles are the hundreds of people who have submitted their lives to the lordship of Jesus Christ. At our last baptism, a couple dozen NCCers publically professed their faith. We ask every baptism candidate to write out the testimony of how they came to faith in Christ, and I could barely read them through my tears. Each one is a testament to God's sovereignty and a trophy of God's grace.

The Genesis

Now let me ask you a sequential question: When did the breakthrough happen for Daniel? Was it the moment Daniel started circling on day one? Or was it the moment he had prayed through and experienced the angelic breakthrough on day twenty-one?

The answer is both/and. Every breakthrough has a genesis and a revelation, literally and figuratively. There is a first breakthrough and a second breakthrough.

Let me retrace the circle.

"The moment you began praying, a command was given."

This one revelation has the power to change your perspective on prayer. It will inspire you to dream big, pray hard, and think long. The answer is given long before it is revealed. It's not unlike the Jericho miracle when God said He had already given them the city, past tense. Do you realize that the victory has already been won? We're still waiting for its future tense revelation, but the victory has already been won by means of the death and resurrection of Jesus Christ. *It is finished.* This isn't just when God made good on grace; it is when God made good on every promise. Every single one is yes in Christ. Past tense. Present tense. Future tense. The full revelation won't happen until His return, the return that Daniel prophesied, but the victory has already been won, once and for all, for all time.

After the miraculous purchase of the last piece of property on

Capitol Hill at 8th and Virginia, I thought God was finished, but God was just getting started. The great danger when God does a miracle is that we get comfortable. That's when we've got to stay humble and stay hungry. If we aren't careful, we can lose faith simply because we already have what we need. That isn't just mismanagement of a miracle; it's gross negligence. One reason God does miracles is to stretch our faith so we can draw bigger circles so He can do bigger and better miracles.

Honestly, I was exhausted from four months of drawing circles around 8th and Virginia, and I was satisfied with our footprint. That's when someone in our congregation with more faith than their pastor said, "We need to believe God for the entire block." At first a city block seemed like too big of a circle to draw, especially with property on Capitol Hill going for $14 million an acre. But it was like there was a sonic boom in my spirit. I knew that God wanted us to go after the auto shop on the corner of 7th and Virginia Avenue. The problem is that it wasn't even for sale.

I knew that the auto shop would be a thorn in the flesh if we didn't buy it, because it was an eyesore. So we started praying, and to be honest, I wanted an easy answer for once. Ironically, the auto shop proved to be even harder. The owners weren't just resistant to offers; our realtor told us that they had torn up contract offers in the faces of those offering them — offers that were nearly $2 million more than our original offer. It felt like an impossible fight unless God was fighting for us, but if God was fighting for us, then I knew the victory was already won.

I knew we couldn't just pray for this miracle. It had to be coupled with fasting, so we did a variety of fasts over several months. I also felt like our entire staff needed to lay hands on this property, so we took a little field trip on September 15, 2010. As we laid hands on those cinder block walls, it was a genesis moment.

For several months, our negotiations remained at an impasse. The problem was that they had all the leverage. They knew we wanted it and needed it, and they didn't want or need to sell it. Our only leverage was prayer, but prayer is a long lever. We circled that property so many times that I'm almost surprised the walls didn't fall down just like at Jericho.

On January 15, 2011, four months to the day after laying hands on it, I was on a flight to Portland, Oregon. When the plane landed, my phone showed a text message from our realtor telling me that the deal was done. I couldn't believe it and I could believe it.

The question, of course, is this: When was it a done deal? Was it a done deal on January 15? Or was it a done deal back on September 15? The answer is both/and. The genesis was laying hands on that auto shop on September 15; the revelation was a signed contract on January 15. As of January 15, 2011, we might be the only church in America that owns both a coffee shop and an auto shop.

One Resolution

Every miracle has a genesis moment.

In the first century BC, it was a circle in the sand drawn by a sage named Honi. For Moses, it was declaring that God would provide meat to eat in the middle of nowhere, even though he had no idea how. For Elijah, it was getting on his knees seven times and praying for rain. For Daniel, I think it traces back to one resolution.

Destiny is not a mystery. For better or for worse, your destiny is the result of your daily decisions and defining decisions.

Daniel made the decision to stop, drop, and pray three times a day. Those daily decisions add up. If you make good decisions on a daily basis, it has a cumulative effect that pays dividends the rest of your life.

Along with daily decisions, there are defining decisions. We only make a few defining decisions in life, and then we spend the rest of our lives managing them. Maybe you've made some bad decisions that have gotten you to where you don't want to be. The good news is that you're only one defining decision away from a totally different life.

Daniel makes one of those defining decisions as a teenager. It doesn't seem like a big deal, but it changes the course of his story and history. Daniel's ascent to power traces all the way back to one resolution.

Daniel resolved not to defile himself with the royal food and wine.

Daniel risked his reputation by refusing the royal food. It was an insult to the king, but Daniel was more concerned about insulting God. Daniel knew it would violate Jewish dietary laws, and while that may not seem like a big deal, if you obey God in the little things, then God knows He can use you to do big things! It was Daniel's unwillingness to compromise his convictions in the little things that led to his big break. Daniel did a ten-day fast that won him favor with the king's chief official and that favor translated into his first job with the administration. Then "the favor of him who dwelt in the burning bush" kept opening doors via a series of promotions until Daniel was second-in-command to the king.

I wonder if Daniel ever had one of those out-of-the-spirit moments when he looked in the mirror and asked himself, "How did I get here?" The answer: daily decisions and defining decisions. Never underestimate the potential of one resolution to change your life. It can be a genesis moment. Daniel's destiny traces all the way back to one resolution not to defile himself, but making the resolution was easier than keeping it. That is where prayer, coupled with fasting, comes into play.

Try, Try Again

In May of 2009, Brian and his wife, Kristina, were watching the movie *Fireproof*. It was both a genesis and a revelation. It was a revelation because Brian knew that his addiction to pornography would tear his marriage apart, just as in the marriage portrayed in the movie. It had been tearing him apart since he was twelve. It was a genesis because Brian, like Daniel, resolved not to defile himself.

Brian and his college sweetheart were married in 1995, but he continued to look at porn while she was at work. He thought he could stop when they had their first child. No such luck. Then, after watching *Fireproof*, he prayed that God would help him quit cold turkey. Six weeks later, he failed. A year later, after winning some battles and losing some battles, he gave it to God once again. Six weeks later, he failed again. Then on June 29, 2010, he nailed it to the cross where Jesus had won the war against sin.

The Enemy of our souls is known as "the accuser of our brethren," and when it comes to the brethren, most of Satan's accusations have to do with sexual sins. For men, the spiritual battle is often won or lost on the battlefield of sexual temptation. And when we lose a battle, the enemy wants us to give up the fight. Can I remind you of something the enemy knows all too well? You may lose some battles, but the war has already been won. And while the Enemy never stops accusing us, our Almighty Ally never stops fighting for us, never gives up on us.

On October 8, 2010, Brian celebrated one hundred days of being porn free. It was the longest period of freedom in a quarter century. That's the night the men's group at his church formed a prayer circle around him and prayed for purity of mind; they prayed for strength of will. Brian hasn't been the same since. It doesn't mean that there won't be more battles to fight. The war never ends. It doesn't mean he can stop circling. He's got to pray through. But Brian is now helping other men as a Life Group leader at his church, leading men through a study of Stephen Arterburn's book *Every Man's Battle*. Brian is winning the battle because Christ already won the war. He is now praying circles around the men that God is bringing into his circle of influence.

What I love about Brian is that despite repeated failures, he kept trying. Most of us quit trying after six circles or twenty days or two failures. In case you missed the message the first time, if you keep trying, you are not failing. The only way you can fail is if you quit trying. If you're still trying, even if you're failing, you're succeeding. God is honored when you don't give up. God is honored when you keep trying. God is honored when you keep circling.

There is an old maxim: If at first you don't succeed, try, try again. The saying dates back to the early 1800s and comes from *The Teacher's Manual* written by American educator, Thomas H. Palmer. It was intended to encourage American schoolchildren to do their homework, even when it gets hard, because persistence pays off.

In every spiritual journey, there are setbacks. And if you listen to the accuser of the brethren, you'll feel like a failure. Too many men have believed his lies. The truth is that the victory has already been won. To seal the victory, all it takes is a defining decision and a daily decision. This doesn't mean it will be easy. In fact, the longer you've been in bondage the harder it will be. And that can be overwhelming when you think long, but part of thinking long is breaking down our dreams, goals, and problems into short-term steps. And it always starts with the first step.

Circle Daniel 1:8.

Make a resolution not to defile yourself.

Then circle it again tomorrow. And the next day. And the day after that.

Some of us don't start fighting the battle because we're not sure we can win the war, but the war has already been won nearly two thousand years ago at Calvary. All you have to worry about is winning the battle today. God can take care of tomorrow.

Can you keep the resolution for a day? Sure you can.

That defining decision will lead to a daily decision, and together, these defining decisions and daily decisions will lead to a different destiny.

The Spirit Versus the Flesh

On the eve of His crucifixion, Jesus was in Gethsemane praying hard and thinking long. He was about to face the greatest test of His life, and He knew He needed to pray through the night. His disciples were supposed to be praying, but instead they were sleeping. They probably pretended to be praying when He awakened them, but drooling and snoring are dead giveaways. You can hear the disappointment in Jesus' voice when He asks them: "Couldn't you men keep watch with me for one hour?"

That challenge is worth circling. Take it literally. Take it personally.

Jesus was always coming through for the disciples, but the disciples couldn't pray through for Him. They didn't even last an hour. The disciples let Jesus down when He needed them most. It didn't just hurt Jesus; Jesus knew it would hurt them as well.

Let me play counterfactual theorist.

I wonder if Peter would have denied Jesus if he had been praying instead of sleeping? Maybe he failed the test three times because he hadn't done his prayer homework? We see those three denials as three temptations, but maybe they were three opportunities to get it right. While I can't prove it, I think Peter would have passed the test if he had prayed through. But he didn't.

Then Jesus hits the bull's-eye, and we live in the crosshairs.

"The spirit is willing, but the flesh is weak."

Is it ever! Never were truer words spoken.

Most people have a willing spirit; it's the weak flesh that gets in the way. The problem isn't desire; the problem is power — more specifically, willpower. This is where fasting comes into play. Fasting gives you more power to pray because it's an exercise in willpower. The physical discipline gives you the spiritual discipline to pray through. An empty stomach leads to a full spirit. The tandem of prayer and fasting will give you the power and willpower to pray through until you experience a breakthrough.

Escape Velocity

On July 16, 1969, Neil Armstrong, Michael Collins, and Buzz Aldrin climbed aboard Apollo 11 on Launch Pad 39A at the Kennedy Space Center. The multistage rocket weighed 102,907 pounds, but it carried 5,625,000 pounds of propellant.

Breaking the sound barrier is one thing; exiting the earth's atmosphere is another thing altogether. At takeoff, the five engines produced 7,500,000 pounds of thrust in order to exceed the gravitational pull of the planet and reach an escape velocity of 17,500 mph. But that only gets you into orbit. If you want to shoot the moon, you've got to top 25,000 mph.

Prayer is the way we escape the gravitational pull of the flesh and enter God's orbit. It's the way we escape our atmosphere and enter His space. It's the way we overcome our human limitations and enter the extradimensional realm where all things are possible.

Without prayer, there is no escape. With prayer and fasting, there is no doubt. Like tandem staging, it will take you to spiritual heights you never imagined possible. You won't just escape our atmosphere;

if you pray a little harder and fast a little longer, you may just shoot the moon.

On Sunday, July 20, 1969, Buzz Aldrin and Neil Armstrong landed their lunar module, the Eagle, on the Sea of Tranquillity. The first thing they did was celebrate Communion. Because of a lawsuit filed by Madalyn Murray O'Hair, when NASA aired the reading from Genesis by the astronauts of Apollo 8, it decided to black out that part of the broadcast.

Aldrin, an elder in the Presbyterian Church (U.S.A.), took out a Communion kit provided by Webster Presbyterian Church in Houston, Texas. In the one-sixth gravity, the wine curled and gracefully came up the side of the cup. Just before eating the bread and drinking the cup, Aldrin read from the gospel of John:

"I am the vine, you are the branches; he who abides in Me and I in him, he bears much fruit, for apart from Me you can do nothing."

It must be hard *not* to dream big when you're 238,857 miles from earth. It must be hard *not* to pray hard when you're traveling 25,000 miles per hour through space. It must be hard *not* to think long and think different when you're watching the earthrise from the surface of the moon.

After the greatest technological feat the world had ever known, Aldrin circled back to an agricultural metaphor about bearing fruit. It's a long way from the garden of Gethsemane to the Sea of Tranquillity, both in terms of miles and in terms of years. But when you plant carob trees, you never know when or where or how they will bear fruit. But bear fruit they will, two thousand years later and 238,857 miles away. They will bear fruit from here to eternity, from here to infinity.

Chapter 15

Life Goal List

On a rainy afternoon in 1940, a fifteen-year-old dreamer named John Goddard pulled out a piece of paper and wrote "My Life List" at the top. In one afternoon, he wrote down 127 life goals. It's amazing what can be accomplished in one afternoon, isn't it? By the time he turned fifty, John Goddard had accomplished 108 of his 127 goals. And they were no garden-variety goals.

- ☑ *Milk a poisonous snake.*
- ☑ *Skin-dive to forty feet and hold breath two and a half minutes underwater.*
- ☑ *Learn jujutsu.*
- ☑ *Study primitive culture in Borneo.*
- ☑ *Land on and take off from an aircraft carrier.*
- ☑ *Run a mile in five minutes.*
- ☑ *Go on a church missions trip.*
- ☑ *Retrace the travels of Marco Polo and Alexander the Great.*
- ☑ *Learn French, Spanish, and Arabic.*
- ☑ *Play the flute and violin.*
- ☑ *Photograph Victoria Falls in Rhodesia.*
- ☑ *Light a match with a .22 rifle.*
- ☑ *Climb Mount Kilimanjaro.*
- ☑ *Study Komodo dragons on the island of Komodo.*
- ☑ *Build a telescope.*
- ☑ *Read the Bible from cover to cover.*
- ☑ *Circumnavigate the globe.*

☑ *Visit the birthplace of Grandfather Sorenson in Denmark.*
☑ *Publish an article in* National Geographic *magazine.*

My favorite Goddard goal is one he never achieved: *Visit the moon.* Now that is dreaming big and thinking long. He set the goal before anyone had ever escaped the earth's atmosphere!

John Goddard has not accomplished every goal he set. He never climbed Mount Kilimanjaro, and his quest to visit every country in the world fell a few countries short. There were also some disappointments along the way. His goal of studying Komodo dragons (the world's largest living lizards) was thwarted when his boat broke down twenty miles offshore. So Goddard hasn't accomplished all of his goals, but I doubt he would have accomplished half of what he did if he hadn't set the goals in the first place. After all, you'll never achieve the goals you don't set.

The brain is a goal-seeking organism. Setting a goal creates structural tension in your brain, which will seek to close the gap between where you are and where you want to be, who you are and who you want to become. If you don't set goals, your mind will become stagnant. Goal setting is good stewardship of your right-brain imagination. It's also great for your prayer life.

When I first read Goddard's list of life goals, I was inspired to come up with my own life goal list. While I started more than a decade ago, I still view my list of 100-plus life goals as a rough draft. Every year I check a few goals off the list; I also add new goals along the way.

Dreams with Deadlines

What do life goals have to do with dreaming big? For that matter, what does goal setting have to do with praying hard and thinking long? The answer is everything. Goal setting is a great way of doing all three simultaneously.

Goals are the cause and effect of *praying hard.* On the front end, prayer is a goal incubator. The more you pray, the more God-sized goals you'll be inspired to go after. But prayer doesn't just inspire godly goals, it also ensures that you keep praying hard because it is the only way you'll accomplish a God-sized goal. Simply put, prayers naturally turn into goals, and goals naturally turn into prayers. Goals give you a prayer target.

In their groundbreaking book *Built to Last,* Jim Collins and Jerry Porras introduced the acronym BHAGs (Big Hairy Audacious Goals). I've substituted a P for the G. I think of my God-sized goals as Big Hairy Audacious Prayers (BHAPs). They force me to work like it depends on me and pray like it depends on God.

Goals are a great way of *thinking long.* I have checked approximately one-quarter of my life goals off my list. Some of them, like speaking for an NFL chapel or coaching a sports teams for each of my children, I've checked off numerous times. But many of my life goals will take a lifetime to achieve. It might take until I'm seventy-five to write twenty-five books. I cannot pay for my grandchildren's college education until I have grandchildren. And I have no idea when I'll be part of baptizing three thousand people in the same place at the same time, like the day of Pentecost, but it's on my life goal list. And that's why they are *life* goals. They might take a lifetime to achieve, but they are worth waiting for and working for.

Finally, setting goals is a practical way of *dreaming big.* If prayer is the genesis of dreams, then goals are the revelation. Goals are well-defined dreams that are measurable. Getting in shape is not a goal; it's a wish. Running a half marathon, however, is a goal because you know you've accomplished it when you cross the finish line.

Goals are dreams with deadlines. And these deadlines, especially if your personality is anything like mine, are really lifelines. Without a deadline, I would never accomplish anything because I'm both a procrastinator and a perfectionist. And that's why so many dreams go unaccomplished. If you don't give your dream a deadline, it will be dead before you know it. Deadlines keep dreams alive. Deadlines bring dreams back to life.

I dreamed of writing a book for thirteen years, but the lack of a deadline nearly killed my dream. It wasn't until I actually set a deadline, my thirty-fifth birthday, that I was able to finish my first manuscript and accomplish a life goal.

Visualization

"Show me your vision, and I'll show you your future."

I was twenty-one when I heard those words, and I'll never forget them. But it's not just the words that impacted me; it's the fact that they were spoken by the pastor of one of the largest churches in the world. His words carried extra weight because he knew whereof he spoke. Very few people have dreamed bigger dreams or prayed harder prayers.

Scripture says that without a vision, people perish. The opposite is true as well. With a vision, people prosper. The future is always created twice. The first creation happens in your mind as you envision the future; the second creation happens when you literally flesh it out.

Vision starts with visualization. In 1995, Alvaro Pascual-Leone did a study validating the importance of visualization. A group of volunteers practiced a five-finger piano exercise while neurotransmitters monitored their brain activity. As expected, neuroimaging revealed that the motor cortex was active while practicing the exercise. Then researchers told the participants to mentally rehearse the piano exercise in their mind. The motor cortex was just as active while mentally rehearsing as it was during physical practice. Researchers came to this conclusion: imagined movements trigger synaptic changes at the cortical level.

That study confirmed statistically what athletes already knew instinctually. Mental rehearsal is just as important or more important as physical practice. It's mind over matter. And that is a testament to the power of right-brain imagination and the importance of well-defined dreams. When you dream, your mind forms a mental image that becomes both a picture of and a map to your destiny. That picture of the future is one dimension of faith, and the way you frame it is by circling it in prayer.

In 1992, a Canadian swimmer named Mark Tewksbury won the gold medal in the 200-meter backstroke at the Barcelona Olympics. When he stepped onto the gold medal stand, it wasn't the first time he had done so. He stood on the gold medal stand the night before the race and imagined it before it happened. He visualized every detail of the race in his mind's eye, including his come-from-behind victory by a fingertip.

The Australian sailing team did the same thing in preparation for the 1983 America's Cup. The coach made a tape of the Australian team beating the American team three years before the race. He narrated the race with the background sound of a sailboat cutting through the water. Every member of the team was required to listen to that tape twice a day for three years. By the time they set sail from San Diego Bay, they had already beaten the American team 2,190 times in their imagination.

The simple act of imagining doesn't just remap your mind; it forms a map. And that is the purpose of goal setting. If dreams are the destination, goals are the GPS that gets you there. So before sharing my life goal list, let me retrace my steps and explain how I arrived at them.

Ten Steps to Goal Setting

Goals are as unique as we are. They should reflect our unique personality and passions. And we arrive at them via different avenues. But these ten steps to goal setting can guide us as we circle our life goals.

1. Start with Prayer

Prayer is the best way to jump-start the process of goal setting. I highly recommend a personal retreat or season of fasting. I came up with my original life goal list during a two-day retreat at Rocky Gap Lodge in Cumberland, Maryland. The relaxed schedule gave me the margin I needed to dream big, pray hard, and think long. My original list only contained twenty-five goals. During a ten-day fast a few years later I revised and expanded the list.

If you set goals in the context of prayer, there is a much higher likelihood that your goals will glorify God, and if they don't glorify God, then they aren't worth setting in the first place. So start with prayer.

2. Check Your Motives

If you set selfish goals, you would be better off spiritually if you didn't accomplish them. That's why you need to check your motives.

You need to take a long, honest look in the mirror and make sure you're going after your goals for the right reasons.

One of our goals — to create a family foundation — was inspired by my role as a trustee for a charitable foundation. The man who created the trust was tragically struck and killed by an automobile while visiting London, but he had written the trust into his will. It's been almost two decades since his death, but his legacy is the hundreds of ministries that have received seed money in the form of a grant. No matter how much or how little money we make, that legacy of generosity is inspiring us to do something similar as a family.

By sharing my list of life goals, I know I'm risking my reputation because the motivation behind some of my goals can be easily misinterpreted. Owning a vacation home, for example, may seem selfish, but our motivation is to use that home to bless pastors who can't afford to take a vacation. Why? Because others have blessed us in that way when we couldn't afford a vacation. Yes, we would love a place to escape to, because we live in an urban setting. Yes, it's one way to diversify our portfolio and save for retirement. But our deepest motive is to simply return the blessing.

For the record, this goal has not been checked off the list because in prioritizing our goals, this one is near the bottom of the list. We won't go after this goal at the expense of our giving goals, because our giving goals take precedence over all other financially related goals. More than a decade ago, I had a paradigm shift when it comes to finances. I stopped setting "getting goals" and started setting "giving goals." All of our financial goals are giving goals because that is our focus. Our motivation for making more is giving more. After all, you make a living by what you get, but you make a life by what you give.

3. Think in Categories

It is hard to pull life goals out of thin air, so I recommend looking at the life goal lists of others. Don't cut and paste someone else's goals, but it's a great way of getting your own ideas.

Another trick that has helped me is thinking in categories. My goals are divided into five categories: (1) family, (2) influential, (3) experiential, (4) physical, and (5) travel. The obvious omission is a category for spiritual goals, but that is by intention. All of my goals have a spiritual dimension to them. Some of them are obviously spiritual, like taking each of my children on a mission trip or reading the Bible from cover to cover in seven different translations, but running a triathlon with my son was a spiritual experience as well. Any goal that cultivates physical discipline will cultivate spiritual disciplines too.

Even the seemingly least spiritual goal on my list, going to a Super Bowl, turned out to have a spiritual component to it. After the Packers won the 2010 NFC championship game, I tweeted that I would preach for tickets. I was half joking, but a pastor-friend in Dallas, Bryan Jarrett, took me seriously. I would never have spent the money to buy tickets myself, but I was happy to preach for them. To top it off, Super Bowl XLV happened to fall on Josiah's birthday, and he got to go with me! For one day, I think I won the Best Dad of the Day award. Of course, the downside is that it's all downhill from there. He'll never get another birthday gift that comes close to that one! Neither of us will ever forget that experience, but what made the experience even more meaningful is that I got to preach the gospel. I was thrilled to be part of the Super Bowl celebration, but that celebration pales in comparison to the celebration in heaven over anyone who put their faith in Christ the morning I preached. That goal ended up being one of the greatest win-win experiences of my life.

4. Be Specific

Just like our prayers, our goals need to be specific. If a goal isn't measurable, we have no way of knowing whether we've accomplished it. Losing weight isn't a goal if we don't have a target weight within a target timeline.

One of the ways I've increased the specificity of my goals is by attaching ages to them. I want to complete a triathlon in my fifties and sixties. Those are two separate goals that are time-stamped. I've also added nuances that make my goals more meaningful. I don't just want to see the Eiffel Tower; I want to kiss Lora on top of the Eiffel Tower.

It was extremely difficult to attach numbers to some of my giving goals and writing goals, but I decided it was better to aim high and fall short than to aim low and hit the target. And it's OK to make revisions to our visions.

I cannot control how many books I sell, and that has never been my focus. I write because I'm called to write. But I was inspired by a goal that was set by Jack Canfield and Mark Hansen, coauthors of the Chicken Soup for the Soul series. Their books have sold more than 80 million copies, and their 2020 vision is to sell a billion books and give $500 million to charity. I love the motivation and specificity of that goal.

One of the life goals that Lora and I have is to eventually live 90/10. In other words, we want to live off of 10 percent of our income and give away 90 percent. That goal was inspired while reading a biography of J.C. Penney, the founder of the department store by the same name. He started out giving 10 percent and living off of 90 percent, but by the end of his life he was giving 90 percent and living off of 10 percent. Each year, Lora and I try to increase the percentage of income we're giving back to God. Living 80/20 and 50/50 are benchmarks along the way. Eventually, our goal is to reverse tithe or give God a 90/10 split.

Since we're on the subject of J.C. Penney, it's worth sharing what he said about the importance of goals. "Give me a stock clerk with a goal, and I will give you a man who will make history," said Penney. "Give me a man without a goal, and I will give you a stock clerk."

5. Write It Down

I have a saying that I repeat to our family and our staff all the time: "The shortest pencil is longer than the longest memory." If you haven't written down your goals, you haven't really set them. Something powerful happens when you verbalize a goal, whether in a conversation or in a journal. And it's more than a good idea; it's a God idea:

"Record the vision and inscribe it on tablets."

On more than one occasion, I've been able to achieve a goal almost immediately after setting it. A few years ago, I blogged about a new goal that I had just added to my list: visiting the Castle Church in Wittenberg, Germany, where Martin Luther posted his ninety-five theses and sparked the Protestant Reformation. The very next day I got an invitation to be part of a gathering of leaders and thinkers to discuss what the next Reformation might look like. The place? Wittenberg, Germany. And our gathering took place on Reformation Day!

At some point in the process of goal setting, you need to muster the courage to verbalize it. That act of verbalization is an act of faith. When you write down a goal, it holds you accountable. The same goes for a prayer journal. I used to think that written prayers were less spiritual because they were less spontaneous. I now think the opposite. A written prayer requires more faith simply because it's harder to write it than to say it. But the beautiful thing about written prayers in particular and prayer journals in general is that you have a written record of your prayer. Too often we fail to celebrate an answer to prayer simply because we forget what we asked for before God answers!

6. Include Others

I used to have a lot of personal goals, but I have replaced most of them with shared goals. Nothing cements a relationship like a shared goal. Goals are relational glue. And God set the standard with the Great Commission. If you want to grow closer to God, go after the God-sized goal He set nearly two thousand years ago. I've also discovered that when you go after a goal with another person, it doubles your joy.

One of my travel goals is to spend a night on Catalina Island with Lora. I fell in love with the idyllic island when I first visited it ten years ago. I strolled the streets and toured the town. I even checked a life goal off my list by parasailing over the Pacific. It was a magical day, but I was by myself, and it wasn't the same without Lora. All day I kept thinking to myself, *I wish Lora was here.* So one of my goals is to take Lora there someday so we can experience it together.

Many of my goals revolve around my family. They are tailored to the unique personality and passions of my wife and children. Josiah is the biggest football fan, so he got in on the goal of going to the Super Bowl. My daughter, Summer, is a gifted swimmer, so I thought swimming the Escape from Alcatraz, a 1.5-mile swim from Alcatraz Island to San Francisco, would be a great goal for us to go after. And Parker has my adventure gene, so he went with me to Peru last year to hike the Inca Trail to Machu Picchu.

One of the most important life goals on my list is creating a discipleship covenant for my sons. I think I've made more mistakes than the average father, but I knew I needed to get this right. When Parker turned twelve, I had circled his birthday in prayer. I spent months praying and planning a discipleship covenant with three components: spiritual, intellectual, and physical. The physical challenge was training for and completing a sprint triathlon. The intellectual challenge was reading a dozen books together. The spiritual challenge included reading through the New Testament, identifying our core values, and putting together his first life goal list.

At the end of that year, we celebrated the completion of the covenant by going after a life goal on both of our lists: hiking the Grand Canyon from rim to rim. Those two days will forever rank as two of the most challenging and fulfilling days of my life. We made the 23.6-mile hike in July as temperatures climbed above 120 degrees Fahrenheit. I lost thirteen pounds in two days! It was one of the hardest things I've ever done, but that is what made it so memorable. I'll never forget the feeling as my son and I ascended the Bright Angel Trail and made it to the top of the South Rim. The first thing we did was get a vanilla ice cream cone at the concession stand. Then we just stood on the rim looking back at the trail we had traversed. No one can take that moment or that memory from us.

7. Celebrate along the Way

When you accomplish a goal, celebrate it. When God answers a prayer, throw a party. We should celebrate with the same intensity with which we pray. One of my favorite Hebrew words is *ebenezer*. It means "thus far the LORD has helped us." When you accomplish a God-ordained goal, it is an *ebenezer* moment. You need to find a unique way to celebrate it and commemorate it. Whenever I write a new book, for example, our family celebrates with a special meal on the day the book is released. And I get to choose the restaurant!

One of my favorite family traditions is dinner at Tony Cheng's in Chinatown on New Year's Eve. We go around the table, sharing our favorite memories from the past year, and it's amazing how many of those memories were once goals. Taking Summer to her first Broadway play, learning to snowboard with Parker, and celebrating an anniversary in Italy with Lora are some of my greatest memories, but like all memories, they started out as imaginations. Setting goals is the way you turn imaginations into memories, and once you do, you need to celebrate them.

8. Dream Big

Your life goal list will include goals that are big and small. It will include goals that are short-term and long-term. But I have one piece of advice: Make sure you have a few BHAGs on the list. You need some God-sized goals that qualify as crazy. Here's why: big goals turn us into big people.

One of my crazy goals is to make a movie. I have no idea how this goal will be accomplished. If I had to guess, it's more likely I'll write a screenplay than land a role as a stunt double. But who knows? I have no idea how it will happen, but this motivation traces all the way back to one of my earliest memories. When I was five years old, I put my faith in Christ after watching a movie called *The Hiding Place*. Somehow God used the medium of a movie to save my soul. I'd like to make a movie that does the same for someone else.

9. Think Long

Most of us overestimate what we can accomplish in two years, but we underestimate what we can accomplish in ten years. If we want to dream big, we need to think long. Big dreams often translate into long goals. My goal of leading National Community Church to give $25 million to missions won't happen next year, but if we give faithfully and sacrificially over the next twenty-five years, we'll get there. And Lora and I want to lead the way with one of our long goals: giving away $10 million over our lifetime.

Remember the question that Honi the circle maker grappled with his entire life? *Is it possible for a man to dream continuously for seventy years?* If you want to dream until the day you die, you need to set goals that take a lifetime to achieve. And it's never too late to start.

My octogenarian uncle, Ken Knappen, always dreamed of writing a book, but he didn't accomplish that goal until he was in his eighties. *Is it possible for a man to dream continuously for seventy years?* Evidently it's possible to dream into your mid-eighties and beyond.

The sad truth is that most people spend more time planning their summer vacation than they do planning the rest of their life. That's poor stewardship of right-brain imagination. Goal setting is good stewardship. Instead of letting things happen, goals help us make things happen. Instead of living by default, goals help us live by design. Instead of living out of memory, goals help us live out of imagination.

10. Pray Hard

Goal setting begins and ends with prayer. God-ordained goals are conceived in the context of prayer, and prayer is what brings them to full term. You need to keep circling your goals in prayer, like the Israelites circled Jericho. As you circle your goals, it not only creates God-ordained opportunities; it also helps us recognize God-ordained opportunities by sanctifying our reticular activating system.

The Reticular Activating System

At the base of the brain stem lies a cluster of nerve cells called the reticular activating system. We are constantly bombarded by countless stimuli vying for our attention, and it is the job of the reticular activating system to determine what gets noticed and what goes unnoticed. Like a radar system, the RAS determines what makes a blip.

When God gave us the dream of starting a coffeehouse, I immediately started noticing everything about every coffeehouse I visited. Before the dream, the only thing I noticed was the taste of my drink. After the dream, I noticed everything from signage and seating to store layout and product branding. The dream of starting a coffeehouse created a category in my reticular activating system, and I started collecting ideas.

This is why goal setting is so important. It creates a category in your reticular activating system, and you start noticing anything and everything that will help you accomplish the goal. Prayer is important for the same reason. It sanctifies your RAS so you notice what God wants you to notice. The more you pray, the more you notice.

It's no coincidence that being watchful and prayerful are coupled by the apostle Paul in his letter to the Colossians: "Devote yourselves to prayer, being watchful and thankful." The word *watchful* is a throwback to the ancient watchmen whose job it was to sit on the city walls and scan the horizon for attacking armies or trading caravans. They saw sooner and further than anyone else. Prayer opens our spiritual eyes so we see sooner and further.

The Aramaic word for *prayer* means "to set a trap." Prayer is the way we take thoughts and dreams and ideas captive. And one way to set prayer traps is by keeping a prayer journal. In my opinion, journaling is one of the most overlooked and underappreciated spiritual disciplines. Journaling is the difference between learning and remembering. It's also the difference between forgetting and fulfilling our goals.

Life Goal List

My life goal list is always morphing, but here is the latest evolution. Some of the goals may seem grandiose, while others seem trivial. Obviously, travel goals are not as significant as financial goals, which aren't as important as family goals. The goals are not ranked in terms of importance or priority. The goals that are italicized are the ones I've already accomplished at the time of this writing.

Family Goals

- ☐ 1. Celebrate our fiftieth wedding anniversary.
- ☐ 2. Dedicate my great-grandchildren to the Lord.
- ☑ 3. *Celebrate an anniversary in Italy.*
- ☐ 4. Celebrate an anniversary in the Caribbean.
- ☐ 5. Take each child on a mission trip.
- ☑ 6. *Coach a sports team for each child.*
- ☐ 7. Pay for our grandchildren's college education.

☑ 8. *Create a family foundation.*

☐ 9. Leave an inheritance for our children.

☐ 10. Write an autobiography.

☑ 11. *Create a discipleship covenant.*

☐ 12. Take each child on a rite of passage pilgrimage.

☑ 13. *Create a family coat of arms.*

☐ 14. Research our family genealogy.

☐ 15. Find and visit an ancestor's grave in Sweden.

☐ 16. Take our grandchildren to a state fair.

☐ 17. Go on a camping trip with our grandchildren.

☐ 18. Take our grandchildren to Disney World.

☐ 19. Celebrate a family reunion on a cruise ship.

☐ 20. Celebrate a family reunion in Alexandria, Minnesota.

Influence Goals

☐ 21. Write twenty-five-plus nonfiction books.

☐ 22. Pastor one church for forty-plus years.

☐ 23. Help 1,000,000 dads disciple their sons.

☐ 24. Speak at a college commencement.

☑ 25. *Speak at an NFL chapel.*

☐ 26. Write a *New York Times* bestseller.

☐ 27. Write a fiction title.

☑ 28. *Start a mentoring group for pastors.*

☐ 29. Create a conference for writers.

☑ 30. *Create a conference for pastors.*

☑ 31. *Teach a college course.*

☐ 32. Lead National Community Church to 10,000-plus in weekly attendance.

☐ 33. Baptize 3,000 people in the same place at the same time.

☐ 34. Build an orphanage in Ethiopia.

☐ 35. Build a vacation home.

☐ 36. Get a doctoral degree.

☐ 37. Start a chain of coffeehouses that give their net profits to kingdom causes.

☐ 38. Help plant 100-plus churches.

☐ 39. Make a movie.

☐ 40. Host a radio or television program.

Experiential Goals

☑ 41. *Take Summer to a Broadway play.*

☑ 42. *Hike the Inca Trail to Machu Picchu with Parker.*

☑ 43. *Go to a Super Bowl with Josiah.*

☐ 44. Spend a night on Catalina Island with Lora.

☑ 45. *Go paragliding with Parker.*

☐ 46. Go skydiving.

☑ 47. *Go cliff jumping.*

☐ 48. Go to a cowboy camp with my boys.

☐ 49. Take Parker to a film festival.

☑ 50. *Learn how to snowboard.*

☐ 51. Learn how to surf.

☑ 52. *Take a helicopter ride over the Grand Canyon.*

☐ 53. Take a rafting trip through the Grand Canyon.

☐ 54. Take a three-month sabbatical.

☐ 55. Do a silent retreat at a monastery.

☐ 56. Go on an overnight canoe trip with one of my kids.

☐ 57. Drive a race car with one of my kids.

☐ 58. Read the Bible from cover to cover
in seven translations.

☐ 59. Take a hot air balloon ride.

☑ 60. *Go horseback riding as a family.*

☐ 61. Spend a night in a tree house hotel.

☑ 62. *Go to a Packers' game at Lambeau Field.*

☐ 63. Hike the Camino de Santiago in Spain.

☐ 64. Run with the bulls in Pamplona.

☑ 65. *Play a round of golf at St Andrews in Scotland.*

☑ 66. *See the Stone of Destiny at Edinburgh Castle.*

☐ 67. Do a stand-up comedy routine.

☐ 68. Take Lora to the Oscars.

☐ 69. Go to a TED Conference.

☐ 70. Take a mission trip to five different continents.

Physical Goals

☑ 71. *Hike the Grand Canyon from rim to rim.*

☐ 72. Climb a 14er (mountain over 14,000 feet tall).

☐ 73. Swim the Escape from Alcatraz with Summer.

☐ 74. Run a 10K with one of our kids.

☐ 75. Run a triathlon with Parker and Josiah.

☐ 76. Dunk a basketball in my forties.

☐ 77. Bench-press 250-plus pounds in my fifties.

☐ 78. Run a triathlon in my sixties.

☑ 79. *Run a half marathon.*

☐ 80. Bike a century (100-mile trip).

☐ 81. Run an urbanathlon (urban obstacle-course race).

Financial Goals

☐ 82. Be debt free by fifty-five.

☐ 83. Give back every penny we've earned from National Community Church.

☐ 84. Live off 10 percent and give 90 percent by the time we retire.

☐ 85. Give away $10-plus million.

☐ 86. Lead National Community Church to give $25,000,000 to missions.

Travel Goals

☐ 87. Retrace one of Paul's missionary journeys.

☐ 88. Take an RV vacation as a family.

☑ 89. *Hike to the top of Half Dome in Yosemite National Park.*

☑ 90. *Stay at the Ahwahnee Hotel in Yosemite.*

☑ 91. *Visit the Biltmore mansion.*

☑ 92. *Stay at Old Faithful Inn in Yellowstone National Park.*

☑ 93. *Hike to Inspiration Point near Jenny Lake in Grand Teton National Park.*

☑ 94. *Go to a Western rodeo.*

☐ 95. Climb to the rock-hewn churches in Lalibela, Ethiopia.

☐ 96. Visit the monasteries of Meteora in Greece.

☐ 97. Go on an African safari.

☐ 98. Walk the Via Dolorosa in the Holy Land.

☐ 99. Visit Jerusalem during a Jewish holiday.

☐ 100. See a kangaroo in Australia.

☐ 101. Snorkel the Great Barrier Reef in Australia.

☐ 102. Kiss Lora on top of the Eiffel Tower in France.

☐ 103. Climb Mount Kilimanjaro.

☐ 104. See the aurora borealis.

☐ 105. Go kayaking in Alaska.

☑ 106. *Visit the Castle Church in Wittenberg, Germany.*

☐ 107. Take a boat cruise down the Rhine River.

☐ 108. Ride a gondola in Venice.

☐ 109. See the sunrise on Cadillac Mountain in Acadia National Park.

☐ 110. Hike the trails in Haleakala National Park in Hawaii.

☑ 111. *Straddle the equator.*

☑ 112. *See the Blue Grotto sea cave in Italy.*

☐ 113. Visit the Parthenon in Athens, Greece.

☐ 114. Take a carriage ride through Central Park in New York City.

☐ 115. Stay at the Grand Hotel on Mackinac Island.

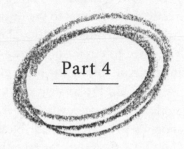

Part 4

Keep Circling

The most recent life goal checked off my list was hiking Half Dome in Yosemite National Park with my son, Parker. In terms of degree of difficulty, it ranks right behind hiking the Inca Trail to Machu Picchu and hiking the Grand Canyon from rim to rim. It was a 15.5-mile hike with a 4,800-foot ascent. But the hardest part wasn't the physical challenge; the hardest part was facing my fear of heights and climbing the cables that scaled the sixty-degree slope to the summit.

On the morning of the hike, I glanced up at Half Dome from the valley floor, and this thought crossed my mind: *How in the world are we going to get up there?* It seemed next to impossible, but the answer was quite simple: *one step at a time.* That's how you accomplish any goal. You can climb the highest mountain if you simply put one foot in front of the other and refuse to stop until you reach the top.

Drawing prayer circles is a lot like climbing a mountain. The dream or promise or miracle may seem impossible, but if you keep circling, anything is possible. With each prayer, there is a small change in elevation. With each prayer, you are one step closer to the answer.

After my hike to Half Dome, I came to this realization: The degree of satisfaction is directly proportional to the degree of difficulty. The harder the climb, the sweeter the summit. The same is true with prayer. The more you have to circle something in prayer, the more satisfying it is spiritually. And, often, the more glory God gets.

Until recently, I wanted God to answer every prayer ASAP. That is no longer my agenda. I don't want easy answers or quick answers because I have a tendency to mishandle the blessings that come too easily or too quickly. I take the credit or take them for granted. So now I pray that it will take long enough and be hard enough for God to receive all of the glory. I'm not looking for the path of least resistance; I'm looking for the path of greatest glory. And that requires high-degree-of-difficulty prayers and lots of circling.

Very rarely does our first prayer request hit the bull's-eye of God's good, pleasing, and perfect will. Most prayer requests have to be refined. Even "the prayer that saved a generation" didn't hit the bull's-eye the first time. Honi refined his request twice: "Not for such rain have I prayed." He wasn't satisfied with a sprinkle or torrential downpour. It took three attempts to spell out exactly what he wanted: "rain of Your favor, blessing, and graciousness." Honi drew a circle in the sand. Then he drew a circle within a circle within a circle.

One of the reasons we get frustrated in prayer is our ASAP approach. When our prayers aren't answered as quickly or easily as we would like, we get tired of circling. Maybe we need to change our prayer approach from *as soon as possible* to *as long as it takes*.

Keep circling!

Chapter 16

Double Miracle

When you live by faith, it often feels like you are risking your reputation. You're not. You're risking God's reputation. It's not your faith that is on the line. It's His faithfulness. Why? Because God is the one who made the promise, and He is the only one who can keep it. The battle doesn't belong to you; it belongs to God. And because the battle doesn't belong to you, neither does the glory. God answers prayer to bring glory to His name, the name that is above all names.

Drawing prayer circles isn't about proving yourself to God; it's about giving God an opportunity to prove Himself to you. Just in case you have forgotten — and to ensure that you always remember — *God is for you*. I can't promise that God will always give you the answer you want. I can't promise that He'll answer on your timeline. But I can promise this: *He answers every prayer, and He keeps every promise.* That is who He is. That is what He does. And if you have the faith to dream big, pray hard, and think long, there is nothing God loves more than proving His faithfulness.

The son of the daughter of Honi the circle maker, Hanan ha-Nehba, carried on his grandfather's legacy in spirit and in deed. When Israel was in need of rain, the sages sent schoolchildren to take hold of the hem of his garment and ask for rain. Hanan ha-Nehba captured his grandfather's heart and the heart of the heavenly Father with a simple prayer: "Master of the universe, do it for the sake of these little ones, who do not know the difference between the Father who can give rain and a papa who cannot."

Despite what skeptics may say, God is not offended by your big dreams or bold prayers. He's a proud Papa. The religious establishment criticized Honi for drawing a circle and demanding rain, but it gave God an opportunity to prove His power and His love. That's what God wants. And that's what prayer does.

Make No Small Plans

"Make no little plans; they have no magic to stir men's blood." These words are attributed to architect and visionary Daniel Burnham. After serving as the principal architect of the Chicago World's Fair in 1893, he set his sights on a grand vision — Washington's Grand Terminal.

It took an army of laborers an entire year and four million cubic yards of fill dirt just to fill in the swamp that would become the foundation of Union Station. That's enough dirt to pack eighty thousand train hoppers stretching six hundred miles. Five years and $25 million dollars later, Burnham's vision became a reality as the Baltimore and Ohio Pittsburgh Express whistled into Union Station at 6:50 a.m. on October 27, 1907.

Over the next century, kings and queens would walk its corridors. During both World Wars, countless servicemen and servicewomen kissed their sweethearts good-bye as they went off to war. And after a $160 million restoration in the early 1980s, the modernized metro stop and mall would become the most visited destination in Washington, DC.

It's hard to walk through Union Station without hearing the echo of Daniel Burnham's words: "Make no little plans." It's almost as though the grand ceilings lift the ceiling on your dreams. For thirteen amazing years, National Community Church met in the movie theaters at Union Station, and that is where we learned to dream big dreams for God. When those movie theaters closed in the fall of 2009, it felt like the train had left the station and we missed it. It was one of the greatest disappointments of my life, and we mourned that loss for months. I honestly didn't believe we would find a replacement that could even begin to compare with the visibility and accessibility Union Station afforded us.

I was wrong.

Standing Room Only

Sometimes we act as though God is surprised by the things that surprise us, but by definition, the Omniscient One cannot be surprised. God is always a step ahead, even when we feel like He's a step behind. He's always got a holy surprise up His sovereign sleeve.

When the doors of the movie theaters closed at Union Station, it felt like we were caught between the Red Sea and the Egyptian army. I didn't understand why God let it happen, and I didn't know where to go or what to do. I was full of questions. I was full of doubts. But I was also standing on the promise I had circled in Exodus 14: "Stand still, and see the salvation of the LORD." I just didn't know we would have to stand still for a year and a half.

We were caught off guard by the theater closure, but God had already perfectly prepared us for what He knew would happen next. As a multisite church with five locations at the time, we had the flexibility to handle the redistribution of our congregation. Plus our coffeehouse, with performance space, was less than a block from the Station. The problem was that our coffeehouse couldn't handle the capacity. We knew it was a temporary solution as we searched high and low for a year and a half, but we found nothing. It was discouraging because we were working like it depends on us and praying like it depends on God, but it was encouraging for the same reason. We had peace because we were praying through. We knew that our inability to find an alternate meeting space wasn't for lack of trying or lack of praying.

We continued to stand still until we had standing room only. At one point, we joked that we wanted to reach everyone on the Hill except the fire marshal, but it wasn't really a joke. We were squeezing twice as many people into the performance space as it was designed for, and we were doing it four times a weekend. When we started turning people away, we got desperate.

Then one day I was driving down Barracks Row, the main street of Capitol Hill, and I noticed The Peoples' Church. It's impossible to miss because of the movie theater marquee that has graced the facade for the last century.

Location, Location, Location

Barracks Row was the first commercial street in the nation's capital because of its proximity to the Navy Yard, which was established in 1799. New arrivals to Washington arrived at those docks and ate their first meal or spent their first night on 8th Street. In 1801, Thomas Jefferson selected 8th Street as the location for barracks for the Marine Corps, giving the area its designation as Barracks Row. The Row flourished for a century and a half, but the 1968 riots in DC drove businesses out of the area and left Barracks Row languishing. It looked like a ghost town from the triple-feature Westerns that once played at the theater on the Row.

In the late 1990s, a revitalization effort culminated with the 2005 Great American Main Street Award from the National Trust for Historic Preservation. Facades were restored to their original grandeur; mom-and-pop shops brought a unique feeling of community back to the area; and a wide variety of creative restaurant concepts reestablished the nightlife.

When the Fourth of July parade route returned to 8th Street a few years ago, Barracks Row was once again the Main Street of Capitol Hill. That parade route begins at our property on 8th and Virginia, passes by The Peoples' Church three blocks north, and ends at 8th and Pennsylvania Avenue.

If God had said, "I'll give you any place you want to relaunch your Union Station location," I would have chosen The Peoples' Church. It had location, location, location. But I felt bad thinking it and almost dismissed the thought for an obvious reason: The Peoples' Church met there. At the same time, I felt prompted to call the pastor, and I learned a valuable lesson after the Holy Spirit prompted me to call Robert Thomas a decade earlier: You never know what answer you might receive if you make the call. That single phone call led to the purchase of 205 F Street, which led to the purchase of 201 F Street, which led to Ebenezer's Coffeehouse. I had no idea that this phone call would lead to a double miracle, but I knew I needed to make the call.

Double Time

I Googled The Peoples' Church and found a phone number for their pastor, Michael Hall. Before I could even introduce myself, he told me that he had heard about our predicament with the closing of Union Station. He was as cordial as cordial can be. In fact, he offered to let us use their church temporarily until we could find a permanent solution. I declined the gracious offer because it wasn't during a time slot that would alleviate our space problems, but I was humbled by the offer.

A few weeks later, we had lunch at Matchbox, one my favorite restaurants on Barracks Row located a few doors down from The Peoples' Church. I immediately knew I had found a new friend. I was shocked to find out that he was seventy-one, because he doesn't look a day over fifty-five. It must be in the genes. His ninety-one-year-old mother is still preaching.

Michael told me that his parents, Fred and Charlotte Hall, had purchased the old Academy Theatre in 1962 and started The Peoples' Church. He told me that the demographics of the church had changed in the past decade, and most members now commuted in from Maryland. And he told me they almost sold the church a few years before for financial reasons, but the deal fell through because the Capitol Hill community didn't want a nightclub going in, plus the church itself voted unanimously against selling.

A month later, we had lunch again. I felt like God was prompting me to ask him if they would consider selling the church. I honestly didn't care whether the answer was yes or no; I just hoped he wouldn't be offended by the question. He wasn't offended at all, but the answer was no.

The more I got to know Pastor Michael Hall and his wife, Terry, the more I liked them and respected them. They told me about the wonderful history of the church. They told me about the unique joys of being white pastors of a primarily African-American congregation. And they told me about their vision for the future. At age seventy-one, most people are slowing down. Not Michael Hall. He has the spirit of Caleb, who was as strong at eight-five as he was at forty.

Six months later, I felt prompted to ask Michael again if they would consider selling the church. Once again, he said no, but he also said, "Mark, if we ever sell the church, we want you to have it." Then in February 2011, I felt prompted to ask one more time. I honestly didn't want to do it. The pressure for space at our church continued to increase as each month went by, but at that point, I valued my relationship with Michael and Terry far more than the real estate. If it wasn't what was best for The Peoples' Church, then it wasn't what was best for National Community Church. If it wasn't a win for them, it wasn't a win for us. It had to be a win-win, and I told them that. For a third time, the answer was no, but Michael also said he would pray about it, and I knew he meant it.

Two days later, on my way to Super Bowl XLV, I got a text from Michael telling me that God changed his heart. He felt it wasn't just the miracle we had been praying for; he felt it was the miracle *they* had been praying for too. I was shocked, not just by the text, but by the fact that a seventy-one-year-old pastor texts! That was the first miracle. The second miracle would be convincing a congregation that a few years before had voted unanimously not to sell. The third miracle would be finding property in Maryland where most of their members live. I thought those miracles could take years, if they happened at all, but when God moves, God moves. After a year and a half of standing still, the second and third miracles happened in less than one week. God did a double miracle in double time.

Double Miracle

On March 23, 2011, I met with Michael to sign the contract to purchase The Peoples' Church. It had only taken them a couple days to find their piece of Promised Land on Branch Avenue, the main artery that runs through the heart of Prince George's County in Maryland. Right as we were getting ready to sign the contract, their realtor called and told them that the owner had knocked $375,000 off the sale price of $795,000.

Only God.

Michael could have gotten that phone call right before or right after our meeting, but God's timing is impeccable. It felt like 375,000 confirmations. And that's not the only miracle. Within twenty-four hours of signing the contract, we received a $1.5 million matching gift that got us halfway toward our purchase price of $3 million. It was like God parted the Red Sea, and both churches walked through on dry ground. We were headed to Barracks Row; they were headed to Maryland. And we passed each other in the middle of the Red Sea, praising God for our double miracle.

We thought it would take at least three years to construct our new campus on the property we had miraculously purchased at 8th and Virginia Avenue. Then God gave us a stepping-stone three blocks away: The Peoples' Church. Here's the great irony. Our phase-one auditorium was going to be an art deco theater. It's almost like God said, "I've already built what you've dreamed of." So God did in three weeks what we thought would take three years. In His providence, God gave a church with a vision to meet in movie theaters at metro stops an old movie theater two blocks from the Eastern Market metro stop.

I pray that I have half the courage of Michael Hall when I'm seventy-one. It took courage to leave the comfort of a place where they had met as a church for forty-nine years. It took courage to start all over again and replant The Peoples' Church in Maryland. But it's as much a miracle for them as it is for us. Not only does the sale cancel all of their existing debt; they can also purchase their property and build their building debt free. But the thing that most excites them is that they'll have enough cash left over to begin giving to missions again, which has been their heartbeat from the very beginning.

Long story short, a miracle for them + a miracle for us = a double miracle.

One footnote.

I wasn't the only one doing a Daniel fast at the beginning of 2011. Michael Hall was doing one too! Coincidence? I think not. As I look back on it, the only way this double miracle goes down is if both of us had been fasting and praying. It was prayer and fasting that gave me the courage to ask him a third time if they would sell, and prayer and fasting gave him the courage to say yes. When Michael told me he would pray, he was in a season of fasting. I believe that his open mind was the result of an empty stomach. And when two people fast and pray like Daniel, it makes double miracles possible.

And one more footnote. This one goes back more than fifty years. Let me retrace the circle.

Prophetic Prayer

In 1960, an evangelist named R.W. Shambach preached a revival in Washington, DC for church planters Fred and Charlotte Hall. Without them even knowing it, Shambach laid hands on the Academy Theatre and prayed that God would give it to them. That prayer was answered in 1962 when The Peoples' Church purchased that old theater and turned it into a place of worship. They faithfully served God and the community there for forty-nine years.

Shambach also prayed what I believe was a prophetic prayer over that theater. As he laid hands on that building, he bound it for God's glory: "May this place always be used for God's glory."

That prophetic prayer resurfaced one day over lunch. Michael said he knew that prayer was the reason that the nightclub deal fell through. He also knew that we were the fulfillment of that prayer. I knew it too.

It's hard to describe the feeling when you know that a fifty-year-old prayer is being answered and you're right in the middle of the miracle. Shambach's prayer was a binding prayer that sealed the theater for God's glory forever. Like a time capsule, it was opened and answered fifty years later.

Every prayer is a time capsule. You never know when or where or how God is going to answer it, but He will answer it. There is no expiration date, and there are no exceptions. God answers prayer. Period. We don't always see it or understand it, but God always answers.

We can live with holy anticipation because God is ordering our footsteps. When R.W. Shambach laid hands on that theater in 1960, he prayed a circle around it. Then I double circled it in 1996 without even knowing it. It didn't even dawn on me until we were about to seal the deal that I had prayed a circle around The Peoples' Church when I did my prayer walk all the way around Capitol Hill. I walked right down 8th Street. I walked right under the marquee. Without even knowing it, I had double circled that double miracle fifteen years before.

After signing the contract, I e-mailed a banker-friend who has financed some of our dreams. I had recently told him about my prayer walk around Capitol Hill, so he knew this was the fourth piece of Promised Land I had walked by — along with our first office at 205 F Street NE, our coffeehouse at 201 F Street NE, and the last piece of property on Capitol Hill at 8th and Virginia Avenue — that God had now given us. He jokingly asked me, "Are there any other properties you walked by that I need to know about?" My response: "I did walk by the Capitol. Who knows?"

You can't never always sometimes tell.

Chapter 17

Bottled Prayer

I love the ending of the book of Daniel. Daniel is thinking long and thinking out loud. In his final vision of the book, he asks the question that all of us want the answer to: "My lord, what will the outcome of all this be?" Well, God always answers, but it's not always a straight answer. This certainly doesn't mean it's not an honest answer; it just means it's far too complicated, with infinite twists and turns, for our logical left brains to comprehend.

"Go your way, Daniel, because the words are rolled up and sealed until the time of the end."

I realize this specifically references the prophecies given to Daniel by the Holy Spirit, but I also believe there is a universal principle in this passage. Our prayers are prophecies, and God Almighty seals them until their designated time. He's never early. He's never late. When the time comes, *kairos*, not *chronos*, the prayer will be unsealed and the answer revealed.

At some point, our spoken words cease to exist because they are subject to the law of entropy. Our spoken words, aka sound waves, run into friction and run out of energy. Our prayers, however, are sealed forever. Our prayers never cease to exist because they aren't subject to natural laws, including the law of entropy. The supernatural laws of prayer defy the natural laws of time and space.

While it's impossible to trace the pinball path of a single prayer, our prayers somehow exit our four dimensions of space-time in order to get to the God who exists outside of the four space-time dimensions He created when He said, "Let there be light." Our prayers don't dissipate over time; our prayers accumulate through eternity.

According to the Doppler Effect, our universe is still expanding. The significance is this: The four words that God spoke at the beginning of time, "Let there be light," are still creating galaxies at the edge of the universe. If God can do that with four words, what are you worried about? There is nothing He cannot do. After all, He created everything out of nothing.

His words never return void. Neither do your prayers when you pray the word of God and the will of God. The same God who hovered over the chaos at the beginning of time is hovering over your life, and you never know when His answer will reenter the atmosphere of your life. But you can know this: The Lord is watching over His word to perform it.

As sure as our prayers reach escape velocity and enter God's orbit, the answer will reenter the atmosphere somewhere, somehow, sometime. A binding prayer in 1960 sealed 535 8th Street for the glory of God, and it was unsealed on March 23, 2011. That was the day we put our signatures on a legally binding contract to purchase The Peoples' Church, but the spiritually binding contract was sealed long before.

Prayers Convey

After we signed the contract to purchase The Peoples' Church, Michael and I were talking about what things would legally convey and what things wouldn't. Then, in a moment of revelation, we realized that every prayer ever prayed in that place would be passed on to us. I was so overcome by that realization that tears welled up in my eyes. If The Peoples' Church is anything, it's a praying church. In fact, Michael's parents almost named it The House of Prayer.

We are going to reap what we have not sown. Why? Because The Peoples' Church planted carob trees on Barracks Row, and we will bear the fruit of the seeds our spiritual fathers planted long ago. And it's not just the prayers that pass on; the visions convey too.

A few days after signing the contract, Michael texted me about a vision he had ten years before we met. In his vision he saw young people raising their hands in worship and packing the theater all the way out the front door and onto the sidewalk. Michael said, "I thought it was for us, but I now realize it was for you."

That vision was fulfilled at our first service on our first weekend. It was standing room only. We literally filled every seat, packed the lobby, and spilled out the front door. I wasn't thinking about the vision when I asked everybody to raise their hands during worship, but Michael said it was the picture the Lord had showed him ten years before.

Double Anointing

Do you remember when Elijah gave his mantle to Elisha? It was more than the conveyance of physical property; it was the conveyance of spiritual anointing. It was no coincidence that Elisha did many of the same miracles that Elijah did. That anointing was far more valuable than the mantle.

When I stood beside my father-in-law's casket the day after he died, I had a flood of thoughts and feelings, but my predominant memory was asking for a double portion of his anointing, just like Elisha received from Elijah. I don't think I even knew what I was asking for, but that hasn't kept God from answering that prayer. His answers are omniscient and omnipresent. I asked for a double portion because I wanted to honor his legacy with my ministry, and I believe God has honored that.

I feel the same way about Michael Hall and The Peoples' Church. I pray for a double portion of their anointing. I love the physical building, and I love where it's located. We'll find ways to leverage it creatively and make it a place where church and community cross paths. Like Ebenezer's Coffeehouse, this movie theater will become a postmodern well where our community gathers and the gospel is preached. But far more valuable than the physical property that is transferred are the prayers that pass on. We're the beneficiaries of forty-nine years of accumulated prayers by the saints of God. And every single one of them conveys. Not one of them is lost on God.

Bottled Tears

One of the most beautiful and powerful images in Scripture is found in Psalm 56:8. It's a precious promise that begs to be circled. It's the last promise I'll circle, but maybe it's a place for you to begin circling.

You have collected all my tears in your bottle.

There are many different kinds of tears. There are the tears shed by the mother of a little boy in ICU who is far too young to fight leukemia, but he fights anyway. There are the tears shed by the father of the bride as he walks his daughter down the aisle on her wedding day. There are tears that stain divorce papers, and tears mixed with sweat that stream down the faces of grown men who have just won a national championship. Then there are the tears shed in prayer.

Each and every teardrop is precious to God. They are eternal keepsakes. The day will come when He wipes away every tear in heaven. Until then, God will move heaven and earth to honor every tear that has been shed. Not a single tear is lost on God. He remembers each one. He honors each one. He collects each one.

In much the same way that God bottles our accumulated tears, God collects our prayers. Each one is precious to Him. Each one is sealed by God. And you never know when He's going to uncork an answer.

Sometimes I struggle with fear.

My greatest fear is that my kids might someday walk away from the faith, but I have learned to rebuke that fear, because fear is not of God. Then I remind myself that I have circled Luke 2:52, and I have circled my children with that blessing thousands of times. Those prayers are bottled by God, and the Holy Spirit will unseal them in the lives of my children long after I'm gone.

Sometimes I struggle with doubt.

I'm afraid that I will someday mishandle the blessings of God. Then I remember that I have circled Psalm 84:11: "No good thing does he withhold from those who walk uprightly." All I have to do is stay humble and stay hungry.

Sometimes I struggle with faith.

I'm afraid that the last miracle might be the last miracle. Then I remind myself that I have circled Deuteronomy 33:16: "The favor of him who dwelt in the burning bush" is upon me. I have no idea what the future holds, but I know who holds the future. Your life is in His hands, and your prayers are in His bottle. And like a message in a bottle, your prayers are carried by the current of His sovereign will. When and where they will land no one knows. But those bottled prayers will be unsealed in God's time, in God's way. He will answer somewhere, sometime, somehow. All you have to do is keep circling.

Dream big.

Pray hard.

Think long.

Chapter 18

Now There Was One

In his epic history *Antiquities of the Jews*, Josephus notes the deeds of Honi the circle maker, aka Onias the rainmaker. He documents the first-century drought and points to Honi as Israel's only hope. Josephus makes one statement that punctuates every turning point in history: "now there was one."

> Now there was one, whose name was Onias, a righteous man he was, and beloved of God, who, in a certain drought, prayed to God to put an end to the intense heat, and whose prayers God had heard, and had sent them rain.

Honi stood alone. Then he knelt down in the circle he had drawn. And that's all it takes to change the course of His-story. In the words of theologian Walter Wink, "History belongs to the intercessors."

After the rain fell and the dust settled, Simeon ben Shatah, the ruling head of the Sanhedrin who threatened excommunication, wrote to Honi:

> Were you not Honi, I should decree excommunication against you … But what can I do to you, for you act petulantly before the Omnipresent and he does whatever you want for you …
>
> A generation that was shrouded in darkness did you illuminate through your prayer … A generation that was sunk down you lifted up with your prayer … A generation that was humiliated by its sin you saved by your prayer.

One Prayer Circle

Never underestimate the power of one prayer circle.

When you dream big, pray hard, and think long, there is nothing

God cannot do. After all, He is able to do 15.5 billion light-years beyond what you can ask or imagine. When you draw a circle and drop to your knees, *you can't never always sometimes tell*. It changes the forecast of your life. It's always cloudy with a chance of quail.

You can't fell a fifty-foot wall, but you can march around Jericho. You can't shut the mouths of lions, but you can stop, drop, and pray. You can't make it rain, but you can draw a circle in the sand.

Don't let what you cannot do keep you from doing what you can. Draw the circle. Don't let who you are not keep you from being who you are. You are a circle maker.

There is a Mother Dabney reading this book, I know it. There is a Harriet Beecher Stowe, a Bill Groves, and a Michael Hall.

Now there was one.

All it takes is one person, one prayer.

Why not you?

It's as simple as drawing your first prayer circle, just like I did when I prayed all the way around Capitol Hill. It might be a promise or a problem. It might be a friend or an enemy. It might be a dream or a miracle. I don't know how it's spelled, but you need to spell it out. Then you need to keep circling.

Don't attempt this by yourself. Israel had an army. You need to invite others into your prayer circle. Together you will form a prayer circle. And when two or three agree in prayer, double circling their God-ordained dreams, all bets are off.

Echo through Eternity

At the end of our prayers, we say "Amen," which means "so be it." It signifies the end of a prayer. But the end of a prayer is always just the beginning. It's the beginning of a dream. It's the beginning of a miracle. It's the beginning of a promise.

The legend of Honi the circle maker began with a prayer for rain. Now it's time to reveal the *amen*.

In 63 BC, Palestine was torn in two by a bloody civil war. Hyrcanus II and Aristobulus II — sons of Alexander Jannaeus, king of Judea — met in battle near Jericho. Aristobulus was forced to flee to the temple in Jerusalem to make his last stand. Hyrcanus and his ally, the Arabian sheik Aretas, surrounded the temple with fifty thousand troops. None but the priests and temple guard stood by Aristobulus.

That is when the army of Hyrcanus found the old rainmaker, Honi, who had been in hiding. The superstitious army brought Honi to Hyrcanus, who commanded him to invoke a curse on the defenders of the temple. Honi could not and would not obey the command, even at sword point. Like the prophet Balaam, who refused to curse Israel and prayed a blessing according to his conscience, Honi drew his last circle in the sand.

In one of history's sad ironies, the man who saved a generation with his prayer for rain was put to death because of a prayer that went against the wishes of Hyrcanus. But Honi stayed true to his convictions, not just in life, but also in death. Many years before, a crowd of thirsty souls surrounded Honi as he drew his circle in the sand. Now he was encircled by savage soldiers whose lives he had saved with his prayer for rain. They compelled him to speak, so Honi uttered his last words while living on this earth, but it's a prayer that will echo through all eternity.

O God, the King of the whole world! since those that stand now with me are Your people, and those that are besieged are also Your priests, I beseech You that You will neither hearken to the prayers of those against these, nor bring to effect what these pray against those.

Then those who surrounded him turned on him and stoned Honi the circle maker to death. It may seem like a tragic ending, but Honi died the way he lived. He prayed until the day he died. In fact, his dying breath was a prayer that ushered him into eternity. I don't think the circle maker would have had it any other way.

What a way to live.

What a way to die.

What a way to enter eternity.

The Chalk Circle

He never received a formal education, yet he lectured at Harvard. He was born in a gypsy tent, yet he was summoned to the White House to meet two presidents. Born in the Epping Forest outside of London in 1860, Rodney "Gypsy" Smith crisscrossed the Atlantic Ocean forty-five times, preaching the gospel to millions. Few evangelists have preached with more passion. His secret? Private prayer. More powerful than his preaching was his praying.

Gypsy's secret was revealed to a delegation of revival seekers, who asked him how God could use them, just as he was using Gypsy. Without hesitation, Gypsy said, "Go home. Lock yourself in your room. Kneel down in the middle of the floor, and with a piece of chalk draw a circle around yourself. There, on your knees, pray fervently and brokenly that God would start a revival within that chalk circle."

My friend Michael Hall told me this story after I had already written *The Circle Maker*. The cover of the book, complete with chalk circle, had already been designed. Honestly, I wasn't sold on the cover design before I heard the story about Gypsy Smith. After I heard the story, I felt like the cover was both historic and prophetic. If a picture is worth a thousand words, then the chalk circle on the cover is worth a thousand prayers. May it inspire you and remind you to draw a prayer circle. That is where every great movement of God begins. May it begin with you, in you.

Acknowledgments

To my wife, Lora — you are the love of my life.

To my kids, Parker, Summer, and Josiah — nothing compares with being your dad.

To my grandparents, Elmer and Alene Johnson — your prayers outlive you.

To my mom and dad, Don and Bonnie Batterson — your prayers are a constant in my life.

To my father-in-law, Bob Schmidgall — you showed me how to kneel.

To my mother-in-law, Karen Schmidgall — your intercessions are priceless.

To my spiritual family, National Community Church — I wouldn't want to be anyplace else, doing anything else, with anyone else.

To Beth, Heidi, Deb, Madeline, Jennifer, and the entire prayer team at NCC — thanks for circling me and circling this book in prayer.

To my agent, Esther — you believed in this book before I did.

To my editors, John and Dirk — you are skilled word surgeons. And on the electronic side, to Jake and the E-Team — thanks for the finishing touches.

To my publishing family — Cindy Lambert, Don Gates, Verne Kenney, and Scott Macdonald — your personal and professional support for this book has gone above and beyond the call of duty.

To the curriculum crew — John Raymond, TJ, Mike, Andy, and Jay — thanks for your "sweat equity" in this project.

Notes

Chapter 1: The Legend of the Circle Maker

Page 9: *His name was Honi*: To read more about Honi, see "The Deeds of the Sages," in *The Book of Legends: Sefer Ha-Aggadah*, ed. Hayim Nahman Bialik and Yehoshua Hana Ravnitzky (New York: Schocken, 1992), 202–3. See also Abraham Cohen, *Everyman's Talmud* (New York: Schocken, 1995), 277, and Henry Malter, *The Treatise Ta'anit of the Babylonian Talmud* (Philadelphia: Jewish Publication Society, 1978), 270. Note: Honi the circle maker is sometimes referred to as Choni the circle maker, Honi Ha-Me'aggel, and Onias the rainmaker.

Chapter 2: Circle Makers

Page 13: *God is for you*: Romans 8:31.

Page 15: *"I'm giving you every square inch"*: Joshua 1:3 MSG.

Page 15: *I had a Honi-like confidence*: Notice that the promise was originally given to Moses. The promise was then transferred to Joshua. In much the same way, all of God's promises have been transferred to us via Jesus Christ. While promises must be interpreted and applied in an accurate historical and exegetical fashion, there are moments when the Spirit of God quickens our spirit and transfers a promise that He had originally given to someone else. While we have to be careful not to blindly claim promises, I think our greatest challenge is that we don't circle as many promises as we could or should.

Chapter 3: The Jericho Miracle

Page 20: *They finally understood why*: Numbers 13:33.

Page 21: *Your entire army is to march*: See Joshua 6:3–4.

Page 22: *"What do you want me to do for you?"*: Matthew 20:31–32.

Page 25: *Then we wrote down our holy desires*: According to Psalm 37:4, God actually downloads new desires in our hearts when we genuinely seek His glory. Those desires are often conceived in the context of prayer and fasting. It takes tremendous discernment to distinguish between holy desires and selfish desires.

Page 29: *If you think of a problem*: Quoted in M. Mitchell Waldrop, *Complexity: The Emerging Science at the Edge of Order and Chaos* (New York: Simon & Schuster, 1992), 29.

Chapter 4: Praying Through

Page 32: *Lord, if you will bless my husband*: Mother Elizabeth J. Dabney, "Praying Through," www.charismamag.com/index.php/newsletters/spiritled-woman-emagazine/22087-forerunners-of-faith-praying-through (accessed June 7, 2011).

Page 34: *Like the story Jesus told*: Luke 18:1 – 8.

Page 37: *"gates of Jericho were securely barred"*: Joshua 6:1 – 2.

Part 1: The First Circle — Dream Big

Page 41: *Is it possible for a man to dream*: Henry Malter, *The Treatise Ta'anit of the Babylonian Talmud* (Philadelphia: Jewish Publication Society, 1978), 270.

Page 42: *"One of the best things about aging"*: Quoted in Sally Arteseros, *American Voices: Best Short Fiction by Contemporary Authors* (New York: Hyperion, 1992), 123.

Chapter 5: Cloudy with a Chance of Quail

Page 46: *"The people of Israel also began to complain"*: Numbers 11:4 – 6 NLT.

Page 47: *"Here I am among six hundred thousand men"*: Numbers 11:21 – 22.

Page 49: *"How far will they go among so many?"*: John 6:9.

Page 50: *"So Moses went out and told the people"*: Numbers 11:24.

Page 52: *"Now a wind went out from the Lord"*: Numbers 11:31 – 32.

Page 54: *"Still other seed fell on good soil"*: Matthew 13:8.

Page 55: *And if you are willing to subtract*: I'm a proud member of the Junky Car Club. I drive a Honda Accord with 230,000 miles on it. Check out www.junkycarclub.com. It's an intentional effort to spend less on a car payment so more money can be given to kingdom causes.

Chapter 6: You Can't Never Always Sometimes Tell

Page 65: *"One day at about three"*: Acts 10:3.

Page 65: *"prayed to God regularly"*: Acts 10:2.

Page 66: *"amazed and perplexed"*: Acts 2:12.

Page 66: *"Surely not, Lord!"*: Acts 10:14.

Page 66: Scripture says he was *"very perplexed"*: Acts 10:17 NLT.

Page 66: *"I have never eaten anything impure"*: Acts 10:14.

Page 69: *"unless the Lord builds the house"*: After our failed church plant in Chicago, I circled Psalm 127:1.

Chapter 7: The Solution to Ten Thousand Problems

Page 71: *"Is there a limit to my power?"*: Numbers 11:23 GNT.

Page 74: *"Is the Lord's arm too short?"*: Numbers 11:23 NIV; *"Is the Lord's hand waxed short?"*: Numbers 11:23 KJV.

Page 74: *"This is the finger of God"*: Exodus 8:19.

Page 75: *"As the heavens are higher than the earth"*: Isaiah 55:9.

Page 79: *"Casting all your care upon him"*: 1 Peter 5:7 KJV.

Part 2: The Second Circle — Pray Hard

Page 81: *"One day Jesus told his disciples a story"*: Luke 18:1 – 5 NLT.

Page 84: *He is praying hard for you*: Romans 8:26.

Chapter 8: Persistence Quotient

Page 85: *The American children lasted, on average, 9.47 minutes*: Malcolm Gladwell, *Outliers* (New York: Little, Brown, 2008), 249.

Page 86: *the average players had logged*: Gladwell, *Outliers*, 38 – 39.

Page 86: *"The emerging picture from such studies"*: Daniel Levitin, *This Is Your Brain on Music: The Science of a Human Obsession* (New York: Penguin, 2007), 193.

Page 87: *it wasn't a light drizzle*: 1 Kings 18:45.

Page 88: *"Blessed is the one who is not offended"*: Luke 7:23 ESV.

Page 89: *"Lord, if you had been here"*: John 11:21 – 22.

Page 92: *"No matter how many promises"*: 2 Corinthians 1:20.

Chapter 9: The Favor of Him Who Dwells in the Burning Bush

Page 98: *has been voted the #1 coffeehouse*: Washington, DC, metro area, *AOL City Guide, 2008*.

Page 99: *Elijah won that sudden-death showdown*: 1 Kings 18:38.

Page 99: *"whatever you bind on earth"*: Matthew 18:18.

Page 100: *Honi was honored for his prayer*: Jacob Neusner, *The Rabbinic Traditions about the Pharisees Before 70: The Houses* (Leiden: Brill, 1971), 179.

Page 100: *The Lord is watching over His word*: Jeremiah 1:12 ESV.

Page 100: *He is actively watching and waiting*: Matthew 8:8 is a great example of this kind of faith. The Roman centurion doesn't ask Jesus to come and heal his child. He simply says, "Just say the word." He had an inherent belief that God's word was His bond. And it says that Jesus "was amazed." If you amaze the Son of God, you've done something significant.

Page 101: *"No good thing does [God] withhold"*: Psalm 84:11 ESV.

Page 101: *"Surely goodness and mercy shall follow me"*: Psalm 23:6 ESV.

Page 103: *"Now is the time of God's favor"*: 2 Corinthians 6:2.

Page 104: *"May the LORD bless his land"*: Deuteronomy 33:13 – 16.

Page 105: *"Let my people go"*: Exodus 5:1.

Chapter 10: The Cattle on a Thousand Hills

Page 107: *Shortly after Dallas Theological Seminary opened*: While the broad strokes of this story are true, there are different versions as it relates to specific details. I've tried to relay the story based on personal research. Most versions attribute the gift to a Texas cattle rancher, but some research indicates it may have been an Illinois banker. Either way, God owns the cattle on a thousand hills and the money in a thousand bank vaults. And it was the amount of the gift and its timeliness that is the true miracle.

Page 109: *He did it with the widow*: 2 Kings 4:1–7.

Page 109: *He did it when the Israelites are trapped*: Exodus 14:21–31.

Page 109: *He did it when the boat is about to capsize*: Matthew 8:23–27.

Page 110: *When God provided the miraculous manna*: Exodus 16:4.

Page 110: *"Do not keep any of it until morning"*: Exodus 16:19 NLT.

Page 110: *"Give us today our daily bread"*: Matthew 6:11.

Page 114: *"Elijah was as human as we are"*: James 5:17–18 NLT.

Page 114: *Elijah didn't just pray against*: 1 Kings 18:22–24; *didn't tell the widow of Zarephath*: 1 Kings 17:13; *in a remake miracle, Elijah didn't pray for*: 2 Kings 2:8.

Page 115: *"When you reach the banks"*: Joshua 3:8 NLT.

Page 117: *"Come"*: Matthew 14:29.

Page 118: *"After Jesus and his disciples arrived"*: Matthew 17:24–27.

Chapter 11: No Answer

Page 124: *"What have I done to you"*: Numbers 22:28.

Page 125: *"I have come here to oppose you"*: Numbers 22:32–33.

Page 126: *"These are the words of him"*: Revelation 3:7–8.

Page 126: *The key of David is an allusion*: Isaiah 22:20–24.

Page 129: *"Don't be afraid. Just stand still"*: Exodus 14:13–14.

Part 3: The Third Circle — Think Long

Page 135: *After a little historical research, it was discovered*: Stewart Brand, *The Clock of the Long Now: Time and Responsibility* (New York: Basic, 1999), 162.

Chapter 12: Long and Boring

Page 139: *"Now when Daniel learned"*: Daniel 6:10.

Page 139: *Daniel prophesied that it would take*: Daniel 9:2.

Chapter 13: The Greatest of Them All

Page 148: *"Go and pray, Connie"*: Conrad Hilton, *Be My Guest* (New York: Simon and Schuster, 1994), 17.

Page 148: *"In the circle of successful living"*: Hilton, *Be My Guest*, 288.

Page 152: *"I will give you every place"*: Joshua 1:3.

Page 153: *New York University psychologist John Bargh*: Cited in Malcolm Gladwell, *Blink: The Power of Thinking without Thinking* (New York: Little, Brown and Company, 2005), 53–57.

Page 154: *"fearfully and wonderfully made"*: Psalm 139:14.

Page 154: *Dutch researchers did a similar priming experiment*: Gladwell, *Blink*, 56.

Page 155: *"In the morning, LORD"*: Psalm 5:3.

Page 155: *"I would rather be able to pray"*: Donald Sweeting and George Sweeting, *Lessons from the Life of Moody* (Chicago: Moody, 2001), 128–29.

Page 156: *He loved to pray early in the morning*: Mark 1:35.

Page 157: *"I will stand upon my watch"*: Habakkuk 2:1, quoted in *The Book of Legends: Sefer Ha-Aggadah*, ed. Hayim Nahman Bialik and Yehoshua Hana Ravnitzky (New York: Schocken, 1992), 202.

Page 157: *"Let God be as original"*: Oswald Chambers, *My Utmost for His Highest* (Grand Rapids: Discovery House, 2006), June 13.

Page 159: *"We try to call Him to mind"*: Frank Laubach, *The Game with Minutes* (Westwood, N.J.: Revell, 1961).

Page 160: *"Last Monday was the most completely successful"*: Brother Lawrence and Frank Laubach, *Practicing His Presence* (Goleta, Calif.: Christian Books, 1973), June 1, 1930 entry.

Chapter 14: The Speed of Prayer

Page 164: *"Do not be afraid, Daniel"*: Daniel 10:12 – 14.

Page 166: *"The moment you began praying"*: Daniel 9:23 NLT.

Page 169: *"Daniel resolved not to defile himself"*: Daniel 1:8.

Page 170: *"the accuser of our brethren"*: Revelation 12:10 KJV.

Page 171: *"Couldn't you men keep watch"*: Matthew 26:40.

Page 172: *"The spirit is willing"*: Matthew 26:41.

Page 173: *"I am the vine, you are the branches"*: John 15:5 NASB.

Chapter 15: Life Goal List

Page 177: *In his groundbreaking book*: Jim Collins and Jerry Porras, *Built to Last* (New York: HarperCollins, 1994), 93.

Page 178: *Scripture says that without a vision*: Proverbs 29:18 KJV.

Page 182: *"Record the vision and inscribe it"*: Habakkuk 2:2 NASB.

Page 184: *"Thus far the LORD has helped us"*: 1 Samuel 7:12.

Page 187: *"Devote yourselves to prayer"*: Colossians 4:2.

Chapter 16: Double Miracle

Page 197: *"Stand still, and see the salvation"*: Exodus 14:13 KJV.

Chapter 17: Bottled Prayer

Page 205: *"My lord, what will the outcome"*: Daniel 12:8.

Page 205: *"Go your way, Daniel"*: Daniel 12:9.

Page 205: *kairos, not chronos*: Both Greek words can be translated "time," but they have very different meanings. The word *chronos* refers to mechanical or linear time. The word *kairos* has more to do with timing. It's the ability to recognize when the right time has come, for example. In fact, it can be translated "opportunity." There is also a providential dimension to *kairos*. If *chronos* is clock time, then *kairos* is divine timing.

Page 205: *"Let there be light"*: Genesis 1:3.

Page 206: *His words never return void*: Isaiah 55:11.

Page 206: *"The Lord is watching over His word"*: Jeremiah 1:12 ESV.

Page 208: *"You have collected all my tears"*: Psalm 56:8 NLT.

Page 208: *God collects our prayers*: Revelation 8:3.

Chapter 18: Now There Was One

Page 211: *"Now there was one"*: Flavius Josephus, *Jewish Antiquities* (London: Wordsworth, 2006), 581.

Page 211: *"History belongs to the intercessors"*: This is one of my all-time favorite sayings, but I want to share the larger context of the statement (from Walter Wink's *The Powers That Be: Theology for a New Millennium* [New York: Doubleday, 1999], 185–86).

> Intercessory prayer is spiritual defiance of what is in the way of what God has promised. Intercession visualizes an alternative future to the one apparently fated by the momentum of current forces. Prayer infuses the air of a time yet to be into the suffocating atmosphere of the present.
>
> History belongs to the intercessors who believe the future into being. This is not simply a religious statement. It is also true of Communists or capitalists or anarchists. The future belongs to whoever can envision a new and desirable possibility, which faith then fixes upon as inevitable.
>
> This is the politics of hope. Hope envisages its future and then acts as if that future is now irresistible, thus helping to create the reality for which it longs. The future is not closed. There are fields of forces whose actions are somewhat predictable. But how they will interact is not. Even a small number of people, firmly committed to the new inevitability on which they have fixed their imaginations, can decisively affect the shape the future takes.
>
> These shapers of the future are the intercessors, who call out of the future the longed-for new present. In the New Testament, the name and texture and aura of that future is God's domination-free order, the reign of God.
>
> No doubt our intercessions sometimes change us as we open ourselves to new possibilities we had not guessed. No doubt our prayers to God reflect back upon us as a divine command to become the answer to our prayer. But if we are to take the biblical understanding seriously, intercession is more than that. It changes the world and it changes what is possible to God. It creates an island of relative freedom in a world gripped by unholy necessity. A new force field appears that hitherto was only potential. The entire configuration changes as the result of the change of a single part. A space opens in the praying person, permitting God to act without violating human freedom. The change in one person thus changes what God can thereby do in that world.

Page 211: *"Were you not Honi"*: Jacob Neusner, *The Talmud: Law, Knowledge, Narrative* (Lanham, Md.: University Press of America, 2005), 183.

Page 213: *"O God, the King of the whole world"*: Lawrence H. Schiffman, *Texts and Traditions: A Source Reader for the Study of Second Temple and Rabbinic Judaism* (Hoboken, N.J.: KTAV Publishing House, 1998), 261.

Draw
the
Circle

Contents

Introduction

The forty-day prayer challenge is going to change your life. In fact, the next forty days have the potential to dramatically alter the *rest* of your life. God is going to begin a good work in you, and He is going to carry it to completion. Miracles that happen in your life decades from now will trace their origin back to this season of prayer. Breakthroughs that happen during these forty days will become generational blessings that live on long after you die.

If you press into God's presence like never before, you will experience God like never before. You'll look back on these forty days as the best forty days of your life. They won't be the easiest forty days; in fact, they may be the hardest. Don't be surprised if you experience spiritual opposition along the way. But if you pray through, God will break through in new ways. It's as inevitable as the tide coming in.

There is nothing magical about forty days, but there is something biblical about it. That's the number of days Jesus spent in the wilderness fasting and praying. It marked a critical chapter in His life — the transition from His earthly father's business to His heavenly Father's business. Jesus was tested like never before, but this experience set the stage for His greatest victories over the enemy. The war against sin and Satan may have been won on Calvary's cross, but a key battle happened in the wilderness three years earlier. When Jesus returned to Galilee, He wasn't the same person. You won't be either. You'll emerge from this forty-day prayer challenge, just like Jesus, in the power of the Holy Spirit.

If you want God to do something new in you, you cannot keep doing the same old thing. You have to do something different. And if you do, God will create new capacities within you. There will be new gifts and new revelations. But you've got to pray the price. You'll get out of this what you put into it.

How to Start a Revival

Draw the Circle is a sequel of sorts. Since the release of *The Circle Maker*, I've heard hundreds of prayer testimonies that have set my faith on fire. Almost every day I hear a new story that makes me want to applaud God. This book is my way of stewarding those testimonies by sharing them. I've also learned more about prayer since *The Circle Maker* was released than the knowledge I had beforehand. I'll share those new discoveries in the pages that follow.

So let me pick up where *The Circle Maker* left off.

Rodney "Gypsy" Smith was born on the outskirts of London in 1860. He never received a formal education, yet he lectured at Harvard. Despite his humble origins, he was invited by two sitting United States presidents to the White

House. Gypsy crisscrossed the Atlantic Ocean forty-five times, preaching the gospel to millions of people, and he never preached without someone surrendering their life to the lordship of Jesus Christ.

Gypsy was powerfully used of God. Everywhere he went, it seemed like revival was right on his heels. But it wasn't his preaching that brought revival. It never is. Preaching may move the hearts of men, but praying moves the heart of God. And that's where revival comes from.

Gypsy revealed his secret to a delegation of revival seekers who sought an audience with him. They wanted to know how they could make a difference with their lives the way he had with his. His answer was simple yet profound — as timely and timeless now as it was a hundred years ago. He gave them this advice:

Go home. Lock yourself in your room. Kneel down in the middle of the floor, and with a piece of chalk draw a circle around yourself. There, on your knees, pray fervently and brokenly that God would start a revival within that chalk circle.

Start Circling

I have a confession to make. Even though I wrote a book on prayer, and my personal prayer life was thriving, I failed to lead our church in corporate prayer for fifteen years. That changed this year, and everything changed with it.

We completed our first forty-day prayer challenge at National Community Church, and on a corporate level, it completely changed our church culture. It ranks as the most significant season of spiritual growth in our fifteen-year history. And on a personal level, I'm not who I was when we started.

As we prepared for the forty-day challenge, I believed that God wanted our church to circle 2 Chronicles 7:14 by hitting our knees every day at 7:14 a.m. I explained to our church that the time in and of itself wasn't significant but offered a daily reminder of the promise we were circling in prayer.

"If my people, who are called by my name, will humble themselves and pray and seek my face and turn from their wicked ways, then I will hear from heaven, and I will forgive their sin and will heal their land."

On the first day of the prayer challenge, I dropped to my knees right after I got out of bed. This daily habit didn't stop on day 40. In fact, I'll do it the rest of my life. Please read this carefully: the goal of the forty-day prayer challenge isn't to get what you want by day 40. In fact, the goal isn't to get what you want at all. The goal is to figure out what God wants, what God wills. Then you start circling it in prayer and don't stop until God answers.

Too often we pray ASAP prayers — *as soon as possible*. We need to start praying ALAT prayers — *as long as it takes*. The goal of the prayer challenge is to establish a prayer habit so you're still praying on day 41, day 57, day 101, day 365.

Logistics

Who should I do the prayer challenge with?
You may want to consider a church-wide challenge or turn

your small group into a prayer circle. You can do this challenge with your family or with your friends. But whatever you do, don't do it alone.

What should I circle?

Don't feel bad if you don't know what to circle on day 1. One of the biggest misconceptions about prayer is that it means outlining our agenda to God as a divine to-do list. The true purpose of prayer is to get into God's presence so He can outline His agenda for us. Here's my advice: pray about what to pray about. God will reveal a promise, a problem, or a person. Then circle whatever God has prompted you to pray for with the same kind of consistency with which the earth circles the sun.

Too often we pray for something once and then completely forget about it. So when God answers, we fail to give Him the glory because we forgot what we asked for. That's one reason why you need to journal during these forty days. Document your prayers and God's answers. If you don't have a journal, pick up a copy of *The Circle Maker Prayer Journal*. It'll help you not just pray, but pray through.

During our forty-day prayer challenge, different people circled different things. We saw prodigals come back to God after years of running away. Marriages were restored. Job opportunities opened up. Provision for financial needs came out of nowhere. Divine appointments happened on a daily basis. And there were even a few miraculous healings.

When should I take the challenge?

You can do this at any time, but the important thing is to establish a start date or end date. A forty-day prayer challenge is a great way to begin a new year or to end a year. At NCC, we approach Lent as a way of beginning the spiritual journey to Easter. This past year, I coined the word *ExperiLent* because we wanted to see what would happen if we circled one promise for forty days, and God delivered. You'll read about it in the devotion for day 34. You can also leverage a birthday or holiday. A forty-day fast leading up to my thirty-fifth birthday was a turning point in my life. I turned my birthday into a self-imposed deadline that yielded my first book.

Where should I pray?

It's important to make a daily appointment with God by determining a *time and place* to pray. If it helps, put the appointment in your calendar or set an alarm. I recommend that you give God the first few minutes of the day. When I pray at the beginning of the day, it's like my whole day becomes a prayer. When I dial into God's frequency in the morning, I hear His still, small voice the rest of the day.

I also recommend a corporate gathering for prayer. Kick it off with a night of prayer and praise. Then sustain the momentum with daily gatherings. Our 7:14 a.m. weekday prayer gatherings not only create tremendous synergy; they also are a way to hold me accountable.

Find Out about Prayer

In 1952, a Princeton doctoral student asked Albert Einstein a question: "What original dissertation research is left?" I'm intrigued and inspired by Einstein's answer: "Find out about prayer."

That is the challenge on the table: find out about prayer.

My prayer for you is that each day on this journey will yield a new discovery. Those discoveries will change the way you pray, and when you change the way you pray, everything else changes.

Few people had a more profound impact on the spiritual climate of America in the last half of the twentieth century than Bill Bright, founder of Campus Crusade for Christ (CRU). He championed evangelism and discipleship from college campuses to foreign mission fields and influenced millions of people through the organization he started and the books he wrote.

In 1994, Dr. Bright felt led to do a forty-day fast for revival in America. The man who went into that prayer circle and the man who came out were two different people. His faith soared. He sensed God's presence like never before. And biblical truths went from his mind to his heart to his soul. In his own words, "This proved to be the most important forty days of my life."

I believe the same thing can be true for you.

Draw the circle!

Day 1

Get Ready

He prayed to God regularly.
ACTS 10:2

Five words tell me everything I need to know about Cornelius: *He prayed to God regularly.* Scripture doesn't record exactly *when* or *where* or *how* he prayed. It doesn't reveal whether he prayed in the morning or the evening. It doesn't tell us what he said or the posture he prayed in. It just says he prayed regularly. And when you pray to God regularly, irregular things happen on a regular basis. You never know when or where or how God will invade the routine of your life, but you can live in holy anticipation, knowing that God is orchestrating supernatural synchronicities.

Like a grandmaster who strategically positions chess pieces on a chessboard, God is always preparing us and positioning us for divine appointments. And prayer is the way we discern the next move. The plans of God are only revealed in the presence of God. We don't get our marching orders until we get on our knees! But if we hit our knees, God will take us places we never imagined going by paths we didn't even know existed.

If history is a chess match between good and evil, then Acts 10 is one of God's epic moves. It reveals how one prayer can change the game. It reveals what can happen when two people pray. It reveals the power of prayer to checkmate the enemy and seal the victory.

Here's the play-by-play.

A man named Cornelius has a vision while praying in Caesarea. Simultaneously, Peter has a vision while praying in Joppa. Those visions collide in a divine appointment that radically alters the course of history. Up to this point, the Way was a sect of Judaism. It isn't until Cornelius, an officer in the Roman army, puts his faith in Jesus Christ that the gospel is opened up to Gentiles. If *he* doesn't get saved, *you* can't get saved. It's not even an option. So if you're a non-Jewish follower of Jesus, your spiritual genealogy traces back to this genesis moment. When Cornelius puts his faith in Christ, the door of salvation swings wide open to the Gentiles. But it started with two people praying. Those two prayers have been answered billions of times over the last two thousand years. In fact, they were answered yet again when you put your faith in Jesus Christ.

Now let me state the obvious: Cornelius and Peter should have never met each other. Never. Ever. They were separated by geography. The thirty-two-mile distance between their two towns may not seem like much to us, but the average person in the first century didn't travel outside a thirty-mile radius of their birthplace. And more significantly, they were separated by ethnicity. Roman soldiers and Jewish disciples didn't hang out. In fact, Peter broke every law in the Jewish books when he entered the home of Cornelius. Stepping through that doorway was like crossing the Rubicon. He went against everything he'd ever known and risked everything he'd ever accomplished. That doorway to the home of Cornelius was like the wardrobe in *The Lion, the Witch, and the Wardrobe* or the rabbit hole in *Alice in Wonderland*. I call it The Door to Whosoever. When Peter entered the house of Cornelius, it literally meant, "Whosoever will may come." And that includes you and me!

Get Ready

It's not every day that a member of the United States Congress requests a meeting with me. At first I was curious. Then I got a little nervous. I hoped it had nothing to do with the fact that I had illegally taken my kids sledding at the Capitol during snowmaggedon a few winters back, but I figured that couldn't possibly warrant a federal investigation. Turns out the congressman just wanted to thank me for writing *Wild Goose Chase*, a book he read during his first run for Congress.

As we sipped lattes in my office above Ebenezer's Coffeehouse, the congressman shared his backstory with me. Not unlike Daniel's improbable rise to political power, Jim's path was full of unpredictable twists and turns. It all started one day in 2007 when the Holy Spirit said in that still, small voice, "Get ready." His initial reaction was, *Get ready for what?* At the time, Jim was directing one of the largest Christian camps in the country and preaching on weekends. He was perfectly content doing what he was doing, but the Holy Spirit kept impressing the same thing on him: "Get ready."

Several months later, Jim was reading the newspaper when he came across an article about the congresswoman who represented his district. Rumors were flying that she was going to make a run for governor, which would leave her seat in Congress vacant. That's when the Holy Spirit said, "This is it."

Jim didn't have a political bone in his body. In fact, he didn't even know the boundaries of his congressional district. He went online to do a little research when his wife walked in and said, "What are you looking at?" He said, "County statistics." She said, "We're running for Congress, aren't we?" They had never talked about it or thought about it. Running for Congress seemed like a wild goose chase. After all, Jim had no background, no network, and no resources. There was no way he could win — unless, of course, the front-runner happened to drop out of the race a few months before the election. That is exactly what happened, and Jim Lankford was elected to represent the 5th Congressional District of Oklahoma.

The Celtic Christians had a fascinating name for the Holy Spirit. They called Him *An-Geadh-Glas*, which means "wild goose." Can you think of a better description of what it's like to live a Spirit-led life than "wild goose chase"? When you follow the leading of the Holy Spirit, you never know who you'll meet, where you'll go, or what you'll do. But one thing is certain: it'll be anything but boring!

At the end of our conversation, Congressman Lankford mentioned that he had also read *The Circle Maker*. And he's putting it into practice. If you visit the Cannon House Office Building on any given morning when Congress is in session, you'll find a camp-director-turned-congressman circling the fifth floor, praying for his constituents, colleagues, and country!

Anything but Routine

If you establish a prayer routine, your life will be anything but routine. You will go to places, do things, and meet people you have no business going to, doing, or meeting. You don't need to seek opportunity. All you have to do is seek God. And if you seek God, opportunity will seek you.

I live in a town, Washington, D.C., where it's all about who you know. *Who you know* is more important than *what you know*. This is certainly true for the children of God. Who you know — the heavenly Father — is far more important than what you know.

Don't worry about meeting the right people. If you meet with God, God will make sure you meet the right people at the right time. After all, there is nobody He doesn't know. It's one degree of separation! And if God can change the heart of Pharaoh, He can help you find favor with anybody and everybody. Let God do the promoting and networking. I'm certainly not suggesting that you don't apply for a promotion or trade business cards, but seek first His kingdom. You've got to do God's will God's way.

Remember when Moses got impatient and took matters into his own hands by killing an Egyptian taskmaster? He thought it would expedite God's plan. In reality, it delayed God's plan by forty years. He thought it would bring relief, but it made the burden on the Israelites almost unbearable. That's what happens when we try to do God's job for Him. It's unbearable. When we try to make things go faster, we usually slow things down. When we try to make things easier, we usually make them harder.

Don't try to manufacture your own miracles.

Don't try to answer your own prayers.

Don't try to do God's job for Him.

Stay humble. Stay patient. Stay focused.

Keep circling.

Draw the Circle

If you pray to God regularly, irregular things will happen on a regular basis.

Established by God

In their hearts humans plan their course,
but the LORD establishes their steps.

PROVERBS 16:9

It may feel like you are sitting still right now, but you are not. You are on a planet that is rotating on its axis at 1,000 miles per hour. Like clockwork, it makes one full revolution every twenty-four hours. And if that isn't amazing enough, planet Earth is moving around the sun at speeds approaching 67,000 miles per hour! So the next time you feel like you've had an unproductive day, remind yourself that you did travel more than 1.5 million miles through space today.

Now let me ask you a question: When was the last time you lost sleep because you were concerned about the Creator keeping the planets in orbit? When was the last time you got down on your knees at night and prayed, "Lord, thanks for keeping the planet rotating. I wasn't sure if we'd make the full rotation today, but You did it again!" I'm guessing the answer to these questions is *never*.

We don't doubt God's ability to keep the planets in orbit, but we have a difficult time believing He can keep our lives in orbit. You tell me which is more difficult — keeping the planets in orbit or determining our steps? The truth is that we already trust God for the big things; now we need to trust Him for the little things, like healing our cancer, getting us out of debt, helping us conceive, or helping us find our soul mate. I'm certainly not suggesting that any of these situations are small. They are giant mountains to us. But prayer can turn them into molehills!

God is great not just because nothing is too big for Him; God is also great because nothing is too small. The Sovereign One cares about every minute detail of our lives.

Every act of obedience, no matter how small, makes our heavenly Father proud. Every act of faith — even a faith as small as a mustard seed — puts a smile on His face. Every sacrifice, no matter how insignificant it may seem to us, makes a difference.

Like a proud parent watching their child take their first steps, God rejoices over every baby step. And He can turn those small steps of faith into giant leaps.

Divine Assignment

I have a handful of prayers I pray all the time. Because of their frequent repetition, I call them prayer mantras. One is that God will put my books into the right hands at the right time. I've prayed this prayer thousands of times, and God has answered it in dramatic fashion countless times. The right book in the right hands at the right time can save a marriage, avert a mistake, demand a decision, plant a seed, conceive a dream, solve a problem, and prompt a prayer. That's why I write. And that's why, for me, a book sold is not a book sold; a book sold is a prayer answered. I don't know the name and situation of every reader, but God does, and that's all that matters.

The other day I got an e-mail from Peter, a man who started reading *In a Pit with a Lion on a Snowy Day* on a flight to Las Vegas. During the first half of his flight, he read chapter 1 and felt challenged and convicted. One sentence arrested his attention: "God is in the business of strategically positioning us in the right place at the right time, but it's up to us to see and seize those opportunities that are all around us all the time." So Peter switched planes in Phoenix and sat down in his new seat assignment. He said hello to the girl next to him, but she shut him down rather abruptly. It was one of those looks that says, *Don't talk to me the rest of this flight, and by the way, the armrest belongs to me!* Peter didn't want to offend her or bother her, but he couldn't shake the feeling that something was wrong. He knew he needed to swallow his pride, face his fears, and seize the opportunity. He leaned over and said, "I know it's absolutely none of my business, but you seem so burdened. If sharing it with a complete stranger might help, I'm all ears."

The seventeen-year-old girl, who was three months pregnant, proceeded to tell him she was running away from home. Her boyfriend told her to take off and "take care of it." She had stolen her dad's credit card that morning to buy a ticket to Vegas to get an abortion. During the flight, Peter spoke words of comfort and encouragement. When they landed in

Vegas, he convinced the girl to call her parents, who were worried sick. Her parents convinced her to grab the next flight and come home.

I'm quite sure one life, perhaps two, were saved that day! All because one man believed that a seat assignment might be a divine assignment. And when we act on those prayer promptings, the Grandmaster can use a single pawn to check-mate the enemy's plans.

At the end of his e-mail, Peter thanked me for writing the book. He wrote, "So that's what happened after chapter 1. I can't wait to see what happens after chapter 2!" Me too! All I know is this: God is setting up divine appointments all the time. Only God can *make* the appointment, but only you can *keep* the appointment. It's your job to recognize and respond to the God-ordained opportunities that come your way.

Choreography

Few promises are more circled in my Bible than Proverbs 16:9: "In their hearts humans plan their course, but the LORD establishes their steps."

God wants us to get where God wants us to go more than we want to get where God wants us to go. And He is awfully good at getting us there. All we have to do is follow the script of Holy Scripture and the improvisation of the Holy Spirit.

We can't create divine appointments. All we can do is keep them.

We can't plan God-ordained opportunities. All we can do is seize them.

We can't perform miracles. All we can do is pray for them. Our job is to hear His voice. His job is to establish our steps. And if we do our job, God will do His!

The Hebrew word *kûn*, translated in Proverbs 16:9 as "establishes," can also be translated as "determines," "prepares," "provides," "sets in place," "directs," "firmly decides," "makes secure." It's a meticulous word that involves careful planning right down to the smallest detail. It's a redemptive word that celebrates God's ability to redeem past experiences and recycle them for future opportunities. It's a calming word that imparts confidence in the fact that God has everything under control. It's a creative word that hints at the beauty of God's artistry.

God is the Composer. Your life is His musical score.

God is the Artist. Your life is His canvas.

God is the Architect. Your life is His blueprint.

God is the Writer. You are His book.

God is great not just because nothing is too big for Him; God is also great because nothing is too small.

Amazing Things

*"Consecrate yourselves, for tomorrow
the LORD will do amazing things among you."*
JOSHUA 3:5

More than a hundred years ago, a British revivalist spoke the words to Dwight L. Moody that would transform Moody's approach to life — words of challenge that echo across every generation: "The world has yet to see what God will do with and for and through and in and by the man who is fully and wholly consecrated to Him."

Why not you?

All of us want to do amazing things for God, but that isn't our job; it is God's job. Our job is simply to consecrate ourselves by yielding our will to His will. And if we do our job, God will do His job. If we consecrate ourselves to God, amazing things will happen. It's absolutely inevitable. Consecration always ends in amazing!

The Israelites were camped on the eastern banks of the Jordan River when God gave them this command: "Consecrate yourselves." And because they obeyed, God delivered on the promise. He parted the Jordan River, and the Israelites walked through on dry ground. We'd rather build a boat or build a bridge. We try to do things for God instead of letting God do things for us. And it's certainly a two-way street. We need to *work like it depends on us*, but we also need to *pray like it depends on God*. That's what consecration is all about. It's letting God do for us what we cannot do for ourselves. And that's how God gets all the glory.

Consecration is a complete surrender to the lordship of Jesus Christ. We relinquish everything to God — our time, talent, and treasure. It's a complete divestiture. Nothing belongs to us, not even ourselves. But the exchange rate is unbelievable. All of our sin is transferred to Christ's account, and all of His righteousness is transferred to our account. God cancels our debt, writes us into His will, and calls it even!

The word *consecrate* means "to set apart." It means "to be designated for a special purpose." It means "to be completely dedicated to God."

The Son of God set the standard. Jesus gave all of Himself at Calvary, and He expects nothing less in return. If Jesus hung on His cross, we can certainly carry our cross. His death demands our lives.

Gate D8

During our prayer challenge at National Community Church, our church gathered for corporate prayer every morning at our coffeehouse. Like clockwork, we hit our knees at 7:14 a.m. sharp. It was such a regular routine that it became second nature. Almost like hunger pangs that hit you after going too long without eating, I couldn't go too long without hitting my knees. Kneeling became almost as instinctual as eating or sleeping.

One day I had to miss our prayer meeting because of an early morning flight to Cleveland. As I got off the plane, I realized it was time to pray. I knew I'd be kneeling at our coffeehouse, but I was in the middle of an airport. And that's when I felt the Holy Spirit throwing down the gauntlet, impressing on me the need to kneel right then and there. To be honest, I resisted: "But, Lord, I'm in the middle of the Cleveland airport." The Lord said, "I know exactly where you are. Gate D8."

At first I rationalized *not* kneeling.

I don't want to feed negative stereotypes about religious fanatics. I can pray just as effectively as I walk toward baggage claim. I can kneel a little later in the privacy of my hotel room.

While all of these things are true, I knew it wasn't the point. I knew the Lord was testing me to see if I'd be willing to obey Him whenever, wherever, whatever. I knew that if I failed this test, I would be standing in God's way of using me in bigger ways. I wanted to prove to Him that I cared more about what He thought than about what people thought. I wanted to prove to Him that I belong to Him everywhere, all the time. And I knew that if God could trust me with the little things, then He could use me to do big things. So after looking both ways down the terminal, I hit my knees at Gate D8. It was one small step in the long journey toward complete consecration. A little piece of my ego died that day at Gate D8.

I shared that story with our congregation, and I was inspired by the response. You've heard of a flash mob? Well, our church became a kneeling mob! I've heard stories of people kneeling in elevators, in classrooms, in banks, and in courtrooms. It isn't about kneeling in strange places at strange times; it's about the willingness to obey the promptings of the Holy Spirit. It's about a willingness to kneel anyplace, anytime.

Veto Power

Consecration means we no longer call the shots. We give God veto power. His word is the final word, whether it's Holy Scripture or the Holy Spirit. Either way, it's no longer a selfish spirituality that asks God to serve our purposes. It's all about serving His purposes so that His glory is revealed.

Consecration is death to self.

I know there is a fear that if we give more of ourselves to God, there will be less of us left, but it's the exact opposite. It's not until we die to self that we truly come alive. The more we give to God, the more we have and the more we become. It's only in losing our lives that we will really find them.

Sometimes prayer is a casual conversation with God. It's like two friends catching up over coffee. But sometimes prayer involves intense intercession, as it was for Jesus praying in Gethsemane on the eve of His crucifixion. It was so intense that Jesus was literally sweating drops of blood. He was facing the greatest test of his life on earth, so He prayed through the night. Three times He prayed a prayer of consecration: "My

Father, if it is possible, may this cup be taken from me. Yet not as I will, but as you will."

Consecration is a process of surrender that never ends. And prayer is the catalyst. It begins with a sinner's prayer. We confess our sins to the Savior and surrender our lives to His lordship. And along the way, our spiritual journeys are marked by decisive moments when we consecrate ourselves to God in our own garden of Gethsemane.

Jonathan Edwards is famous for his sermon "Sinners in the Hands of an Angry God," which helped spark the first Great Awakening. Along with his pastorate in North Hampton, Massachusetts, he served as the president of Princeton University. Of his known descendants, there are more than 300 ministers or missionaries, 120 university professors, 60 authors, 30 judges, 14 college presidents, 3 members of Congress, and 1 vice president. That's an impressive family lineage! And that legacy, like every spiritual genealogy, traces back to a moment of consecration.

On January 12, 1723, Jonathan Edwards made a solemn dedication of himself to God. He consecrated himself, all of himself, to God.

> I made a solemn dedication of myself to God, and wrote it down; giving up myself, and all that I had to God; to be for the future, in no respect, my own; to act as one that had no right to himself, in any respect. And solemnly vowed, to take God for my whole portion and felicity; looking on nothing else, as any part of my happiness, nor acting as if it were.

If we give more of ourselves to God,
God will give more of Himself to us.

Don't Pray Away

*"This happened so that the works of God
might be displayed in him."*
JOHN 9:3

My friends John and Tricia Tiller experienced a parent's worst nightmare nearly a decade ago. Their three-year-old son, Eli, was playing by himself in his room when Tricia became concerned because it was too quiet. When she walked into his room, Eli was nowhere to be seen. That's when she saw a table out of place. It had been pushed beneath his second-story bedroom window, and the window screen was conspicuously missing. Tricia's worst fears were realized when she ran to the window, looked down, and saw Eli lying thirteen feet below.

Eli was medivaced to the hospital, where he fought for his life in the ICU for three weeks. He miraculously survived, but not without significant brain damage. He has virtually no peripheral vision on his right side, and the left side of his body has very little motor skills or muscle development. Eli speaks with a severe stutter and walks with a pronounced limp. Yet twelve-year-old Eli Tiller has as sweet a spirit and as courageous an attitude as anybody I've ever met. He recently sang at National Community Church, and there wasn't a dry eye in the place.

John and Tricia have thanked God countless times for saving their son, but their prayers for complete healing have gone unanswered. In the aftermath of the accident, John dueled with doubt.

> *I began to interrogate God. "Why, God? Why do little boys fall from windows?"*
>
> *Why did my little boy fall from that window? Why him? Why me? I looked to Scripture for an answer, and it turns out that "Why, God?" is not a new question at all.*

In John 9, Jesus encountered a man who was born blind, and the people falsely assumed it was the result of sin. They asked Jesus, "Who sinned, this man or his parents?" Jesus told them it was neither! The people assumed it was a generational curse or a lack of faith. But Jesus set the record straight by revealing the real reason: "This happened so that the works of God might be displayed in him."

> *Since Eli's accident, Tricia and I have done everything humanly possible to make our son well. We've spent tens of thousands of dollars on uninsured medical equipment. For the first three years after the accident, Tricia and Eli literally spent 80 percent of their waking hours in therapy. We had faith that he would be completely healed. We knew it was going to happen, so we just kept praying and kept waiting. We waited and waited. We knew that one day we'd be standing in front of crowds saying, "Look what the Lord has*

done! He has completely healed our son." But that's not what happened.

After three years of doing everything we could for our son, it was time to accept his current condition and choose to live life with disability. This disability was something we couldn't remove, and evidently God was choosing to not completely heal Eli. So we had to burn our old scripts and look for what God could do with our new script. So for the past five years, we've accepted life with disability. That doesn't mean I've stopped praying for my son. Like any father, I'd give my right arm to see my son healed. But instead of getting discouraged or getting angry, I choose to look for what God can do.

Sometimes the purpose of prayer is to *get us out of* circumstances, but more often than not, the purpose of prayer is to *get us through* them. I'm certainly not suggesting we shouldn't pray deliverance prayers, but there are times we need to pray prevailing prayers. We need to ask God to give us the grace to sustain, the strength to stand firm, and the willpower to keep on keeping on.

Praying Away versus Praying Through

There is a big difference between *praying away* and *praying through*.

We're often so anxious to get out of difficult, painful, or challenging situations that we fail to grow through them. We're so fixated on *getting out of them* that we don't *get anything out of them*. We fail to learn the lessons God is trying to teach us or cultivate the character God is trying to grow in us. We're so focused on God changing our circumstances that we never allow God to change us! So instead of ten or twenty years of experience, we have one year of experience repeated ten or twenty times.

Sometimes we need to pray "get me out" prayers. But sometimes we need to pray "get me through" prayers. And we need the discernment to know when to pray what.

If we're being completely honest, most of our prayers have as their chief objective our own personal comfort rather than God's glory. We want to pray away every problem, but those shortsighted prayers would short-circuit God's perfect plan. There are seasons and situations when we need to simply pray through.

My prayer batting average is no better than anyone else's. I swing and miss all the time, but I have determined that I'm going to "go down swinging." Even when a prayer isn't answered the way I want, I have a peace that passes under-standing because I know that God heard me. It just means the answer is no. And I've learned to praise God when the answer is no, not just when the answer is yes. It simply means I'm asking for the wrong thing or for the wrong reason or at the wrong time. And I'm convinced that the day will come when we thank God for the prayers He did *not* answer as much as the ones He did because He had a better answer. And the best answer is very rarely what is most convenient or comfortable for us. The best answer is always what brings God the most glory!

Can our prayers change our circumstances? Absolutely! But when our circumstances don't change, it's often an indication that God is trying to change us. The primary purpose of prayer is not to change circumstances; the primary purpose of prayer is to change us! But either way, the chief objective remains the same: to glorify God in any and every situation.

Sometimes God delivers us from our problems; sometimes God delivers us through our problems.

Write It Down

"Write down the revelation."

HABAKKUK 2:2

I have a handful of sayings that our staff can recite from memory because I repeat them all the time. One of them is this: *the shortest pencil is longer than the longest memory.* That's why I keep a prayer journal. Next to my Bible, nothing is more sacred to me than my journal. It's the way I mark my trail. It's the way I process problems and record revelations. It's the way I keep track of the prayers I've prayed so that I can give God the glory when He answers.

Journaling is one of the most overlooked and undervalued spiritual disciplines. In my estimation, it's on a par with praying, fasting, and meditating. It's the way we document what God is doing in our lives. In Habakkuk 2:2, the Lord states, "Write down the revelation." Why? Because we have a natural tendency to remember what we should forget and forget what we should remember. Journaling is the best antidote, maybe the only antidote, to spiritual amnesia.

This year I started taking my journal with me everywhere I go. When I'm in a meeting, I write things in my prayer journal so I can double back and pray about them later. If I'm listening to someone speak, I take notes so I can process them in prayer. And of course, I always have my prayer journal handy when I'm praying. I pray about current situations and future dreams. I have a prayer list for my children that helps me pray consistently and strategically. And I often journal my meditations on Scripture. Then, every once in a while, I go back through my journal and circle the things I need to keep praying through.

My prayer journal doubles as my prayer genealogy. I can trace many of the blessings, breakthroughs, and miracles back to their genesis prayers. As I look back through my journals, I'm able to connect the dots between my prayers and God's answers. Connecting these dots inspires my faith like nothing else because it paints a picture of God's faithfulness.

We kicked off this calendar year with a sermon series on *The Circle Maker*, and I encouraged everyone in our congregation to get a prayer journal. I've been amazed at how many people's prayer lives have been revolutionized by the simple act of journaling. I'm convinced it is the key to consistency and specificity in prayer. And it even adds an element of fun. It turns prayer into a game of watching and waiting to see how God will answer!

Journal like a Journalist

One of our church attenders recently shared with me one of the most well-documented prayer testimonies I've ever received. It seems particularly appropriate that this testament to journaling came from a journalist. After I read it, this thought fired across my synapses: we all need to journal like a journalist.

Kimberly's lifelong dream was to work at a major network covering politics. Not only did she end up at the largest network; she got to cover the most famous address in the country, 1600 Pennsylvania Avenue. As a member of the White House travel pool, she often accompanies the president on Air Force One. In fact, her first trip was April 29, 2011 — the same day that President Obama authorized the Osama bin Laden mission.

Kimberly is living her dream, but like every dream, it took a lot of prayer and a lot of patience. During our sermon series on *The Circle Maker*, she went back through dozens of her journals from the past decade. As she retraced her steps, she saw the hand of God on every page. Kimberly's prayer genealogy started in 2001. As a college senior, she penned this fragile yet faith-filled prayer:

> *Dare I ask for my dreams? Dare I see the imagination of the soul? Dare I risk? What if I ask and receive? So then, I risk. I ask of my King, "May I impact others with news and knowledge?"*

After college, Kimberly thought about grad school, considered pursuing library science, and contemplated moving to Chicago or New York. It was during this season of wandering that she created a prayer map — a sheet of paper in her journal with a verse at the top and prayer requests written below. On one of those pages, she circled Psalm 37:4: "Delight yourself in the LORD; and He will give you the desires of your heart." That was a critical promise at a critical time.

On November 4, 2003, she wrote out this prayer:

Where do you want me to go? Where can I represent you? Where is your will? Tug at my heart. I am willing and waiting.

Fast-forward to April 15, 2004.

Kimberly was sitting on a bench overlooking Lake Michigan, depressed by how much money she wasn't making. In that moment, the dream of working at a major network was birthed in her spirit. She also knew she needed to take a step of faith and move to Washington, D.C. So with no job and very little money, Kimberly made the move to D.C. She slept on a friend's floor for several months until she could get on her feet financially. To make ends meet, she worked for a temp agency filing papers while she sent out hundreds of résumés and made hundreds of cold calls.

After numerous dead ends, Kimberly finally got her first break working for a small news bureau during the graveyard shift. Her first night as a full-time journalist was the day Hurricane Katrina hit.

As awful as those overnights were, turns out those overnights were the best thing to hone my journalistic skills. This was also the height of the Iraq War so everything was happening overnight. I got to see how the early morning shift can set the agenda for the entire news cycle.

About a year into the overnight shift, Kimberly wanted to

get a day job so she could get a life! It was killing her social life and spiritual life, so she applied for a day job with a major network. She thought her dream job was finally at her fingertips. She got an interview, but the door slammed shut. It was devastating. That's when many of us give up on our dreams, but Kimberly kept circling her dream job while working her night job for another year! Then she got another interview with the same network, and this time the door opened.

Long story short, it took a decade of working like it depended on her and praying like it depended on God for her dream to come true. But because she journaled her prayers, Kimberly is able to look back and see how God determined her steps. God's fingerprints were on every page!

I'm the granddaughter of farmers. One of my grandmothers only got an eighth-grade education because she had to leave school to help out on the farm. She was told, "All you'll ever do is milk cows."

Now her granddaughter works at the White House. She can be in the Oval Office and say, "Excuse me, Mr. President."

What a country. What a God.

Draw the Circle

The shortest pencil is longer than the longest memory.

Shameless Audacity

"... yet because of your shameless audacity
he will surely get up and give you
as much as you need."

LUKE 11:8

I was doing a radio interview shortly after *The Circle Maker* was released, and the host of the show told an amazing story about his missionary friend, Dr. Bob Bagley. Bob's church in Africa didn't have a church building, so they literally met under the shade of a single tree near the village — that is, until the local witch doctor cursed the tree, and it withered. The church didn't just lose their shade; they were overshadowed by the curse. It undermined the authority of their message. Bob knew their status in the village was in jeopardy if he didn't do something about it, so he called for a public prayer meeting. Not unlike Elijah, who challenged the prophets of Baal to a prayer duel, Bob confronted the curse and called down a blessing on the tree. He literally laid hands on the tree and prayed that God would resurrect it.

Now *that's* shameless audacity!

If God doesn't answer his prayer, he would have dug an

even deeper hole. That is the risk of prayer, isn't it? But if we don't ask, we'll never know. We accumulate lots of wouldas, couldas, and shouldas. Here's what I know for sure: God won't answer 100 percent of the prayers we don't pray.

There is an old adage: *Desperate times call for desperate measures.* Every prayer is a calculated risk, but sometimes God calls us to ante up all the faith we have, and then let the chips fall where they may! That's what Bob did. He asked God to resurrect a tree, and then he added a little tagline to his prayer: "It's not my name that's at stake."

When we act in faith, we aren't risking our reputation; we are risking God's reputation because He's the one who made the promise in the first place. But if we aren't willing to risk our reputation, we'll never establish God's reputation. We'll also never experience miracles like the one Bob saw. Not only did God break the curse and resurrect the tree; it became the only tree of its type to yield its fruit, not once, but twice a year. A double crop! A double blessing!

Why do we mistakenly think that God is offended by our prayers for the impossible? The truth is that God is offended by anything less! God is offended when we ask Him to do things we can do ourselves. It's the impossible prayers that honor God because they reveal our faith and allow God to reveal His glory.

Shameless Audacity

In Luke 11, Jesus tells a story about a man who won't take no for an answer. He keeps knocking on his friend's door until he gets what he came for. It's a parable about prevailing in prayer. And Jesus honors his bold determination: "… yet because of your shameless audacity he will surely get up and give you as much as you need."

I love this depiction of prayer. There are times when you need to do whatever it takes. You need to grab hold of the horns of the altar and not let go. You need to dare demonic forces to a duel. You need to do something crazy, something risky, something different.

The epitome of shameless audacity is the circle maker himself. When a severe drought threatened to destroy a generation of Jews, Honi drew a circle in the sand, dropped to his knees, and said, "Lord of the universe, I swear before Your great name that I will not move from this circle until You have shown mercy upon Your children."

It was a risky proposition. Honi could have been in that circle a long time! But God honored that bold prayer because that bold prayer honored Him. And even when God answered that prayer for rain, Honi had the shameless audacity to ask for a specific type of rain. "Not for such rain have I prayed, but for rain of Your favor, blessing, and graciousness."

The moral of this parable is to prevail in prayer, but it also reveals the character of Him who answers prayer. The request is *not* granted simply because of repeated requests. Prayer is answered to preserve God's good name. After all, it's not our reputation that is on the line; it's His reputation. So God doesn't answer prayer just to give us what we want; God answers prayer to bring glory to His name.

The beauty of obedience is this: it relieves us of responsibility. It takes all the pressure off of us and places it squarely on God's sovereign shoulders.

When we give God the tithe, for example, our finances are no longer our responsibility; they become God's responsibility. God even says, "Test me in this." And if we test God, we'll find that He can do more with 90 percent than we can do with 100 percent. It turns financial management into a giving game that gets more fun the more we give. And the more we give away, the more we can enjoy what we keep.

When we pray, we relieve ourselves of responsibility. We let go and let God. We take our hands off and put our concerns into the hands of Almighty God. And trust me, He can handle whatever we put in His hands.

Sometimes we're afraid of praying for miracles because we're afraid that God won't answer, but the answer isn't up to us. We never know if the answer will be yes, no, or not yet. But the answer isn't up to us. It's not our job to answer; it's our job to ask. And Jesus exhorts us to ask.

> "Ask and it will be given to you; seek and you will find; knock and the door will be opened to you."

These three words — *ask*, *seek*, and *knock* — are present imperative verbs. In other words, they aren't something we do once; they are actions that are repeated over and over and over again.

Keep asking. Keep seeking. Keep knocking.

And, I might add, keep circling!

*The greatest tragedy in life
is the prayers that go unanswered
simply because they go unasked.*

Day 7

Put on Waders

They went forth and preached every where, the Lord ...
confirming the word with signs following.

MARK 16:20 KJV

The first testimony I received after writing *The Circle Maker*—and one of my favorites—made reference to a drought in Mississippi fifty years ago. Not unlike Honi the circle maker, whose prayer ended a first-century drought in Israel, one man's faith rose to the occasion in the land of the Delta.

When a drought threatened to destroy a season of crops, a rural church with many farmers in the congregation called for an emergency prayer meeting. Dozens of farmers showed up to pray. Most of them wore their traditional overalls, but one of them wore waders! He got a few funny looks, just like Noah did when he was building the ark, but isn't that faith at its finest? If we genuinely believe God is going to answer our prayer for rain, isn't that exactly what we would wear? Why not dress for the miracle? I love the simple, childlike faith of that old, seasoned farmer. He simply said, "I don't want to walk home wet." And he didn't. But everyone else did.

I can't help but wonder if that act of faith is what sealed the miracle. I don't know for sure, but this I do know: God is honored when we act *as if* He is going to answer our prayers! And acting *as if* means acting on our prayers. After hitting our knees, we need to take a small step of faith. And those small steps of faith often turn into giant leaps.

Like Noah, who kept building an ark day after day, we keep hammering away at the dream God has given us. Like the Israelites, who kept circling Jericho for seven days, we keep circling God's promises. Like Elijah, who kept sending his servant back to look for a rain cloud, we actively and expectantly wait for God's answer.

$85 Faith

A year before we purchased the old crack house on Capitol Hill that we turned into Ebenezer's Coffeehouse, I took an $85 step of faith. And I believe this $85 step of faith set us up for the $3 million miracle that happened many years later.

I was at an auction where items were being sold off to benefit our children's school. Most people were bidding on class projects or tickets to sporting events or vacations. Not me. I had my eye on one item: a book on Capitol Hill zoning codes donated by the Capitol Hill Restoration Society.

I knew I could buy a copy for less money *after* we got a contract on the property, but I felt I needed to demonstrate my faith and purchase it *before* we got the contract. If we weren't able to get the property, it would be a complete waste of money. But I believed that God was going to give it to us, so I acted on it by making an $85 bid. I got the book, and a few months later we got the contract on the property.

Sometimes we need to take an $85 step of faith just to show God that we're serious. It proves our faith.

Don't just pray about your dream; act on it. Act *as if* God is going to deliver on His promise. Maybe it's time to put on waders and act as if God is going to answer. Maybe it's time to make an $85 down payment on your dream.

Buy a ticket to the Broadway show you're auditioning for. Buy a new suit for the dream job you've applied for. Buy a piece of furniture for the dream home you've been saving for. Buy a share of stock. Buy a subscription. Buy a book.

This isn't some "name it, claim it" scheme. If it's not in the will of God, if it's not for the glory of God, it's a waste of time, energy, and money. But if the dream is ordained by God, then that $85 step of faith honors God. And God will honor your $85 faith. Think of it as a down payment on your dream.

Signs Following

The last two words of Mark's gospel are "signs following."

We wish it said "signs preceding."

We want God to go first. That way we don't need to exercise any faith at all. But we've got it backward. If we want to see God move, we need to make a move. If it seems like God isn't moving in our lives, maybe it's because we aren't moving. But if we make a move, God will move heaven and earth to honor our faith.

There comes a moment when we need to make a statement

of faith. I'm not talking about a collection of theological truths written on paper; I'm talking about a statement of faith written with our lives. *Faith* is not a noun; it's a verb — an action verb. The greatest and truest statement of faith is a life well lived. It is faith fleshed out through risks and sacrifices. It is daring to go after a dream that is destined to fail without divine intervention.

We can pray until our knees are numb, but if our praying isn't accompanied by acting, then we won't get anywhere. We need to put feet to our faith. After kneeling down, we need to stand up and step out in faith. There is an old adage: *the journey of a thousand miles begins with the first step.* Based on my experience, that first step is always the hardest and longest step. It will require the most faith. It will feel the most awkward. But if we step out in faith, signs will follow. In fact, an avalanche of blessing will overtake us and overwhelm us. We'll be buried in God's blessings.

Wet Feet

When the Israelites were on the verge of entering the Promised Land, God commanded the priests to step into the river. It's one of the most counterintuitive commands in Scripture: "When you reach the banks of the Jordan River, take a few steps into the river."

I don't know about you, but I don't particularly like getting my feet wet. I'd much rather have God part the river, and then I'll step into the miracle. That way I don't get my feet wet, but if we aren't willing to get our feet wet, we'll never walk through parted rivers on dry ground.

At flood tide, the Jordan River was approximately two hundred feet wide. That was all that separated the Israelites from their four-hundred-year-old promise. Their dream was practically a stone's throw away. But if the priests hadn't stepped into the river, they may well have spent the rest of their lives on the eastern banks of the Jordan River. And that's where many of us spend our lives. We're so close to the dream, so close to the promise, so close to the miracle. But we're waiting for God to part the river, while God is waiting for us to get our feet wet.

We'll never see God part the Jordan River if our feet are firmly planted on dry ground. But if we step into the river, God will part it.

If you want to see God move,
make a move.

Day 8

One God-Idea

"Speak to the earth, and it will teach you."

JOB 12:8

Around the turn of the twentieth century, the agricultural economy of the South was suffering as the boll weevil devastated cotton crops. The soil was being depleted of nutrients because farmers planted cotton year in and year out.

Enter George Washington Carver, one of the most brilliant scientific minds of the twentieth century. Carver introduced the concept of crop rotation and encouraged farmers to plant peanuts instead of cotton. The rotation of crops revived the soil, but it didn't revive the economy because there was no market for peanuts. The abundant peanut crop rotted in warehouses because supply was greater than demand. When frustrated farmers complained to Carver, he did what he had always done: he took a long walk and had a long talk with God.

George Washington Carver routinely got up at 4:00 a.m., walked through the woods, and asked God to reveal the mysteries of nature. Job 12:7 – 8 was one of the most-circled promises in his Bible.

"But ask the animals, and they will teach you,
or the birds in the sky, and they will tell you;
or speak to the earth, and it will teach you,
or let the fish in the sea inform you."

Carver took that promise at face value. He literally asked God to reveal the mysteries of nature. And God answered his prayer. Carver is famous for discovering more than three hundred uses for the peanut, but the genesis of those revelations was one conversation with God. In his own inimitable fashion, Carver shared the story behind the story.

I asked God, "Why did you make the universe, Lord?"
"Ask for something more in proportion to that little mind of yours," replied God.
"Why did you make the earth, Lord?" I asked.
"Your little mind still wants to know far too much. Ask for something more in proportion to that little mind of yours," replied God.
"Why did you make man, Lord?" I asked.
"Far too much. Far too much. Ask again," replied God.
"Explain to me why you made plants, Lord," I asked.
"Your little mind still wants to know far too much."
"The peanut?" I asked meekly.
"Yes! For your modest proportions, I will grant you the mystery of the peanut. Take it inside your laboratory and separate it into water, fats, oils, gums, resins, sugars, starches, and amino acids. Then recombine these under my three laws of compatibility, temperature, and pressure. Then you will know why I made the peanut."

On January 20, 1921, George Washington Carver testified before the House Ways and Means Committee on behalf of the United Peanut Association of America. The chairman, Joseph Fordney of Michigan, told him he had ten minutes. An hour and forty minutes later, the committee told Carver he could come back whenever he wanted and take as much time as he needed. Carver mesmerized the committee by demonstrating a myriad of ingenious uses for the peanut — everything from glue to shaving cream to soap to insecticide to cosmetics to wood stains to fertilizer to linoleum to Worcestershire sauce.

The next time you shave or put on makeup, the next time you stain the deck or fertilize your garden, the next time you enjoy a good old-fashioned PBJ, remember that all of those things trace back to a man who had a habit of praying at 4:00 a.m.

Those three hundred uses of the peanut were *not* good ideas; they were God-ideas. And one God-idea is worth more than a thousand good ideas.

Good ideas are good, but only God-ideas change the course of history.

God-Ideas

Every year, we have an annual theme at National Community Church. It's not just some catchy phrase that rhymes with the year, like "Learning to Lean in 2013." It's the by-product of pressing into God's presence and discerning what God wants to do in us and through us. The theme this year is simply this: *Get into God's presence.*

That is the solution to every problem. That is the answer to every question.

We don't get a vision from God by going to conferences. We might get some good ideas, but God-ideas are only revealed in the presence of God.

Everyone needs counseling of some sort at some point in their lives, but our biggest problems are only solved in the presence of God.

Go ahead and do a planning meeting. After all, failing to plan is planning to fail. But don't just brainstorm; praystorm. The best plans are birthed in the presence of God.

At some point in our lives, the best we can do isn't good enough. Our best solutions, ideas, and efforts aren't good enough. That's when we need to hit our knees and trust God to do what only God can do. After all, *prayer is the difference between the best you can do and the best God can do.* And that's a big difference!

If we hit our knees, the Holy Spirit will do the heavy lifting. If we hit our knees, the Holy Spirit will reveal things that can only be discovered in the presence of God. If we hit our knees, the Holy Spirit will give us God-ideas for our ministry, family, business — for our lives.

The Solution to 10,000 Problems

The modern mystic A. W. Tozer believed that a low view of God is the cause of a hundred lesser evils, but a high view of God is the solution to ten thousand temporal problems. If that's true, and I believe it is, then your biggest problem isn't an impending divorce or a doctor's diagnosis or a failing business. Please understand, I'm not making light of your relational, financial, or health issues. I certainly don't want to minimize the overwhelming challenges you may be facing. But in order to regain a godly perspective on your problems, you must answer this question: *Are my problems bigger than God, or is God bigger than my problems?*

Our biggest problem is our small view of God. That is the cause of all lesser evils. And a high view of God is the solution to all other problems.

Until we come to the conviction that God's grace and God's power know no limits, we will draw small prayer circles. But once we embrace the omnipotence of God, we'll draw ever-enlarging circles around our God-given, God-sized dreams.

How big is your God?

Is He big enough to heal your marriage or heal your child? Is He bigger than a positive MRI or a negative evaluation? Is He bigger than your worst sin, greatest fear, or biggest dream?

If He is bigger than all of those things, then pray like it.

One God-idea is worth more than a thousand good ideas.

Day 9

Dream Factory

We take captive every thought
to make it obedient to Christ.

2 CORINTHIANS 10:5

I have a friend who is out to change the world, one malnourished child at a time.

In fall 2008, Mark Moore was working on Capitol Hill after spending ten years in Africa as a missionary. That's when a briefing from a UNICEF representative changed the trajectory of his life. The rep shared about a revolutionary food supplement called RUTF — Ready-to-Use Therapeutic Food — and showed a *60 Minutes* clip featuring Anderson Cooper, who called it "the most important advance ever to cure and treat malnutrition." For Mark, discovering RUTF was like discovering the cure for cancer. It was more than a good idea; he knew it was a God-idea.

The primary ingredient in RUTF is peanut paste. Peanuts are high in calories and rich in proteins, which support the immune system. And the combination of vitamins and minerals are easily digestible for those whose stomachs have shrunk because of malnutrition. It's the perfect food, the miracle food.

I'm not sure George Washington Carver knew that peanut paste would become the single greatest weapon in the fight against malnutrition, but God knew. And the revelation that saved the agricultural economy of the South a hundred years ago has the potential to save millions of lives today. That is the potential of one God-idea. That is the by-product of one prayer.

On October 16, 2009, Mark launched MANA, which stands for Mother Administered Nutritive Aid. But the acronym is really a double entendre. Like the manna that God provided for the Israelites in the wilderness, it's a miracle for those who receive it!

After stepping into the Jordan River and launching MANA, Mark set out to build a facility that could produce mass quantities of RUTF at cheap prices — but he knew God would have to part the waters. He targeted Georgia since it was the peanut capital of the country, and he identified a town called Fitzgerald. When he shared the vision of MANA with the mayor, the mayor said he'd do everything in his power to facilitate and expedite the building permits if Mark could raise $1 million. One trip to Houston, and one angel donor, took care of the $1 million. And within two weeks, they broke ground on a 30,000 square-foot facility that can produce up to 18,000 packets of RUTF every hour. Last month, MANA produced more than one million lifesaving packets!

Dream Factory

Now here's the rest of the story.

Not long after this God-idea got into his spirit, Mark sent

me an e-mail with the subject line "A Million Lives Saved at Ebenezer's." That got my attention! Mark explained that the vision for MANA was conceived at our coffeehouse. And the official launch, which took place on World Food Day, happened at Ebenezer's as well. So I felt like an accomplice to a holy conspiracy.

Then I remembered a prayer we had prayed many years before. And I connected the dots between that prophetic prayer and its fulfillment.

On March 13, 2006, we dedicated Ebenezer's Coffeehouse to the Lord. We laid hands on the walls, wrote prayers on the floors, and prayed for every person who would walk through our doors — which would have included Mark.

The most memorable moment, however, was when one of our staff members specifically prayed that Ebenezer's would be a *dream factory*. It was one of those moments when you almost open your eyes during prayer to see if it impacted everyone else the same way. It was a specific prayer, a prophetic prayer. This one prayer has been answered hundreds of times since it was first prayed. And Mark is an example of how God can answer one prayer in a way that will affect millions of lives. This is what Mark wrote:

The dream of MANA was formed in the dream factory of Ebenezer's Coffeehouse. Its great coffee and free Wi-Fi made for the perfect office. As that dream began to gel and I began to pull together resources and relationships to pursue the dream, Ebenezer's became the meeting place. Meeting after meeting occurred there. Many were planned and scheduled, as in "meet me at Ebenezer's at 2:00 p.m.," but many more happened by accident. Those meetings led to new ideas, new partnerships, new opportunities, and new relationships that eventually brought us to where we are today.

Severe acute malnutrition will not be stopped by one organization putting peanut paste in a pouch, but we can launch the greatest attack ever on malnutrition and the needless death it brings.

This idea, conceived in Mark's spirit at Ebenezer's Coffeehouse, was more than a good idea; it was a God-idea. And when you get a God-idea, you need to take it captive. In the words of Paul, "Take captive every thought to make it obedient to Christ."

Growing up, I consistently heard this verse interpreted in negative terms. Take captive sinful thoughts and make them obedient to Christ. And that is half the battle. But if we see only the negative implications and not the positive possibilities, it becomes a half-truth. This verse is not just about capturing sinful thoughts and getting them out of our minds; it's also about capturing creative thoughts and keeping them in our minds. It means stewarding every word, thought, impression, and revelation inspired by the Spirit of God.

The first half is taking captive every thought. One of the best ways to capture thoughts is a prayer journal. The second half is making it obedient to Christ — and that requires blood, sweat, and tears.

When I was nineteen years old, I heard a message about Benaiah, King David's bodyguard who chased a lion into a pit on a snowy day and killed it. When I listened to that message, a thought fired across my synapses: *If I ever write a book, I want to write one about that verse in the Bible.* I held captive that thought for nineteen years! Then I made it obedient to Christ by setting my alarm very early in the morning, sitting down at my keyboard, and writing a book titled *In a Pit with a Lion on a Snowy Day.* That book started out as a God-idea, but writing it was an act of obedience.

Nolan Bushnell, the creator of the Atari video game system, once stated, "Everyone who's ever taken a shower has had an idea. It's the person who gets out of the shower, dries off, and does something about it who makes a difference."

Draw the Circle

Never underestimate the power
of a single prayer.

Crazy Faith

"This woman is driving me crazy."
LUKE 18:5 NLT

I love the parable of the persistent widow. I don't mean any disrespect, but I think *persistent* is a nice word for *crazy*. This woman is crazy, but when the cause is a righteous one, it's a holy crazy!

We aren't told what injustice took place, but she was on a mission. Maybe her son was falsely imprisoned for a crime he didn't commit. Maybe the man who molested her daughter was still on the streets. We don't know for sure. But whatever it was, she wouldn't take no for an answer. And the judge knew it. The judge knew she would circle his house until the day she got justice or the day she died. The judge knew there was no quit in the crazy woman.

Does *the Judge* know that about you?

How desperate are you for the blessing, the breakthrough, the miracle? Desperate enough to pray through the night? How many times are you willing to circle the promise? Until the day you die? How long will you knock on the door of opportunity? Until your knuckles are raw? Until you knock the door down?

Like Honi the circle maker, the persistent widow's methodology was unorthodox. She could have, and technically should have, waited for her day in court. Going to the personal residence of the judge crossed a professional line. I'm almost surprised the judge didn't file a restraining order against her. But this reveals something about the nature of God. *God couldn't care less about protocol.* If He did, Jesus would have chosen the Pharisees as His disciples. But that isn't who Jesus honored.

Jesus honored the prostitute who crashed a party at a Pharisee's home to anoint His feet. Jesus honored the tax collector who climbed a tree in his three-piece suit just to get a glimpse of Him. Jesus honored the four friends who cut in line and cut a hole in someone's ceiling to help their friend. And in this parable, Jesus honored the crazy woman who drove a judge crazy because she wouldn't stop knocking.

The common denominator in each of these stories is crazy faith. People took desperate measures to get to God, and God honored them for it. Nothing has changed. God is still honoring spiritual desperadoes who crash parties and climb trees. God is still honoring those who defy protocol with their bold prayers. God is still honoring those who pray with audacity and tenacity. And the crazy woman is selected as the gold standard when it comes to praying hard. Her unrelenting persistence was the only difference between justice and injustice.

The viability of our prayers is not contingent on scrabbling the twenty-six letters of the English alphabet into the right combinations like *abracadabra*. God already knows the last punctuation mark before we pronounce the first syllable. The viability of our prayers has more to do with intensity than vocabulary. It has more to do with what we do than what we say.

Don't just pray about it; act on it.

There are defining moments in life when we need to prove to God that we mean business — and I don't mean "business as usual." In fact, it's only when "business as usual" goes out of business that we're in business — the Father's business. That's when we're on the verge of a spiritual breakthrough.

Crazy Is Normal

Josh Sexton pastors a church plant in North Carolina called Relevant Truth Church. God is doing amazing things at RTC. People who wouldn't darken the doorway of a church are finding a relationship with Jesus Christ at an indoor skate park that has been converted into a sanctuary. But like many church plants, there is more vision than money. RTC was facing the termination of their lease if they couldn't come up with the $3,500 rent when Josh got an idea while reading *The Circle Maker*. One of the leaders at RTC relayed what happened.

> *Josh asked me to come to the front during a worship service. He handed me a can of spray paint and asked me to paint a circle on stage. That's when Josh told us he wasn't going*

to leave the circle until God made provision for the church. With his wife's blessing, he brought in a bed and ordered a Port-a-John. All he had was his Bible and his prayer journal. Three times a day, his wife brings him meals. My wife and I live down the street, so we're helping with the kids.

I think Josh came to the place of desperation. If this thing was going to work, God was going to have to show up and show off. I really think he is planning on staying in that circle until God does something huge. Crazy huh?

Crazy?

Or maybe it's not crazy!

Maybe our normal is so subnormal that normal seems abnormal. Maybe we need a new normal. Bold prayers and big dreams are normal. Anything less is subnormal. And when bold prayers become the norm, so do the miraculous breakthroughs that follow.

I know there may be naysayers who find fault with Josh's approach, but sometimes you need to do something crazy, something risky, something dramatic. That's what Honi the circle maker did when he drew a circle in the sand and declared that he wouldn't come out until it rained. The Sanhedrin almost excommunicated him because they thought his prayer was too bold. But you cannot argue with a miracle, can you? His radical prayer resulted in rain. And Honi was ultimately honored for "the prayer that saved a generation."

For the record, the Sanhedrin still exists in every organization, every denomination, and every church. But don't let the nitpickers and naysayers keep you from doing something crazy if you know God has called you to do it. For the record, RTC didn't just get a new lease on their building; they got a new lease on their faith!

There is a pattern repeated in Scripture: crazy miracles are the offspring of crazy faith. Normal begets normal. Crazy begets crazy. If we want to see God do crazy miracles, sometimes we need to pray crazy prayers.

Bold prayers honor God and God honors bold prayers.

Day 11

First-Class Noticer

Devote yourselves to prayer,
being watchful and thankful.

COLOSSIANS 4:2

The word *watchful* is a throwback to the Old Testament–era practice of sitting on a city wall and keeping watch. Watchmen were the first ones to see attacking armies or traveling traders. They had the best vantage point. They saw things no one else saw. They saw things before others saw them. And this is precisely what happens when we pray. We see things no one else sees. We see things before others see them. We become God's watchmen.

Prayer is the difference between seeing with our physical eyes and seeing with our spiritual eyes. Prayer gives us a God's-eye view. It heightens our awareness and gives us a sixth sense that enables us to perceive spiritual realities that are beyond our five senses.

In their classic book *Geeks & Geezers*, business gurus Warren Bennis and Robert Thomas make an interesting observation about a common denominator among successful leaders in every field. Bennis and Thomas call them "first-class noticers."

Being a first-class noticer allows you to recognize talent, identify opportunities, and avoid pitfalls. Leaders who succeed again and again are geniuses at grasping context. This is one of those characteristics, like taste, that is difficult to break down into its component parts. But the ability to weigh a welter of factors, some as subtle as how very different groups of people will interpret a gesture, is one of the hallmarks of a true leader.

Prayer turns us into first-class noticers. It helps us see what God wants us to notice. The more you pray, the more you notice; the less you pray, the less you notice. It's as simple as that.

Let me explain how it works from a neurological perspective. There is a cluster of nerve cells at the base of our brain stem called the reticular activating system that monitors our environment. We are constantly bombarded by countless stimuli vying for our attention, and it is the job of the RAS to determine what gets noticed and what goes unnoticed.

So you download a new ringtone. And you'd swear you've never heard it before, but after downloading it, it seems like everybody else has the same ringtone. It's not that lots of people went out and downloaded it when you did. It's the simple fact that when you downloaded that ringtone, it created a category in your RAS. That ringtone went unnoticed by you before you downloaded it because it wasn't important to you. Once you downloaded the ringtone, the RAS recognized it as relevant.

When you pray for someone or something, it creates a category in your reticular activating system. You start noticing anything related to those prayers. Have you ever noticed that when you pray, coincidences happen? And when you don't, they don't. It's more than coincidence; it's providence. Prayer creates divine opportunities. But prayer also sanctifies the reticular activating system and enables you to see the God-ordained opportunities that are all around you all the time. And once you see them, you have to seize them.

The Aramaic word for prayer *(slotha)* means "to set a trap." Opportunities are like wild animals. They are tough to capture. If you're going to seize them, you've got to set prayer traps.

We often think of prayer as nothing more than words spoken to God, but maybe it's more than that. Prayer is not a monologue; it's a dialogue. We speak to God with everything from words to groans to thoughts. And God speaks to us through dreams, desires, promptings, impressions, and ideas.

The Sixth Sense

There is an old adage: *Beauty is in the eye of the beholder.* In reality, *everything* is in the eye of the beholder. The emotions we experience don't reflect our external reality; they reflect our internal reality. We don't see the world as it is; we see the world as we are. That's why prayer is so critical. It's a way of seeing reality — and, more specifically, the reality that is beyond that reality we can perceive with our five senses.

Some things cannot be perceived with the five senses; they can only be conceived by the Holy Spirit. Some things cannot be deduced via deductive reasoning; they can only be imagined by the Holy Spirit. Some things cannot be learned by logic; they can only be revealed by the Holy Spirit.

The Holy Spirit compensates for our sensory limits by enabling us to conceive of things we cannot perceive with our five senses. Think of it as a sixth sense. The revelation of the Spirit gives us extrasensory perception, in the truest sense of that phrase. He helps us see the invisible and hear the inaudible. But that sixth sense has to be cultivated, much like our five senses do. Our spiritual vision develops much like our physical vision does.

When babies make their grand entrance into the world, their visual resolution is one-fortieth of that of a normal adult. They lack depth perception. And their visual range is only about thirteen inches. The world is low-definition, two-dimensional, and only thirteen inches in diameter. Slowly yet sovereignly, the world begins to take on width and breadth and depth. By four months, a baby can perceive stereoscopic depth. By six months, visual acuity has improved fivefold. Their black-and-white world has burst into a kaleidoscope of colors, and they have volitional control of their eye movements. And by his or her first birthday, the child sees the world almost as well as an adult.

Our spiritual eyes develop in much the same way. And prayer is the key to perception. Before our spiritual eyes are opened, the world is only thirteen inches in diameter. It's like living in a low-definition, two-dimensional world. Then the Holy Spirit gives us depth perception. He opens our eyes to see the ordinary miracles that surround us, the ordinary miracles that are us. It's like our spiritual cataracts are removed to reveal a reality that was always there. Like Jacob, we come to the ultimate realization: "Surely the LORD is in this place, and I was not aware of it."

When we open our spiritual eyes, we start seeing God everywhere we look. We see the image of God in others. We see His fingerprints on His creation. We see God-ordained opportunities all around us all the time.

It's something like what happens when we watch a film with 3D glasses; when we pray, God comes at us in ways that startle and thrill us.

Draw the Circle

We don't see the world as it is;
we see the world as we are.

Day 12

Sow a Seed

*"If you have faith as small as
a mustard seed ..."*
MATTHEW 17:20

Standing beneath a giant sequoia is like standing in the shadow of the Creator. It was absolutely awe-inspiring on my first visit to Yosemite National Park. These magnificent creations can measure more than twenty feet wide and three hundred feet tall. The root system goes down about twelve feet and stretches out into an area about eighty feet in diameter. Their resistance to disease, insect damage, and fire make them almost indestructible. And their built-in ability to recycle and regenerate contributes to their two-thousand-year life span.

Now here is the amazing thing: the giant sequoia was once a seed. And that sequoia seed is no bigger than the seed that produces a tomato plant. That is the power of a single seed. And one sequoia, when it matures, will produce 400,000 seeds of its own every year. So in every seed, there isn't just a tree; there is a forest of trees.

Then God said, "Let the land sprout with vegetation — every sort of seed-bearing plant, and trees that grow seed-bearing fruit. These seeds will then produce the kinds of plants and trees from which they came."

And we just keep reading the Genesis account as if nothing happened. Granted, there are more spectacular creations than the simple seed — the sun, moon, and stars, for example. But the seed may be the most amazing example of God's prolific creativity. And we certainly owe God a thank-you for every kind of seed every time we bite into the fruit they produce — orange seeds, apple seeds, strawberry seeds, grapefruit seeds, pomegranate seeds, watermelon seeds.

Can you imagine life without any of these seeds?

William Jennings Bryan, famous for his role in the Scopes Monkey Trial in 1925, once likened the mystery of God to a watermelon seed:

I have observed the watermelon seed. It has the power of drawing from the ground and through itself 200,000 times its weight: and when you can tell me how it takes this material and out of it colors an outside surface beyond the imitation of art, and then forms in it a white rind and within that again a side of red heart, thickly inlaid with black seeds, each one of which in turn is capable of drawing through itself 200,000 times its weight — when you can explain to me the mystery of a watermelon, you can ask me to explain the mystery of God.

Mustard Seed

If we are going to understand the potential of faith, we have to understand the power of a seed. Jesus spoke of our faith in relation to a mustard seed, the smallest known garden seed in that culture. Like every seed, it needs to germinate, and this particular seed can take up to ten days to germinate. Some plants, like some dreams, take a lot longer. My dream of writing had to germinate for thirteen years! And some of my goals will take decades to accomplish! Faith is what keeps those dreams alive, even when it seems as though they are dead and buried. But that is the very nature of seeds. They go underground. They disappear. And while it may seem like they are dead, they are not. They're just germinating beneath the surface!

If you saw a mustard seed but didn't know what it was, you would have a hard time imagining what it could become. The potential is disguised in an awfully small package. You would have no clue that the mustard you put on your hot dog is the by-product of a tiny seed that was planted in the ground. You would have no idea what the seed would grow to become or how big it could get. And that is true of every seed. Would you guess that an acorn would become an oak? You'd never guess that a black seed would become a green watermelon with a red interior that tastes amazing!

In case you were wondering, the tiny mustard seed contains all the nutrients you need to survive. It's packed with vitamins B1, B6, C, E, and K. It's a source of calcium, iron, magnesium, phosphorus, potassium, selenium, and zinc.

Faith is a lot like that. It doesn't look like much, but we never know what it can become. A little faith goes a long way; in fact, a little faith will last an eternity.

The Speed of a Seed

Toward the end of his life, Honi the circle maker was walking down a dirt road when he saw a man planting a carob tree. Honi questioned him. "How long will it take this tree to bear fruit?" The man replied, "Seventy years." Honi said, "Are you quite sure you will live another seventy years to eat its fruit?" The man replied, "Perhaps not. However, when I was born into this world, I found many carob trees planted by my father and grandfather. Just as they planted trees for me, I am planting trees for my children and grandchildren so they will be able to eat the fruit of these trees."

This incident led to an insight that changed the way Honi prayed. In a moment of revelation, the circle maker realized that praying is planting. Each prayer is like a seed that gets planted in the ground. It disappears for a season, but it eventually bears fruit that blesses future generations. In fact, our prayers bear fruit forever.

Even when we die, our prayers don't. Each prayer takes on a life, an eternal life, of its own.

Because we are surrounded by technologies that make our lives faster and easier, we tend to think about spiritual realities in technological terms. We want to reap the very second we sow. We want God to microwave answers, MapQuest directions, and Twitter instructions. We want things to happen at the speed of light instead of the speed of a seed planted in the ground, but almost all spiritual realities in Scripture are described in agricultural terms. We want our dreams to become reality overnight. We want our prayers answered immediately. But that isn't the way it works in God's kingdom.

We need the patience of the planter.

We need the foresight of the farmer.

We need the mind-set of the sower.

We worry far too much about outcomes instead of focusing on inputs. We cannot make things grow. Period. All we can do is plant and water. But if we plant and water, God promises to give the increase.

This is both bad news and good news. We cannot break the law of sowing and reaping any more than we can break the law of gravity. No farmer would plant beans and expect to harvest corn!

If you sow kindness, you will reap kindness.

If you sow generosity, you will reap generosity.

If you sow love, you will reap love.

All of us go through times of spiritual, relational, or financial famines. It seems like the harvest will never come. And the temptation is to stop planting, but my advice is simple: sow a seed. Keep praying, keep obeying, keep giving, keep loving, keep serving. And if you keep sowing the right seeds, the harvest of blessing will come in God's time, in God's way!

If we do the little things like they are big things, then God will do the big things like they are little things.

One Day

*One day
at about three in the afternoon
he had a vision.*

ACTS 10:3

I love the two-word phrase in Acts 10:3: *one day*. It is pregnant with hope. Why? Because one day could be today. Today could be the day that God answers the prayer, performs the miracle, or keeps the promise!

In *one day*, God can deliver from an addiction that has held a person captive for years. In *one day*, God can bring back a prodigal child who has run away and been gone for decades. In *one day*, God can provide more than someone has accumulated in a lifetime. But if we are going to experience a miracle *one day*, we need to pray every day. Too many people pray like they are playing the lottery. Prayer is more like an investment account. Every deposit accumulates compound interest. And *one day*, if we keep making deposits every day, it will pay dividends beyond our wildest imagination.

$3 Million Miracle

One reason I love Acts 10:3 is because one of the greatest miracles I've ever experienced happened "one day at about three in the afternoon." I received a phone call on a Wednesday afternoon that changed the trajectory of my life personally and the life of our church corporately. Nothing could have prepared me to hear these words: "We want to give you three million dollars." I was absolutely speechless. And I'm a preacher! The caller graciously broke the awkward silence. He told me there were no strings attached and they wanted to remain anonymous. Then he explained the rationale behind the gift: "Pastor Mark, we love your vision and trust your leadership. There are some churches we wouldn't feel comfortable investing in because they wouldn't know what to do with the money, but you have vision beyond your resources."

That phrase will echo in my auditory cortex forever: *vision beyond your resources.*

That phrase has become a mantra at National Community Church and is inspiring us to continue dreaming irrational dreams. We certainly practice sound financial management, count the cost of every vision, and steward every penny in a way that honors God, but we refuse to let our budget determine our vision. That would be poor stewardship because it's based on our limited resources rather than on God's unlimited supply. Too often we butcher our God-given dreams because we forget the simple fact that God owns the cattle on a thousand hills. Don't let fear dictate your decisions. Letting your budget determine your vision is backward. Faith is letting your vision determine your budget. And if your vision is God-given, it will most definitely be *beyond your ability* and *beyond your resources*. Why? Because then God will get all of the glory! And I promise you this: *the God who gives the vision is the same God who makes provision.*

One Better

Our church is amazingly generous, but our median age is twenty-eight, which means most of our attendees are nowhere near their peak earning potential. They are faithfully tithing on their income as Hill staffers or inner-city schoolteachers or coffeehouse baristas, but they don't have the income or savings accounts to give large financial gifts. They are focused on paying off school loans or saving for a wedding. Over the course of thirteen years, the largest single gift we had ever received was a $42,000 tithe on the sale of a home. I honestly had no idea that anybody in our congregation had the means to give this kind of gift. I've since learned that the miracle is already in the house!

On March 15, 2006, we opened the doors to our coffeehouse on Capitol Hill. The total cost of building Ebenezer's Coffeehouse was about $3 million, and our mortgage was $2 million. One day, as I was praying, I felt prompted to pray for a $2 million miracle. The first thing I had to do was decipher whether this prompting was just my own desire to be debt-free or whether it was the Holy Spirit who dropped that promise into my heart. It's tough to discern between wishful thinking and prayerful promptings, but I was about 90 percent sure it was the Holy Spirit who put that promise in my heart. I had no idea how God would do it, but I knew I needed to circle that promise in prayer. I mentioned the $2 million miracle to four people in my prayer circle, and we started praying for God's provision.

Certainly weeks went by when I failed to even think or pray about the promise, but we did circle that $2 million promise off and on for four years. At one point, I got a little impatient and tried to manufacture the miracle with a start-up business. Unfortunately, what I thought was a $2 million idea turned into a $15,000 personal loss. I was tempted to give up when my plan failed, but we kept circling that promise in prayer. Then one day at about three in the afternoon, I got the phone call. The amazing thing is that we weren't even in a capital campaign. We weren't asking for money publically; we were just praying for it privately.

The moment I heard those words, "We want to give you three million dollars," I knew it was a fulfillment of the promise God had given us. I was, however, a little confused by the amount. We had been praying for $2 million, not $3 million. That's when the Holy Spirit seemed to say in a playful tone, *Mark, I just wanted you to know that I can do one better.* And, of course, He meant $1 million better!

Degree of Difficulty

Whenever I'm praying for something that is way beyond my ability or resources, I tend to pray longer and louder. I'll pull out the biggest theological words I know and pray in King James language. I mistakenly think my combination of words will somehow unlock the miracle, but I'm learning that God listens more to our hearts than our words. And what God loves more than anything else is childlike faith. It's our child-like faith, not our theological vocabulary, that moves the heart of our heavenly Father. It's simple childlike trust. It's the bedrock belief that God is bigger than our problem, bigger than our mistake, bigger than our dream.

When we pray, we tend to rank our requests by degree of difficulty. We see our requests as big or small, easy or difficult, simple or complex. But let me remind you of this simple yet profound truth: to the infinite, all finites are the same.

When Jesus walked out of the tomb, the word *impossible* was removed from our vocabulary. The size of your prayers depends on the size of your God. If your god is small, you'll pray man-sized prayers. But if your God knows no limits, then neither will your prayers. The God we pray to exists outside of the four space-time dimensions He created, and maybe we should pray that way!

I love the story about the man who sized up God in prayer one day. "God, how long is a million years to you?" God said, "A million years is like a second." Then the man asked, "How much is a million dollars to you?" God said, "A million dollars is like a penny." The man smiled and said, "Could you spare a penny?" God smiled back and said, "Sure, just wait a second."

A three million dollar gift was way beyond what I would have asked for or imagined, but then the miracle happened.

And even larger gifts have been given since that $3 million miracle. Please don't miss or dismiss what you're about to read: the way you steward the miracles of God is by believing for bigger and better miracles. God stretches your faith so you can dream bigger dreams.

God can accomplish more in one day than you can accomplish in a lifetime.

Speak to the Mountain

"Say to this mountain,
'Move from here to there,'
and it will move."
MATTHEW 17:20

There comes a moment when you must quit talking to God about the mountain in your life and start talking to the mountain about your God. You proclaim His power. You declare His sovereignty. You affirm His faithfulness. You stand on His Word. You cling to His promises.

Goliath held an entire army captive through fear. His weapon was intimidation. And that is how our enemy operates. He prowls around *like* a roaring lion. But the important word is *like*. He's an imposter. Jesus *is* the Lion of the tribe of Judah. And when He roars, everything is shaken. All authority under heaven and on earth is His. And we are His children. Why don't we live like it, love like it, give like it, serve like it, and pray like it?

If God is for us, who can be against us?
The one who is in you is greater than the one who is in the world.

I can do all things through Christ who strengthens me.
In all things God works for the good of those who love him,
who have been called according to his purpose.

What did Jesus do when Satan tempted Him in the wilderness? He fell back on the word of God. He used it like a skilled swordsman. And He wasn't just defending Himself; He was delivering blows by citing chapter and verse!

Maybe we need to quit playing defense and start playing offense. Maybe we need to quit letting our circumstances get between us and God and let God get between us and our circumstances. Maybe we need to stop talking to God about our problem and start talking to our problem about God.

More Than Conquerors

It's time to claim the victory that has already been won at Calvary. We are *not* conquerors; we are *more than conquerors* through Christ.

Jesus proclaimed the victory when He said, "I will build My church, and the gates of Hades shall not prevail against it." Let me make two observations. First, notice the pronouns. He did not say, "*You* will build My church"; He said, "*I* will build *My* church." The key pronouns are *I* and *My*. The church belongs to Jesus Christ. So does the battle. So does the victory.

Second, it says that the gates of Hades will not prevail. Gates are defensive measures, which means, by definition, that the church is on the offense. It's high time for an all-out attack on the enemy! The battlefield is the prayer closet. And secret prayer is our secret weapon.

When we hit our knees, we pick a fight with the enemy. We are immediately transported to the front lines of the kingdom, where we wage war with principalities and powers. That is where the battle is won or lost — on our knees! And when we hit our knees, God fights our battles for us.

Praying for Pharaoh

When we purchased the crack house that we turned into our coffeehouse on Capitol Hill, it took two miracles. The first miracle was getting the property; the second was getting it rezoned from residential to commercial.

For eighteen months, we met with everybody from the Historic Preservation Office to the Office of Planning to the Capitol Hill Restoration Society. We had overwhelming community backing. After all, we were investing $3 million to turn a crack house into a coffeehouse. But during the rezoning process, some influential neighbors decided to oppose our rezoning efforts because of misinformation about what we planned to do. I followed a link to a website where they were slandering our motives. To be honest, I was so upset I was ready for a throwdown! Their opposition had the potential to short-circuit our dream of building a coffeehouse, and I got angrier every time I thought about it. That's when I discovered the power of praying circles around the pharaohs in your life. And for the record, there will always be pharaohs who get in the way of what God wants to do in your life.

All of us have impossible people in our lives. All we can do is circle them in prayer. It's the only way to keep our attitude in check. And prayer has the power to change the heart of Pharaoh. So every time I got angry, I converted it into a prayer. I think it's the closest I've ever come to praying without ceasing because I was angry all the time.

I prayed for those neighbors for several months leading up to our hearing before the zoning commission. I'll never forget the feeling as we walked into the hearing room and sat down at our tables on either side of the aisle. I had absolutely no animosity toward the people who were opposing us. I felt an unexplainable compassion for the people who opposed us, and I wasn't worried about what they said or did because I had circled them in prayer. I had also circled the zoning commissioners. Not only did we win unanimous approval from the zoning commission, which is a testament to God's favor, but one of our opponents is now a regular customer at our coffeehouse!

The two-year ordeal of rezoning was emotionally and spiritually exhausting, but that is how to increase spiritual endurance. When it was all over, I thanked God for the opposition we encountered because it galvanized our resolve and unified our church. I learned that we don't have to be afraid of the enemy's attacks. These attacks are counterproductive when we counteract them with prayer. The more opposition we experience, the harder we have to pray. And the harder we have to pray, the more miracles God does.

*Quit talking to God about your problem
and start talking to your problem about God.*

Contend for Me

Contend for me,
my God and Lord.
PSALM 35:23

G od loves it when we fight for Him. But God loves it even more when we let Him fight for us! How do we do that? When we hit our knees, God extends His mighty right hand on our behalf. When we pray, He fights our battles for us. So keep fighting the good fight, but let God fight for you.

Prayer is the way we let go and let God. Prayer is the way we take our hands off and let God put His hands on. Prayer is the difference between you fighting for God and God fighting for you.

> Contend, LORD, with those who contend with me;
>   fight against those who fight against me …
> Awake, and rise to my defense!
>   Contend for me, my God and Lord.

I love the Hebrew word translated "contend" in these verses. It's two-dimensional. It refers to both physical combat and verbal combat. So it runs the gamut from cage fighting to courtrooms.

In terms of physical combat, God is like the mother grizzly that protects her cubs. It is God's instinctive nature because we are the apple of His eye. If anyone messes with us, they are messing with our heavenly Father.

In terms of verbal combat, God is like the defense attorney that pleads our case, pleads our cause. When our backs are against the wall, God has our backs. When everything is on the line, God steps in. Satan is the accuser of the brethren, but he's no match for the Paraclete.

The New Testament depiction of this is a little more defined. We actually have two intercessors. The Holy Spirit is interceding for us with groans that cannot be uttered. Long before we woke up this morning and long after we go to sleep tonight, the Holy Spirit was and is circling us in prayer. And if that doesn't infuse us with holy confidence, I don't know what will. But it isn't just the Holy Spirit who is interceding for us; the Son of God is interceding for us as well. They are interceding for the will of God to be accomplished in our lives. We are double circled. They are circling us all the time with songs of deliverance.

I made a determination a few years ago that I wasn't going to defend myself against any and every criticism that comes my way. Life is too short, and the mission is too important. And I'm called to play offense, not defense. God is my defender. And I believe He is contending for me if my cause is just and my heart is right.

It's important for us to have people in our lives who can speak words of rebuke and exhortation. But they will typically be someone with whom we have a relationship. When discerning whether to respond to criticism, I try to discern the spirit of the person doing the criticizing. Is the purpose redemptive or vindictive? And I put the criticism through the filter of Scripture. If it passes through the filter, then I need to repent. If it doesn't, then I don't let it pierce my heart. And I let God defend and contend on my behalf.

There are some battlefields I'm willing to die on, but there are some I'm not willing to die on. I won't engage in the combat of criticism. It is sideways energy, and it doesn't have a redemptive purpose. I overlook the offense so I can keep playing offense.

The First Official Prayer

On September 7, 1774, the Continental Congress held its first official meeting at Carpenter's Hall in Philadelphia. Their first official act was prayer. And it wasn't some perfunctory prayer that was nothing more than protocol; it was a good old-fashioned prayer meeting. Our founding fathers prayed with fervency and intensity. Earwitnesses heard them interceding several blocks away. Eyewitnesses said Henry, Randolph, Rutledge, Lee, and Jay were doubled over as they bowed in reverence before God. John Adams later recounted that it "has had an excellent effect upon every body here." And not surprisingly, General George Washington ended up on his knees. These revolutionaries knew their cause was doomed to fail without divine intervention. They prayed like it depended on God because they knew it did.

The pastor who led them in prayer that morning was

Dr. Jacob Duche. The Scripture he turned to? Psalm 35. He prayed that just as the Lord contended for David, God would contend for their cause if it were a righteous one. Dr. Duche's prayer is more than just a piece of our history; it's a piece of our destiny.

> *O Lord, our heavenly Father, high and mighty King of kings and Lord of lords, who dost from thy throne behold all dwellers on the earth, and reignest with power supreme and uncontrolled over all the kingdoms, Empires, and Governments; look down in mercy, we beseech thee, on these our American states who have fled to Thee from the rod of the oppressor and thrown themselves on Thy gracious protection, desiring to be henceforth dependent only on Thee . . .*
>
> *Be Thou present, O God of wisdom, and direct the councils of this honorable assembly . . . Shower down on them and the millions they here represent, such temporal blessings as Thou seeist expedient for them in this world and crown them with everlasting glory in the world to come. All this we ask in the name and through the merits of Jesus Christ, Thy Son and our Savoir. Amen.*

Our prayers don't have expiration dates. That's why I believe this prayer is still being answered 238 years later. It is part of our prayer genealogy as Americans. This was a genesis prayer. It was the very first prayer uttered at the start of the revolution. It was a prayer for every American henceforth. And it is still being answered. There is no other explanation for the improbability of America. God contended for our cause.

That is our history. That is our destiny.

I'm certainly not suggesting that America is always right and never wrong. Like every nation's history, ours is dotted with grievous sins. But the only explanation for the blessings we've experienced is the favor of God.

If you are on God's side, then God is on your side.

God will fight for you as you fight for Him.

And you can live with holy confidence, knowing that when God is contending for your cause, your cause is destined to succeed. This doesn't mean there won't be setbacks and sacrifices along the way; it just means the war has already been won.

Prayer is the difference between you fighting for God and God fighting for you.

Lord, Surprise Me

"The wind blows wherever it pleases."
JOHN 3:8

A few years ago, a rather routine staff meeting turned into a prayer meeting. All of our staff ended up on their knees. I ended up on my face on the floor. And I prayed a prayer that has been repeated hundreds of times since then. In fact, it has become a prayer mantra: *Lord, surprise us.*

In one respect, this feels like a dangerous prayer because we have to put our plans on the altar. We have to relinquish control. We have to trust God's timing. But that prayer was motivated by a genuine desire to see God do something unprecedented — something that superseded our plans, something that we could not take credit for or control. And God has answered this prayer a thousand times in a thousand ways!

One of the most dramatic surprises happened a few weeks after praying that prayer for the first time. Our family was vacationing at a friend's cabin at Lake Anna, about ninety miles south of Washington, D.C. On the first day we heard a knock on the door. It was a neighbor named Harry, who asked if he could see the cabin. He looked harmless enough, so I invited him in. Within five minutes Harry had offered to let us use his pontoon boat for the week. When we went to his cabin to get the keys, I noticed a book on his coffee table written by a former senator who attended our church. I had a hunch when I saw the book that he might know the senator's good friend and my mentor, Dick Foth. Sure enough, Harry knew Dick. So I told Harry I would send him a copy of a book I had dedicated to Dick titled *Wild Goose Chase*. The week after our vacation ended, I sent Harry a copy, and he liked it enough to recommend it to his friend Tom.

Nearly a year after meeting Harry, I got a call from Tom, a deacon at Glen Echo Baptist Church. He introduced himself and explained that GEBC was once a thriving witness in their community but had dwindled to a dozen members. Then he told me they wanted to consider giving their two properties, valued at approximately $2 million, to National Community Church. I couldn't have been more surprised if he'd said I'd won the lottery without even buying a ticket. And that's what it felt like.

What profoundly impacted me was the fact that GEBC was courageous enough to recognize that the church was dying and generous enough to give its building to another church. We were surprised and humbled beyond words. Then I remembered our prayer: *Lord, surprise us.*

Can I make an observation? And I mean this with all due respect. Baptist churches don't give their churches to non-Baptist churches. To the best of my knowledge, it's unprecedented. But God always has a holy surprise up His sovereign sleeve. And when we pray, God throws surprise parties!

Every miracle, every blessing, every divine appointment has a genealogy. If we trace them back, we'll find a genesis prayer that set in motion the sovereign act of God. Am I saying that God *cannot do it* without us? No, I'm not saying He cannot; I am simply saying He *will not*.

In His omniscience and omnipotence, God has determined there are some things He will only do in response to prayer. The Bible puts it bluntly: "You do not have because you do not ask God." *If we don't ask, God can't answer.* It's as simple as that. The greatest tragedy in life is the prayers that go unanswered because they go unasked. I don't pretend to understand where the sovereignty of God and free will of humans meet, but it motivates me to work like it depends on me and pray like it depends on God. And if we do these two things, God will keep surprising us.

God Knows Every Tom, Dick, and Harry

Our family has a handful of sayings that have been passed down from generation to generation. They are part of our family folklore. I'm not sure where this one originated, but I remember my grandma stating it more than once: *you can't never always sometimes tell.* That tongue twister is a mind bender, so here's the translation: *anything could happen!*

Now let me redeem this saying and give it a prayer twist. When you circle a promise in prayer, you can't never always sometimes tell. Anything could happen. You never know when or how or where God will answer it. Prayer adds an element of surprise to your life that is more fun than a surprise party or surprise gift or surprise romance. In fact, prayer turns life into a party, into a gift, into a romance.

God has surprised me so many times that I'm no longer surprised by His surprises. That doesn't mean I love them any less. I'm still in awe of the strange and mysterious ways in which God works, but I have come to expect the unexpected because God is predictably unpredictable. The only thing I can predict with absolute certainty is this: *the more you pray, the more you will experience holy surprises.*

I love the reference to wind in John 3. I can't think of a better description of the way the Holy Spirit works. He is uncontrollable, unpredictable — which can cause angst or excitement. The choice is ours. About the wind, Jesus states, "You cannot tell where it comes from or where it is going." So it is with the Holy Spirit, says Jesus. In other words, *you can't never always sometimes tell.* But one thing is certain: if we follow Jesus, our lives will be anything but boring.

When I think about the degree of probability of what happened, it's mind-boggling. I have no idea what prompted Harry to knock on our door that day. If he hadn't knocked, I would not have gone over to his cabin, seen a book on his coffee table, mentioned Dick Foth, or sent him a copy of *Wild Goose Chase.* And, of course, I didn't know Tom from Adam! But God knows every Tom, Dick, and Harry! And He can orchestrate divine appointments with anyone, anytime, anywhere.

Lord, surprise us!

*God always has a holy surprise
up His sovereign sleeve.*

Do Not Delay

"O Lord, pay attention and act.
Delay not, for your own sake, O my God."
DANIEL 9:19 ESV

During our forty-day prayer challenge at National Community Church, our prayer circles were interceding for healing, jobs, marriages, deliverance, and salvation. And we saw each of those miracles happen, but there were speed bumps along the way. Praying hard is not the path of least resistance; it's usually the path of most resistance because we engage in spiritual warfare. In fact, when we begin interceding for others, we better make sure that others are interceding for us. We need a prayer circle that provides a prayer covering.

Very rarely are our prayers answered as quickly or easily as we'd like. By definition, praying hard is hard because it's hard. But it's the prayers you pray when you feel like you want to quit praying that can bring the greatest breakthroughs.

One woman in our church decided to circle her husband, who was applying for a job with the United States Attorney's office. On day two of the prayer challenge, Kelly went in for a second interview, but he didn't get the job. It was a bitter disappointment, and that is when most of us quit praying. But Kelly's wife, Charmaigne, kept circling.

The first day of the forty-day prayer challenge, I was praying about Kelly's job application at the U.S. Attorney's office in Alexandria. I prayed, "God, do not delay," but not through Daniel's prayer. Though it was frustrating that Kelly didn't get the job, I continued praying. I prayed that God would sustain us for the entire prayer challenge.

On the last three days of the prayer challenge, I was encouraged to read the book of Daniel. The Circle Maker teaches about praying through the Bible so I decided to do it. I prayed Daniel's prayer in 9:19: "O Lord, hear; O Lord, forgive. O Lord, pay attention and act. Delay not, for your own sake, O my God, because your city and your people are called by your name."

On the last day of the prayer challenge, God prompted me to do a full-day fast, and I prayed again for Kelly's job. I prayed using Daniel's prayer with a faith that God would not delay His answers. Indeed, God did not delay. The next day, the day after the prayer challenge ended, I got a voice mail from my husband that he got a job offer from D.C. Superior Court to clerk for a judge beginning in September. I immediately fell on my knees next to our dining table and thanked God for the miracle He had given us! It was the best gift ever after my constant praying and fasting. And guess what happened next? Another job was offered to him this week that started immediately and ends when his new job starts! God gave us more than what we asked for! Not one job, but two!

Our most powerful prayers are hyperlinked to the promises of God. When we know we are praying the promises of God, we can pray with holy confidence. We don't have to second-guess ourselves, because we know that God's word does not return to Him empty. This doesn't mean we can claim the promises of God out of context. But our problem typically isn't overclaiming the promises of God; it's underclaiming them.

Every spiritual blessing is ours in Christ.
No matter how many promises God has made, they are "Yes" in Christ.
No good thing will God withhold from those whose walk is blameless.

If we stand *on* God's word, God will stand *by* His word.

I recently got an e-mail from a couple who put this principle into practice in a rather ingenious way. They went to Home Depot and bought paver stones. They inscribed ten biblical promises on the stones with white paint and laid them in their patio, and they stand on those promises every day in prayer. "One day when we have children of our own," they wrote, "we hope to give them these stones as a reminder of what it means to pray and to stand on the promises of God."

ALAT

Until recently, I attached an ASAP to every prayer. I wanted God to answer *as soon as possible*. But this is no longer my agenda. I don't want easy or quick answers because I have a tendency to mishandle the blessings that come too easily or too quickly. I take the credit for them, or I take them for granted. So now I pray it will take long enough and be hard enough for God to receive all of the glory.

I'm not looking for the path of least resistance; I'm looking for the path of greatest glory. And that requires high-degree-of-difficulty prayers and lots of circling.

Very rarely does our first prayer request hit the bull's-eye of God's good, pleasing, and perfect will. Most prayer requests have to be refined. Even "the prayer that saved a generation" didn't hit the bull's-eye the first time. Honi refined his request twice: "Not for such rain have I prayed." He wasn't satisfied with a sprinkle or torrential downpour. It took three attempts to spell out exactly what he wanted: "rain of Your favor, blessing, and graciousness." Honi drew a circle in the sand. Then he drew a circle within a circle within a circle.

I'm not praying ASAP prayers; I'm praying ALAT prayers. *As long as it takes.* I'm going to get in my prayer circle, and I'm not coming out until God answers. This doesn't mean I'm forcing God's hand. After all, we can't force God to do anything! It just means I'm praying with confidence. I believe that God never overpromises or underdelivers. He always delivers on His promises, but He does it on His timeline!

God is never early. God is never late.
God is always right on time.

Day 18

Keep Circling

"On the seventh day,
march around the city seven times."
JOSHUA 6:4

I have a friend who moved to Washington, D.C., in 1994 to fight for a noble cause on Capitol Hill. Tony was deeply concerned that innocent children were being introduced to pornography simply because adult channels were one click away from cartoon channels, so he authored legislation that would force the cable industry to fully scramble pornography channels. As Tony prepared to visit all 435 House offices and 100 Senate offices, he decided to circle the Capitol in prayer seven times. He even let out a Jericho shout after the seventh circle!

Tony knew he couldn't win this fight without prayer. He also knew that prayer is the difference between *us fighting for God* and *God fighting for us.*

After praying seven circles, Tony started knocking on doors and asking for an audience with every member of Congress. Some of the offices applauded his efforts, but Tony was repeatedly told his efforts were too little, too late. The telecommunications bill he was trying to amend had already gone to markup. Tony was told there was no way the chairman of the congressional committee would reopen the bill to include his amendment because he'd have to reopen it to everybody else's amendments. Tony walked out of the 220th congressional office depressed and defeated. He was ready to throw in the towel and give up the fight when he had a burning bush moment.

I was on the second floor of the Longworth Building. I went over to a window, sat on its cold marble sill, and hung my head in defeat. I said to myself, "Stop wasting your time and go home to San Diego." Never before, and never since, has God spoken to me so clearly. While I sat there looking down at the marble-tiled floor, totally dejected, these words were spoken to me as clear as a bell: "Who is doing this — you or Me?" I can't explain how I felt when I heard those words, but I straightened up and responded, "You are, Lord!" Instantly I was filled with more excitement than when I had first begun. At each of the following 215 offices, my presentations were given with renewed faith.

Tony made his last presentation at the Canon Congressional Building. His amendment still seemed like a lost cause, but it's not over till God says it's over. If your cause is ordained by God, then the battle belongs to the Lord. It's His victory to win, not yours.

I am not exaggerating when I tell you this. As my leg crossed the threshold as I exited the 435th office, my pager went off.

Chairman Dingle had just agreed to allow my amendment to be added to his telecommunications bill.

Sometimes God shows up; sometimes God shows off!

God's timing is impeccable isn't it? He's never late. He's never early. God is right on time all the time! Is it a coincidence that Tony's pager went off just as he exited the last office? I think not. I don't believe in coincidences; I believe in providence. I believe there is a God in heaven who directs our steps, who prepares good works in advance, who causes all things to work together for good, who fights our battles for us! And if you pray through, there will be a breakthrough!

Don't lose heart. Don't lose hope. Don't lose faith. Don't lose patience.

Maybe you've been interceding for a child who has walked away from the faith. Maybe you've been believing for reconciliation in your marriage. Maybe you've been waiting for a healing miracle, a financial miracle, or an opportunity miracle.

Keep asking. Keep seeking. Keep knocking.

God rarely does things how or when we expect Him to, and it leads us to question His strange and mysterious ways. I'm sure the Israelites questioned God's battle plan at Jericho. They would have preferred to storm the gates or scale the walls, but God told them to circle the city for seven days! It didn't make any sense. It had to feel like forever. But they kept circling!

Sometimes God will push us to our absolute limits — the limits of our faith, of our patience, of our gifts. That is how

God stretches our faith and builds our character. Remember when God told Abraham to sacrifice his son Isaac? When God intervened and provided a ram in the thicket? God's intervention didn't take place until Abraham had put Isaac on the altar, tied him down, and raised the knife. God pushed Abraham to the precipice of logic. He tested Abraham to see if Abraham trusted Him. Abraham passed the test and got a testimony!

There is a branch of history called counterfactual theory that asks "what if" questions. It imagines how history would have unfolded differently if certain things had or had not happened. Let me play counterfactual theorist with biblical history.

What if the Israelites had stopped circling Jericho on day six? For that matter, *what if* Elijah had quit praying for rain after his sixth request? Or *what if* Naaman had only dipped in the river six times? And while we're on the subject, *what if* Tony had quit his door-to-door campaign after the 220th office?

The answer is obvious: *the miracle would have been forfeited right before it happened.*

I don't know what you've been circling for the past forty days or forty weeks or forty years. I don't know if you've gotten a *yes*, a *no*, or a *not yet*. You've got to praise God if the answer is *yes* and trust Him if the answer is *no*. If the answer is *not yet*, you've got to keep circling. It's always too soon to give up! What other option do you have? To pray or not to pray. Those are the only options.

None of my dreams have happened quickly or easily. There was nothing glamorous or glorious about the early days of our church plant adventure. There were certainly moments when I felt like quitting, when I was tempted to think all of our efforts wouldn't make much difference. After all, our average attendance was twenty-five people — and those twenty-five people could have found a much better church to attend. But I was thinking in present-tense terms. When you quit circling, you don't just compromise the present. Every promise, every miracle, every blessing in your future is forfeited. If I had called it quits, I would have bailed not only on the twenty-five people I was pastoring at the time; I would have bailed on the thousands we're influencing now and the tens of thousands we'll influence in the future!

If the Israelites had stopped circling Jericho, they would have forfeited their first victory in the Promised Land. But there was much more at stake than that. They would have forfeited the Promised Land altogether. But they didn't stop. They kept circling. And if you keep circling, the walls *will* come down. If you pray through, the breakthrough is inevitable.

Go ahead. Keep circling!

If you don't get out of the boat,
you'll never walk on water.

Memorial Offerings

"Your prayers and gifts to the poor
have come up as a memorial offering
before God."

ACTS 10:4

My grandfather had a prayer ritual that involved kneeling next to his bed at night, taking out his hearing aid, and praying for his family. He couldn't hear himself without his hearing aid, but everyone else in the house could. Few things leave a more lasting impression than hearing someone intercede for you by name. These prayers are some of my earliest memories.

Grandpa Johnson died when I was six years old, but his prayers did not. Our prayers never die! When we pray, our prayers exit our four dimensions of space-time. Our prayers have no space or time limitations because the God who answers them exists outside of the four dimensions He created. You never know when His timeless answer will reenter the atmosphere of our lives, and that should fill us with holy anticipation. Never underestimate His ability to answer anytime, anyplace, anyhow. He has infinite answers to our finite prayers. He can answer them more than once. And He answers them forever.

Acts 10:4 declares that our prayers are memorial offerings. I cannot promise that God will answer your prayers *how you want* or *when you want*, but I can promise that God will answer. He always answers! At critical points in my life, the Spirit of God has whispered to my spirit: *Mark, the prayers of your grandfather are being answered in your life right now.* Those sacred moments rank as the most humbling and exhilarating moments of my life.

Like a parent who collects their children's elementary artwork and displays it prominently on a refrigerator door, the heavenly Father loves our prayers. Each one is a keepsake. Each one functions like a memorial that jogs the memory of the Almighty.

If our prayers are that precious to God, shouldn't they be more significant to us? Aren't they worth collecting like snapshots in a family photo album? Shouldn't they be treated with respect and dignity, like the monuments that grace the nation's capital?

Every prayer we utter is like the marble stones used in the building of the Washington Monument or Lincoln Memorial. When we pray, we are building a monument to God, a memorial to Him. And those prayers are not perishable. They aren't wood, hay, or straw. They are a foundation of gold, silver, and costly stones.

They will not be forgotten. They will not go unanswered.

Eternal Prayers

I recently met with a pastor-friend who is a circle maker. I've met very few people who pray with more intensity, more specificity, more consistency. Over lunch, Wayne told me a story about his grandmother, and it was evident that the apple didn't fall far from the tree. Intercession is part of their spiritual DNA as a family.

Wayne's grandmother raised twelve children while managing their household. After every meal she prepared, she would go to her bedroom to pray. Three times a day, the children could hear her interceding for them by name. When she was on her deathbed at the age of ninety-one, the entire family gathered at the family home. She invited them into the bedroom where she prayed three times daily. Then she prophetically declared to her twelve children, "I'm going to die, but the power of my prayers will come to pass in each of your lives."

Her predominant prayer was that every member of her family would surrender their lives to the lordship of Jesus Christ. At the time, six children were following Christ, and six weren't. That was fifteen years ago. The tally is now ten *yes* and two *no* — or maybe I should say in faith, *not yet*. Wayne shared with me how the tenth *yes* (the oldest child) came to Christ.

My grandmother's oldest son is named Johnny. A month ago, his next-door neighbor had a dream in the middle of the night about Johnny. The neighbor felt compelled to invite him to church, and he accepted the invitation that Sunday, which happened to be Palm Sunday. When he walked into that church, all he could hear was his mother's voice calling out his name in prayer. The pastor asked if anybody wanted to put their faith in Jesus, and Johnny raised his ninety-two-year-old hand. He got baptized the next weekend on Easter Sunday.

I did the math. Wayne's grandmother passed away when Johnny was seventy-seven years old. From the day he was born until the day she died, she prayed for him three times a day. If you add it up, that is 84,315 memorial offerings. She didn't get to see the answer to her prayers on this side of the space-time continuum, but she will be one of the first people to greet her son when he steps into eternity!

Did her prayers have anything to do with the neighbor's middle-of-the-night dream? I cannot imagine they were unrelated. And that is the beauty of prayer. We never know when our prayers will be answered, and we never know when we are the answer to someone else's prayer. You might be the answer to 84,315 prayers! When we live by faith, we will harvest prayer seeds that have been planted for decades, for centuries, for millennia. When we live by faith, those memorial offerings turn into crowns of glory. Prayer offerings turn into praise offerings.

Draw the Circle

Our prayers don't die when we do.
God answers them forever.

Go. Set. Ready.

He [Abraham] did not know where he was going.

HEBREWS 11:8

You'll never be ready.

You'll never be ready to get married. You'll never be ready to have kids. You'll never be ready to start a business or go back to school or move to the mission field. You'll never be ready financially, emotionally, or spiritually. You'll never have enough faith, enough cash, or enough courage. And if you are looking for an excuse, you will always find one.

I never have been, and I'm sure I never will be, ready for anything God has called me to do. This doesn't mean I haven't prepared myself. I've worked hard getting an education, but I've come to terms with the fact that I'll never be ready for anything God has called me to. And that's OK. God doesn't call the qualified; He qualifies the called.

If you wait until you're ready, you'll be waiting for the rest of your life.

The author of Hebrews writes, "By faith Abraham, when called to go to a place he would later receive as his inheritance, obeyed and went, even though he did not know where he was going" (11:8).

Abraham didn't know the final destination, but it didn't keep him from taking the first step in the journey. What's the first step or next step you need to take in your journey? If you take the first step, God will reveal the second step. The problem is that most of us want the twenty-five-year plan before we're willing to step out in faith. We want to know exactly where we're going and exactly when we'll get there, but God doesn't operate that way. He gives us just enough revelation, just enough grace, just enough strength. Why? So we will live in daily dependence on Him. He doesn't want us to rely on the revelation; He wants us to rely on Him.

Without knowing where he was going, Abraham took the first step. And God honored it. There are moments in life when you need to quit a job, make a move, or end a dating relationship. And you need to take that step without knowing what the next step will be. Don't wait for more revelation; be obedient to the amount of revelation God has given you.

Why Not?

There is an old adage: *ready, set, go*. And I know it's predicated on the importance of preparation. But I think it's backward. You'll never be ready. You'll never be set. Sometimes you just need to go for it. The sequence of faith is this: Go. Set. Ready.

Some people spend their entire lives getting ready for what God wants them to do, but they never end up doing it because they never come to the realization that they'll never be ready. This is where so many of us get stuck. Our failure to act on what we know God is calling us to do not only breeds doubt and discouragement; it's a form of disobedience.

Nearly two thousand years ago, Jesus said "Go." So why do we operate with this red-light mentality? Why are we waiting for the green light we've already been given?

The vision of National Community Church is to have twenty locations by the year 2020. Launching new locations is part of our DNA. But when we launched our first multisite location, there was a little resistance to the idea. Some people asked why. And on one level, this is a fair question. But I honestly think it's the wrong question. The real question is, "Why not?"

Why wouldn't we continue to launch new locations and try to reach more people? Why wouldn't we continue to do more of what God is blessing? Why wouldn't we multiply?

As Christ-followers, we are called to take a *why not* approach to life. It's an approach to life that dares to dream. It's an approach that's bent toward action. And it doesn't look for excuses not to do something. Don't get me wrong. It's awfully difficult to discern the will of God. Even after prayer and fasting, it usually entails making tough decisions. And I'm certainly not advocating a thoughtless or prayerless approach to decision making. We need to know that God is calling us to devote our lives to missions, take the internship offer, quit our job, or make the move. But I wonder if we're so afraid of doing the wrong thing that it keeps us from doing the right thing.

Get Off the Ship

My friend Dr. George Wood has an amazing painting in his office of an African man standing on a high hillside overlooking the ocean. There is a large steamship on the horizon and a smaller canoe coming toward the shoreline. In this instance, the story is worth a thousand paintings. It symbolizes the importance of going before we're set or ready.

In 1908, newly commissioned missionaries John and Jessie Perkins were on board a steamship rounding the coast of Liberia. They knew God had called them to Africa, but like Abraham, they didn't know exactly where God wanted them to go. So they purchased tickets and trusted that God would tell them where to get off. As the ship made its way around Garraway Point, they sensed the Holy Spirit was prompting them to get off the ship.

Unknown to the Perkinses, there was a young man living in the region named Jasper Toe. He was a God-fearing man who practiced the religious rituals passed down by his ancestors, but he had never heard the name of Jesus. One night he looked into the night sky and prayed a simple prayer: "If there is a God in heaven, help me find You."

As Jasper stood under the stars, a voice he had never heard before spoke to him. "Go to Garraway beach. You will see a box on the water with smoke coming out of it. And from that box on the water will come some people in a small box. These people in this small box will tell you how to find Me."

Jasper Toe traveled seven days on foot to Garraway beach, arriving on Christmas Day, 1908. From the shore he saw a black box — a steamship — floating on the water with smoke coming out of it. And that is when John Perkins and his wife sensed the Holy Spirit saying, "Get off the ship here. This is where I want you to go."

When they went to the captain of the ship and asked him to let them get off the ship, he said, "I can't let you off the boat here. This is cannibal country. People go in there and never come back."

John Perkins insisted, "God wants us to get off the boat."

The captain brought the steamship to a halt, and the Perkinses were placed in a mammy chair that swung them over the side of the ship. They got into a canoe along with all of their belongings, and they rowed to shore in that little box. When they got to the shore, Jasper Toe was waiting to welcome them. He motioned for them to follow him, and they did. They could not speak each other's language, but the Perkinses followed Jasper Toe all the way back to his village. They eventually learned the language of the people there. They started the first church in that village. And Jasper Toe was their first convert.

Those who knew Jasper Toe described him as one of the godliest men they had ever met. And his legacy is the hundreds of churches he helped to establish in the country of Liberia.

What if the Perkinses had ignored the prompting of the Holy Spirit? What if they had dismissed that God-idea as a bad idea? What if they had asked *why* instead of *why not*? What if they had decided to play it safe and stay on the ship?

I'm sure God could have intervened in another way. And

I would like to think He would have. But who can calculate the opportunity costs when we ignore the promptings of the Spirit, thereby missing divine appointments? Faith is not faith until it is acted on.

Go. Set. Ready.

If you are looking for excuses,
you will always find one.

Set Your Foot

"I'm giving you every square inch
of the land you set your foot on."

JOSHUA 1:3 MSG

Since the release of *The Circle Maker*, I've received a steady stream of e-mails and letters from readers who have started circling their dreams, homes, and workplaces in prayer. An inner-city teacher circles her classroom; a real estate agent prays circles around the properties she represents as a listing agent; a team of doctors and nurses have turned their patient rounds into prayer circles. A member of Congress is circling the Capitol, and an NFL chaplain is circling his team's practice facility. One reader even circled his bank, praying for a financial miracle — until law enforcement intervened. They thought he was casing the joint!

There is nothing magical about physically circling something in prayer, but there is something biblical about it. The Israelites circled the city of Jericho until the wall came down. That's what a forty-day prayer challenge is all about. Too often we quit circling almost as soon as we start. Drawing prayer circles is a metaphor that simply means "praying until God answers." It's a determination to pray as long as it takes, even if it takes longer than you ever imagined.

Drawing prayer circles isn't some magic trick to get what you want from God. God is not a genie in a bottle, and your wish is not His command. His command better be your wish. If it's not, you won't be drawing prayer circles; you'll end up walking in circles.

Drawing prayer circles starts with discerning what God wants, what God wills. And until His sovereign will becomes your sanctified wish, your prayer life will be unplugged from its power supply. And getting what you want isn't the goal; the goal is glorifying God by drawing circles around the promises, miracles, and dreams He wants for you.

Pray a Perimeter

Over the years, I've drawn prayer circles around promises in Scripture and promises the Holy Spirit has conceived in my spirit. I've drawn prayer circles around impossible situations and impossible people. I've drawn prayer circles around everything from life goals to pieces of property. But let me go back to my first prayer circle and retrace my steps.

When I was a twenty-two-year-old seminary student, I tried to plant a church on the north shore of Chicago, but that plant never took root. Six months later, fresh off a failed church plant, Lora and I moved from Chicago to Washington, D.C. The opportunity to attempt another church plant presented itself, and my knee-jerk reaction was to say no, but God gave me the courage to face my fears, swallow my pride, and try again.

There was nothing easy about our first year of church planting. Our total church income was $2,000 a month, and $1,600 of that went to rent the D.C. public school cafetorium where we held Sunday services. On a good Sunday, twenty-five people showed up. That's when I learned to close my eyes in worship because it was too depressing to open them. I felt underqualified and overwhelmed, which put me right where God wanted me. It is how we learn to live in raw dependence, and raw dependence is the raw material out of which God performs His greatest miracles.

One day as I was dreaming about the church God wanted to establish on Capitol Hill, I felt prompted by the Holy Spirit to do a prayer walk. I often paced and prayed in the spare bedroom in our house that doubled as the church office, but this prompting was different. I was reading through the book of Joshua at the time, and one of the promises jumped off the page and into my spirit:

> "I'm giving you every square inch of the land you set your foot on — just as I promised Moses."

As I read this promise given to Joshua, I felt that God wanted me to stake claim to the land He had called us to and pray a perimeter all the way around Capitol Hill. I had a Honi-like confidence that just as this promise had been transferred from Moses to Joshua, God would transfer the promise to me if I had enough faith to circle it. So one hot and humid August morning, I drew my first prayer circle. It still ranks as the longest prayer walk I've ever done and the biggest prayer circle I've ever drawn.

Starting at the front door of our row house on Capitol Hill, I walked east on F Street and turned south on 8th Street. I crossed East Capitol, the street that bisects the NE and SE quadrants of the city, and turned west on M Street SE. I then completed the circle, which was actually more of a square, by heading north on South Capitol Street. I paused to pray in front of the Capitol for a few minutes. Then I completed the 4.7-mile circle by taking a right turn at Union Station and heading home.

The prayer circle had taken nearly three hours to complete because my prayer pace is slower than my normal pace, but God has been answering that three-hour prayer for the past fifteen years. Since the day I drew that prayer circle around Capitol Hill, National Community Church has grown into one church with seven locations around the metro D.C. area. And all of the properties we own — Ebenezer's Coffeehouse, our theater on Barracks Row, and an $8 million piece of property that we own debt free — are right on that circle.

Coincidence?

More like providence!

When the Israelites circled Jericho, they had no idea how God would give them the city. But they didn't let what they didn't know keep them from obeying the command they had been given. So they circled the promise over and over and over again. They circled the promise thirteen times over seven days! Why? Because even though they didn't know *how* God would deliver on the promise, they knew that God would come though somehow, someway!

And God didn't just show up; God showed off His power. He toppled the wall of Jericho like it was a game of Jenga!

God is not a genie in a bottle,
and your wish is not His command.
His command better be your wish.

Prayer Fleece

"I will place a wool fleece on the threshing floor."
JUDGES 6:37

Anna is a twenty-three-year-old professional dancer from England whose life was turned upside down after reading *Wild Goose Chase* three years ago. Anna now runs a dance studio in Serbia that ministers to the poorest of the poor, but let me tell you how she got there.

Psalm 37:4 states that when you take delight in the Lord, God will give you the desires of your heart. The word *give* means "to conceive." As you press into God's presence, old sinful desires die, and new holy desires are birthed in your spirit. These single-cell desires ultimately become lifelong dreams if we nurture them in prayer.

Anna was living her dream, making a living by doing the very thing she loved most. Then she got a distinct impression one day that she needed to use her dancing for God. She wasn't sure what it meant, but she couldn't shake it. It kept her company during the day and kept her awake at night. Her friends assured Anna that she was making a difference right where she was, but she knew there was something else, something more. Then one day she read about a ministry project in Serbia, and something came alive in her spirit. She felt she needed to go visit, but she didn't know the first thing about Serbia. In fact, she had never met a Serbian. That's when Anna put a prayer fleece before the Lord: *Lord, if You want me to visit this ministry in Serbia, then let me meet a Serbian this week.*

Anna shared her prayer fleece with her friends, and even though they thought it was a crazy prayer, they agreed to circle it with her. Two days later, a tall, dark-haired gentleman walked into the dance studio where Anna was practicing. Anna was sure he was Italian, but she went ahead and asked him where he was from. When he told her he was from Serbia, she said, "You're the one I've been waiting for."

Six months later, Anna packed a suitcase and her guitar, bought a one-way ticket, and moved to Serbia. She works with the lowest-income Serbians, teaching English, the Bible, and dance to the children. Anna has gone from performing on stage for the *Who's Who* of Great Britain to choreographing dance performances for children with disabilities. And she's loving every second of it. But it started with a prayer fleece.

Her next God-idea? To open an Ebenezer's-styled coffeehouse in Serbia. That's why she sent me a letter. Actually, she called it a *prayer letter*. I think it was another fleece of sorts. I was so impacted by Anna's prayer letter that I shared her story, and Anna's dream made its way into the hearts of others. A handful of people stepped up and said they wanted to be shareholders in that ministry. And with the exchange rate, a few American dollars can turn into quite a few Serbian dinar.

Caution

There are moments when we need to turn our desires, ideas, and dreams into prayer fleeces. Now, we have to be very careful when it comes to putting fleeces before the Lord. Generally speaking, signs don't precede our steps of faith; signs follow. But there are occasions when it's OK to ask God for confirmation because of our uncertainty. I don't think we should do it often, and we shouldn't approach it in a haphazard manner that amounts to nothing more than picking petals off a daisy, saying, "She loves me; she loves me not."

So here are a few cautions when it comes to fleeces. First, if God has already answered your question in Scripture, then you don't need to even ask it. Don't seek revelation when God has already given it. Second, check your motives to make sure they aren't selfish. The fleece must come out of a genuine desire to honor God and do His will. Third, you have to be willing to accept whatever answer you receive without second-guessing it.

When God called Gideon to become a judge in Israel, he was filled with insecurity. When the angel addressed him as "mighty warrior," I bet Gideon looked over his own shoulder to see who he was talking to because there was no way it could be him! He thought God was making a mistake. "How can I rescue Israel? My clan is the weakest in the whole tribe of Manasseh, and I am the least in my entire family!"

But I love God's answer: "I will be with you."

That's all we need to know, isn't it? If we could come to grips with two fundamental truths, they would transform our lives: *God is with us*, and *God is for us*. That is all you ever need to know. God is with you, and God is for you. Let it sink into your spirit. And as Romans 8:31 states, "If God is for us, who can be against us?"

The angelic encounter wasn't enough for Gideon. He needed more confirmation, so he devised a test. He put a fleece before the Lord not once but twice. And God patiently reassured Gideon because Gideon asked out of genuine humility.

> "If you are truly going to help me, show me a sign to prove that it is really the Lord speaking to me."

In 2003, when National Community Church was preparing to become a multisite church and launch our second location, I was filled with uncertainties and insecurities. We were venturing into uncharted territory without a map. During an all-day prayer and planning meeting, we concluded we wanted to launch in the movie theaters at Ballston Common Mall in Arlington, Virginia. We closed our daylong meeting asking God for favor and a sign, a prayer similar to the one that Gideon prayed. We had been negotiating with Regal Cinema for three months but had kept hitting a wall. They only wanted to give us early morning access, and the additional time was cost prohibitive. After months of getting nowhere in negotiations, and the day after we put a prayer fleece before the Lord, Regal changed its corporate pricing structure. It's safe to say that in the world of leasing, if you want more time, you pay more money. And if you mysteriously get more time for less money, it has to be a sign from the Lord. It was just the sign we needed, and it catapulted us into one church with two locations.

Ask God

One of my prayer heroes is George Müller. Along with pastoring one church for sixty-six years, he established the Ashley Down orphanage. Müller cared for 10,024 orphans while establishing 117 schools for their education throughout England. In today's dollars, George Müller raised somewhere in the neighborhood of 150 million dollars. That is an amazing feat, but what makes it even more amazing is that he never asked anyone for a penny. He felt compelled to only ask God when he had a need. He trusted that God knew exactly what he needed, so he turned every need into a prayer. When he needed a pipe fixed, he prayed for a plumber. When he needed food or money or books, he prayed that God would provide. It is estimated that more than 30,000 specific prayers recorded in his journals were answered. And just for the record, the most impressive and most important statistic may be this one: Müller read the Bible cover to cover more than 200 times!

Müller prayed like it depended on God, but he also worked like it depended on him. Müller wrote, "This ... is one of the great secrets in connection with successful service for the Lord; to work, as if everything depended upon our diligence, and yet not to rest in the least upon our exertions, but upon the blessing of the Lord." The key to kingdom productivity is this: work really hard at what God has called you to do, but do not trust in your work; trust in God.

Oswald Chambers once wrote, "Let God be as original with other people as He is with you." This piece of advice has become a personal mantra. *Be yourself.* So I'm not prescribing George Müller's approach to prayer for everyone. It was a personal covenant he felt led to make with God. But we can learn from his example. Maybe we've been asking the wrong person — a boss, spouse, friend, or colleague. Maybe we need to ask God.

Don't seek answers; seek God. And the answers will seek you.

When God gives a vision,
He always makes provision.

Not Now

"Wait for the gift my Father promised."
ACTS 1:4

When God says no to a prayer, it doesn't always mean *no*; sometimes it means *not yet*. It's the right request but the wrong time.

A few years ago, Lora and I were house hunting on Capitol Hill. We had lived on the Hill since 1996 when we were fortunate enough to buy a hundred-year-old row home during a buyers' market. As our kids got bigger, our fifteen-foot-wide row home seemed to get smaller, so we started looking for a little larger place. We discovered our dream home less than a block away, and we decided to make an offer, but we also knew our financial limits. After praying about it, we came up with our best offer and felt like it was a fleece. If God wanted us to have the house, the owner would accept our offer. With the real estate market lagging and the time on market increasing, we were confident the seller would accept our offer. He did not. And as much as we wanted the house and as tempted as we were to go beyond our predetermined offer, we walked away. We had already done the interior decorating in our imaginations, so we were definitely disappointed. But we also had complete peace because we had prayed about it.

We stopped looking at homes for a year. Then one night, as we drove by the house we had tried to purchase, Lora said, "Do you ever feel like that is the house that got away?" We had driven by the house a hundred times, and Lora had never said a thing. But her casual comment must have been a subconscious prayer because the next morning a For Sale sign went up in the yard. That's when I had a holy hunch that God's *no* a year earlier was really a *not yet* and was about to turn into a divine *yes*.

What Lora and I didn't know is that the owner had never sold the house! It sat on the market for 252 days with no buyer and then was taken off the market. When the same owner put the house back on the market, we decided to make the *same offer*. It was a calculated risk because he'd already said no once, but it was another prayer fleece. We told our real estate agent it was our final offer. We were willing to walk away a second time, but this time the owner accepted the offer — and God answered our prayer one year after we thought He would. What we thought was a *no* was actually a *not yet* that turned into a *yes*!

Sometimes we have to be willing to give something up *to God* in order to get it back *from God*. Like Abraham's willingness to sacrifice Isaac, it will probably be something that is precious to us. It may even be a gift from God, just like Isaac was to Abraham. But God will test us to make sure the gift isn't more important than the Gift Giver, the dream isn't more important to us than the Dream Giver. He'll test us to make sure it's not an idol. If it is, that dream, gift, or desire might need to die so that it can be resurrected. But God often takes things away to give them back so that we know they are gifts to be stewarded for His glory.

Going through a death and resurrection makes us appreciate our house more than we would have otherwise. And the beautiful thing isn't that *we own the house*; it's that *the house doesn't own us*. When something is given back after it is taken away, whether it's a house or our health, we don't take it for granted.

Now here's the icing on the cake. By waiting a year to buy the house, our house actually went up in value by 10 percent because the real estate market in D.C. had rebounded. So we got our dream house for the same amount of money and sold our old house for a lot more money than we would have a year earlier! It was definitely worth the wait. And tithing on the sale of our house was one of the easiest checks we've ever written because God's hand of blessing was so evident.

Wait

I hate to wait. I don't like waiting at red lights. I don't like waiting at the doctor's office. I don't like waiting in drive-throughs for fast food. It's never fast enough. I don't even like waiting for December 25, so we start opening gifts on Christmas Eve!

You name it, I don't want to wait for it. But waiting is part of praying, and praying is a form of waiting. Prayer will sanctify our waiting, so we wait with holy expectancy. And waiting doesn't delay God's plans and purposes. It always expedites them. Waiting is the fast track to whatever it is that God wants to do in our lives. And we'll discover that on God's timeline, a day is like a thousand years, and a thousand years are like a day.

In our impatience, we often try to do God's job for Him. We treat Sabbath observance like a luxury instead of a commandment. We only obey it when it's convenient, and then we discover that it's never convenient. We work as though the world revolves around us and relies on us. Maybe it's time to rest as though the world revolves around and relies on the Creator who hangs the stars and spins the planets.

Let me come right out and say it: we're way too busy. In the words of the apostle Paul, we're "busybodies." We're constantly trying to do more and more in less and less time. The net result is that we don't have any margins in our lives. And that is when prayer gets marginalized. We think we have too much to do to pray, but the exact opposite is true: we have too much to do *not* to pray! Martin Luther once declared, "I have so much to do that I shall spend the first three hours in prayer." The more you have to do, the more you have to pray!

After the ascension of Jesus, the disciples didn't immediately "go into all the world." Why? Because Jesus left explicit instructions: "Do not leave Jerusalem, but wait for the gift my Father promised." Instead of immediately embarking on their mission, they waited in Jerusalem for the Holy Spirit. They didn't try to get ahead of God. They gathered in an upper room and prayed for ten days. Those ten days have been paying dividends for two thousand years.

After we pray like it depends on God, we need to work like it depends on us. But if we don't pray first, our work won't work. We can't do something for God until we let God do something for us. He wants to fill us with His Holy Spirit, but we need to empty ourselves first. From the depths of our hearts to the depths of our minds, the Holy Spirit wants to fill every crevice that already exists and create new capacities within us. And when the Holy Spirit comes on us, we will think new thoughts and feel new feelings. It's part of the package deal.

But you have to wait for it.

The question is this: How long are you willing to wait?

What would happen if we holed up in an upper room, knelt at an altar, or locked ourselves in a prayer closet and said, "I'm not coming out until I receive the gift my Father promised." I'll tell you exactly what would happen: Pentecost would happen all over again.

You cannot plan Pentecost. It's not like Peter woke up on the day of Pentecost and had "speaking in tongues" on his to-do list. He didn't plan on baptizing three thousand people that day. But if you pray for ten days, Pentecost is bound to happen.

Draw the Circle

Sometimes God's no
simply means not yet.

Find Your Voice

The word of the LORD came to me.
JEREMIAH 1:4

When I was nineteen years old, the Holy Spirit awakened me from my sleep in the middle of the night. It had never happened before, and it has never happened since. I grabbed my Bible and knelt at the foot of my bed. When I flipped the Bible open, it landed on Jeremiah 1. I started reading it, and it started reading me. In the original context, God was speaking to Jeremiah, but it was as though the Holy Spirit was speaking directly to me. Jeremiah's calling is my calling.

I didn't fully understand the ramifications or implications of this singular event that took place more than two decades ago. In fact, I still don't. God's callings aren't understood or accomplished in months or years or decades. It usually takes a lifetime. And one verse in particular always confused me.

> "Before I formed you in the womb I knew you,
>   before you were born I set you apart;
>   I appointed you as a prophet to the nations."

It's the last sentence that didn't make sense: "I appointed you ... to the nations."

It confused me because I've never felt called to be a missionary. I didn't know how that part of the calling would be fulfilled. That's when a friend sent me an e-mail that opened my eyes and helped me connect the dots.

I'm speaking at a national leadership conference for the nation of Malaysia and visited the largest bookstore in Kuala Lumpur today. I was thrilled to see your book in a very visible place in the religious section. I stopped to praise God for the influence He has given you to the nations!

It was the last phrase that caught my attention: *to the nations*.

I feel as called to write as I do to pastor, but I never viewed my writing as being *prophetic* or *international*. Then it dawned on me that my books are translated into more than a dozen languages. In a moment of revelation, I realized that God had fulfilled His promise, and I didn't even know it. I was appointed to the nations, but not by moving to a mission field. My books are like messages in a bottle that land on distant shores.

I've received countless letters from readers all around the world, but I never connected the dots. I just didn't know that God would fulfill this part of my calling in this particular way. But that's how God works, isn't it? He tricks us. We think we're going somewhere to do something, but God always has ulterior motives. There is a rhyme and reason to His will that we aren't even aware of.

Voiceprint

All of us have a unique voiceprint, not just physically but spiritually as well. God wants to speak through you differently than through anyone else. Your life is a unique translation of Scripture. It doesn't matter what you do — politician, preacher, entertainer, homemaker, teacher, musician, lawyer, or doctor. You are called to be a prophetic voice to the people God places in your life. But the key to discovering your prophetic voice is cultivating a prophetic ear. If you want to find your voice, you need to hear the voice of God.

During a recent trip to Ethiopia, I met several amazing leaders. A group of about a dozen political, medical, and business leaders meet regularly as part of a Bible study. God is using them to shape a country and a continent. I met a woman who plays a pivotal role in the African Union, a doctor who is building a hospital in a rural region of Ethiopia, and a developer who is designing the first PGA-quality golf course of its kind in East Africa. What I discovered during my visit is that they have one thing in common: all of them spend one day a week in prayer and fasting. Many of them don't even go into work on that day! We may be tempted to think they're less productive because they give up a day of work, but maybe they are more productive because they waste far less time on nonproductive pursuits.

We live in a culture in which everybody wants to be heard, but many people have nothing to say. Don't worry about building a platform. If you listen to God, people will listen to you. Why? Because you'll have something to say! And God will give you a platform to speak from.

So how do we hear the voice of God?

The first thing to do is open your Bible. When you open your Bible, God opens His mouth. The surest way to get a word from the Lord is by getting into God's Word. God will speak *to* you. Then God will speak *through* you.

In the process, make sure you have no unconfessed sin in your life. Sin doesn't just harden the heart; it also hardens our hearing. In fact, it makes us turn a deaf ear to God because we don't want to hear the convicting voice of the Holy Spirit. But if you aren't willing to listen to the convicting voice of the Spirit, you won't hear His comforting voice, forgiving voice, or merciful voice either. Sin creates relational distance, and distance makes it harder to hear the still, small voice of the Holy Spirit. But if you get close to God, you won't miss a thing He says. And if you incline your ear to God, God will incline His ear to you.

When too much white noise invades my life and I'm having a hard time hearing the voice of God, I'll often go into a season of fasting. Fasting is like noise cancellation. It helps me tune out the voices I shouldn't be listening to and tune into His frequency. It's still difficult to distinguish between our own thoughts and the inaudible voice of the Holy Spirit, but just like a relationship with a loved one, we begin to discern His voice more accurately. Eventually, it'll be like the voice of a spouse or child. We'll be able to interpret even the subtlest intonations.

If you want to find your voice,
you need to hear the voice of God.

A Prophetic Voice

"I wish that all the LORD's people were prophets."
NUMBERS 11:29

During the 2012 NCAA basketball tournament, I heard a postgame interview with Buzz Williams, coach of the Marquette Screaming Eagles. Following a victory that advanced their team to the Sweet Sixteen, Coach Williams referred to his players as "lion chasers." That caught my attention because I use this phrase repeatedly in my book *In a Pit with a Lion on a Snowy Day*. It turns out that his pastor, who went to college with me, gave Buzz a copy of the book. He and many of his players read it right before March Madness began.

During the off-season, Buzz flew out to D.C. so we could spend a few hours together. We discovered that pastors have something to learn from coaches, and coaches have something to learn from pastors. Buzz is the first person to admit he's a "work in progress." So am I. But I love the fact that his intensity for Jesus matches his intensity for basketball. And he's not just interested in how his kids perform on the court; he's investing in them for eternity.

Only four of the kids on Buzz's current squad know their biological father. Only two of them come from a family with an intact marriage. Many of the kids on his team didn't have a father's voice of love or discipline, so Buzz is that voice.

During the first one hundred days of a freshman's involvement in his program, Buzz meets with them on a daily basis. They come to his office, and he prays with them, even the kids who don't believe in God. Buzz told me he's had a few awkward silences! After praying with each other, they embrace each other. And Coach Williams tells them he loves them.

I think Buzz sees his squad of twelve the way Jesus saw His twelve disciples. And isn't that how we should see every person whom God has intentionally put in our lives — family members, friends, colleagues, and neighbors? Buzz is more than a coach who sees athletic potential in his players; he is a prophet who sees the spiritual potential. And he knows that those two things are not unrelated.

Personal Prophecies

Prayer isn't just the way we cultivate our own potential; prayer is the way we recognize potential in others. Like Paul, who saw gifts in Timothy that Timothy couldn't see in himself, we, through prayer, are enabled to see with prophetic eyes. We are given supernatural insight. Then we are prepared to speak with prophetic boldness into the lives God has positioned in our path.

Jewish philosophers did not believe that the prophetic gift was reserved for a few select individuals; they believed that becoming prophetic was the crowning point of mental and spiritual development. The more we grow in grace, the more prophetic we become.

This doesn't mean we will start predicting the future; it means we'll start creating it. How? Through our prayers! Prayer is the way we write the future. It's the difference between letting things happen and making things happen. And when we speak prophetic words into someone's life, it gives them a new lease on life.

According to 1 Corinthians 14:3, a prophet speaks words of comfort and encouragement as prompted by the Holy Spirit. And prophets come in all sizes and shapes. But the common denominator is prophetic insight that is the by-product of intercessory prayer. The more we pray, the more prophetic we will become. And I know it's a play on words, but the less we pray, the more pathetic we will become. Sorry, I couldn't resist, because it's true.

Laurie Beth Jones has stated that at least 40 percent of our lives are based on personal prophecies. I'm not sure how to substantiate this statistic, but I find it very believable. The right word spoken at the right time can make an eternal difference. In *The Power of Positive Prophecy*, Jones gives a great example of how one prophetic word can change a person's destiny:

> I grew up in an alcoholic household where I never heard a positive word. On my way home from school I would always stop in at Jimmy's, the local dry cleaner, because he kept candy on the counter. He got to know me, and told me one afternoon, "Michael, you are a very smart

boy. Someday you are going to run a very big business." I would listen to him in disbelief and return home only to get called a "dog" and knocked around by my dad. But you know ... Jimmy the dry cleaner was the only person I can remember believing in me ... Today I run a multimillion-dollar health care organization, just like Jimmy predicted. I guess you could say that a dry cleaner was the prophet in my life.

You may not see yourself as a prophet, but you are one. You're a prophet to your friends. As I write about in *Praying Circles around Your Children*, parents are prophets to their children. You're a prophet at work and a prophet at home. And your words have the potential to change lives by helping people discover their identity and destiny in Jesus Christ.

Sometimes you need the courage to rebuke. When you catch kids doing something wrong, for example, lovingly remind them of this: *that's not who you are*. And when you catch them doing something right, reinforce it. Celebrate what you want to see more of. That's one way to fan into flame the gift of God.

You don't have to influence thousands of lives to make a difference. Maybe you're called to influence one person who will influence thousands. You sow into their life so they can reap a harvest. The fruit of their life is your reward.

I've always been inspired by something that the former Secretary-General of the United Nations Dag Hammarskjöld said: "It is more noble to give yourself completely to one individual than to labor diligently for the salvation of the masses."

At critical junctures in my life, God has sent prophets across my path. They were ordinary people — a missionary named Chris Smith, a college professor named Opel Reddin, a mentor named Dick Foth. God used them to speak the right word at the right time. God gets all the glory for everything He does in us and through us, but there are people along the way who get some credit as well.

Prayer is the way we recognize potential in others.

Game with Minutes

Pray without ceasing.
1 THESSALONIANS 5:17 NASB

On January 30, 1930, Frank Laubach began a prayer experiment he called "the game with minutes." He was dissatisfied with his lack of intimacy with God and decided to do something about it. One of the inspirations for Laubach's experiment was Brother Lawrence, a seventeenth-century monk whose singular purpose in life was to live in the presence of God. For Brother Lawrence, this didn't mean retreating from the routine of life; it meant redeeming every routine and turning it into a prayer. For decades, Brother Lawrence worked in the kitchen of his Carmelite Monastery, washing dishes and preparing meals, but he turned his chores into prayers. After many years of practicing the presence of God, prayer became a way of life. In the words of Brother Lawrence, "The time of business does not with me differ from the time of prayer; and in the noise and clatter of my kitchen, while several persons are at the same time calling for different things, I possess God in as great tranquility as if I were upon my knees at the blessed sacrament."

Inspired by the example set by Brother Lawrence, Laubach embarked on his prayer experiment. The driving motivation was a question that consumed every waking moment: *Can we have contact with God all the time?* His life became a quest to answer that question. Like an explorer embarking on a voyage of discovery, Laubach set sail on his prayer experiment. He chose to make the rest of his life an experiment in answering that question.

Laubach described "the game with minutes" in these terms:

> We try to call Him to mind at least one second of each minute. We do not need to forget other things nor stop our work, but we invite Him to share everything we do or say or think. Hundreds of us have experimented until we have found ways to let Him share every minute of our waking hours.

One of the ways that Laubach played this game was shooting people with silent prayer. He didn't cock his thumb, use his index finger to fire, and then blow away the imaginary smoke; he simply prayed for people while looking at them. Some people would walk by without any reaction, but others would do a sudden about-face and smile at him. Sometimes a person's entire demeanor would change. The simple act of praying for everybody he encountered turned the routine of life into a daily adventure.

I discourage using an actual shooting motion, but what a great way to pull the trigger on 1 Timothy 2:1: "I urge, then, first of all, that petitions, prayers, intercession and thanksgiving be made for all people." Putting this passage into practice is as simple as praying for people before or after meeting with them. Before walking into a meeting, pray for the people you are meeting with. Ask God for favor, discernment, and grace. Then when you leave, pray a blessing on them. A prayer of blessing isn't just something for pastors to pronounce over congregations at the end of services. If you are a child of God, you are a priest. It's your right and responsibility to pronounce blessings over everyone in your life — from your children to your colleagues to your customers, and everyone in between.

Prayer Routines

The key to praying without ceasing is turning everything into a prayer. It usually starts with the big things like problems and dreams. Then it graduates to little things like chores and routines. And eventually, your entire life becomes a continuous prayer.

Every thought. Every action. Every moment.

If you are a worrier by nature, I have good news for you. You have tremendous prayer potential. The apostle Paul writes, "Don't worry about anything; instead, pray about everything." If you worry about everything, you'll have a much higher likelihood of praying without ceasing if you simply learn to turn your worries into prayers. The Holy Spirit can redeem your anxious thoughts by using them as prayer triggers. Think of worry as a prayer alarm. Every time it goes off, you put it to prayer. And when you do, you'll discover that your anxieties will evaporate like early morning fog. So quit wasting your worries. Redeem them by recycling them. Turn your worries into prayers!

What if you stopped reading the newspaper and started praying it? What if you turned lunch meetings into prayer meetings? What if you turned your chores into prayers?

You'd come a lot closer to the goal of praying without ceasing!

When you are folding your children's laundry, pray that they would be clothed with the righteousness of Christ. When you're commuting to and from work, cast your cares on Him. When you tuck your kids into bed at night, let the last words they hear be your prayers for them.

One of my newest and most meaningful prayer routines is kneeling by my bed at the beginning of every day. It's the first thing I do. I climb out of bed and get on my knees. I want God to have my first thoughts, my first words.

It dials me into God's frequency. It sets the tone. It postures me for the entire day.

Holy Experiment

Six months into his game with minutes, Laubach wrote about his holy experiment in his prayer journal.

> Last Monday was the most completely successful day of my life to date, so far as giving my day in complete and continuous surrender to God is concerned ... I remember how as I looked at people with a love God gave, they looked back and acted as though they wanted to go with

me. I felt then that for a day I saw a little of that marvelous pull that Jesus had as He walked along the road day after day "God-intoxicated" and radiant with the endless communion of His soul with God.

The reason most people don't feel intimacy with God is that they don't have a daily prayer rhythm. They may have a weekly rhythm of going to church, which is wonderful, but doing so in and of itself won't produce intimacy with God. Can you imagine talking with your spouse or child once a week? God wants a day-by-day, hour-by-hour, minute-by-minute relationship with you.

The good news is this: God is only a prayer away. The shortest distance between you and God is the distance between your knees and the floor. But you don't have to hit your knees or bow your head or fold your hands to be heard. Prayer isn't something we do with our eyes closed; prayer is something we do with our eyes wide open. Prayer isn't a sentence that begins with "Dear Jesus" and ends with "Amen." In fact, the best prayers don't even involve words at all. The best prayer is a well-lived life, day in and day out.

Turn your prayer life into a game. Try experimenting with a new posture like walking or kneeling. Try experimenting with different types of fasts — from food to television to sleep to Facebook — but remember that the key is giving something up and replacing it with prayer. Try praying at different times, like first thing in the morning or last thing at night. Try experimenting with different techniques. Create a prayer list or begin journaling your prayers.

If you want God to do something new in your life, you cannot keep doing the same old thing. My advice is simple: do something different. And you'll see what a difference it makes!

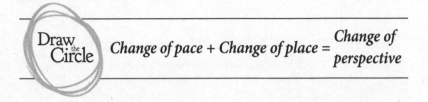

Draw the Circle

Change of pace + Change of place = Change of perspective

Day 27

Double Circle

"This kind goeth not out but by prayer and fasting."
MATTHEW 17:21 KJV

For thirteen years I was a frustrated writer. I had a half-dozen half-finished manuscripts on my computer, but I couldn't seem to finish a book. I started to think that the dream of writing a book might be nothing more than a mirage. Finally, when my level of frustration hit an all-time high, I decided to do a forty-day media fast out of desperation. That fast was the turning point in my writing career. I needed a breakthrough, but it took more than prayer; it took prayer plus fasting. In the process, I found that my writing became a form of praying. I don't type on a keyboard; I pray on it. And by the time I was done, I had completed my first self-published book.

There are times when circling something in prayer isn't enough. We need to double-circle it with prayer and fasting. Matthew 17:21 tells us that certain miracles only happen in response to prayer and fasting. In the same way we open a double combination lock, we need to both pray and fast to unlock the miracle. And the combination of these spiritual disciplines doesn't just add up; it multiplies their effectiveness. Fasting will take us further into the presence of God than praying, and it will get us there much faster. We still need patience and endurance, but fasting has a way of fast-tracking our prayer life like a hyperbolic chamber that speeds healing or a hyperlink that gets us someplace with one click. Fasting is hyperprayer.

There are many different kinds of fasts. I do a twenty-one-day Daniel fast at the beginning of every year that consists of just fruits and vegetables. I sometimes fast from sunrise to sundown. And I occasionally do a complete food fast for short periods of time. But while the most obvious kind of fast involves food, a media fast can be just as powerful. If we want to hear the voice of God, we've got to get rid of the white noise in our lives. A television fast or Facebook fast may be precisely what we need to hear God's voice more clearly.

No matter what we fast, we need to establish a time frame and an objective. If we don't determine exactly when the fast starts and finishes, we'll find excuses to compromise and probably quit. So we must establish a start date and an end date and then figure out what we're fasting for.

We can fast for deliverance from the yoke of bondage. We can fast for the discernment to make a decision. We can fast for favor. We can fast to dedicate something to God — a new year, new job, or new business. We can fast for a financial, relational, or emotional breakthrough. Or we can fast simply to seek the heart of God.

The Flesh

On the eve of his crucifixion, Jesus was in Gethsemane praying hard. His disciples were supposed to be praying, but they were sleeping instead. You can hear the disappointment in Jesus' voice when He asked them, "Couldn't you men keep watch with me for one hour?"

That challenge is worth circling. Take it literally. Take it personally.

I'm convinced that one hour of prayer will revolutionize our lives in ways we can't even begin to imagine. It will help us tap into new dimensions of God's power. It will help us reach out in love, even to the most difficult people. And it will give us the wisdom we need to navigate our greatest challenges.

The disciples let Jesus down when He needed them most. Their failure didn't just hurt Jesus; Jesus knew that it would hurt them. Let me play counterfactual theorist with a question: Would Peter have disowned Jesus if he had been praying instead of sleeping? Maybe he let Jesus down because he wasn't prayed up? While I can't prove it, I think Peter would have passed the temptation test if he had prayed through. His betrayal started when he fell asleep in the garden instead of praying through. That is where the battle is won or lost.

Then Jesus gets to the heart of the matter: "The spirit is willing, but the flesh is weak."

Truer words were never spoken.

Most people have a willing spirit. It's the weak flesh that gets in the way. The problem isn't desire; the problem is power and, more specifically, willpower. That's where fasting comes into play. The reason fasting gives us more power to pray is because it's an exercise in willpower. Physical discipline gives us the spiritual discipline to pray through.

To be honest, I struggle with fasting more than any other spiritual discipline for one simple reason: I love food. But fasting is the way I say to God, *I crave You more than I crave food.* I've also found that saying no to food helps me say no to whatever my flesh craves. It's like a spiritual workout that strengthens my willpower. If I can say no to food, I can say no to other forms of temptation.

When we work out, we break down our muscle fibers so they can be built back up even stronger. In much the same way, fasting breaks down our pride, our bondages, our will. It helps us break bad habits and build good habits. Fasting is the way we break down our spiritual calluses and regain sensitivity to the Holy Spirit.

And if we will live in a place of brokenness, God will build us back up in the power of the Holy Spirit. After forty days of fasting, Jesus' body was undoubtedly in a weakened state. But Scripture states, "Jesus returned to Galilee in the power of the Spirit."

Empty Stomach

I'm more and more convinced that the answer to every prayer is more of the Holy Spirit. Need more power? Then you need more of the Holy Spirit. Need more wisdom? Then you need more of the Holy Spirit. Need more love, joy, peace, patience, kindness, goodness, faithfulness, gentleness, or self-control? Then you need more of the Holy Spirit.

We need to be filled with the Holy Spirit, but we have to empty ourselves first. And one of the best ways to empty ourselves is through fasting.

When I have a big decision to make, I circle it with a fast. It doesn't just purge my body; it purges my mind and spirit as well. It also purges my motives. When I need a breakthrough, I circle it with a fast. It doesn't just break down the challenges I'm facing; it also breaks down the calluses in my heart.

An empty stomach may be the most powerful prayer posture in Scripture. It's even more powerful than kneeling! It shows God that we mean business. And when we fast, God makes our business His business!

Maybe there is something you've been praying for that you need to start fasting for. You need to take it to the next level. Draw a double circle by fasting for a friend or a family member. During our forty-day prayer challenge, small groups turned into prayer circles by fasting for friends who were battling cancer or applying for jobs or fighting to save marriages. And the answers were absolutely amazing. If you double-circle things with prayer and fasting, don't be surprised if you receive a double blessing!

Draw the Circle

If you want to break the sin habit, you've got to establish a prayer habit.

Day 28

Quit Praying

"Well done, good and faithful servant!"
MATTHEW 25:23

One of the defining moments in my prayer life happened a decade ago. I was in a small group with a friend who worked for InterVarsity Christian Fellowship at Georgetown University. Jeremy was working on a shoestring budget, and their campus ministry needed a computer. He shared the request at the end of our meeting, and I agreed to pray for it, but when I started praying for it, I felt that the Lord wanted me to stop praying. It was like the Holy Spirit said, "Why are you asking Me? You're the one with the extra computer!" I quit praying in midsentence. I told Jeremy we didn't need to pray about it because I had an extra computer he could have.

I wonder how many of our prayer requests are within our own power to answer? Yet we ask God to do what we can do ourselves. And then we wonder why God doesn't respond. Maybe it's because God won't do for us what we can do for ourselves. God isn't honored by prayers that are within the realm of human possibility; God is honored when we ask Him to do what is humanly impossible. That way, God gets all the glory!

There are some things we don't need to pray about. We don't need to pray about loving our neighbors. We don't need to pray about giving generously or serving sacrificially. We don't need to pray about blessing someone when it is in our power to do so. We don't have to pray about turning the other cheek or going the extra mile. God has already spoken on those subjects.

There comes a moment when praying becomes a form of spiritual procrastination. It's time to stop praying and start acting.

Quit praying about the program and fill out an application. Quit praying for the friend you hurt and make a phone call. Don't just complain to God about your coworker; circle them in prayer. Don't just pray for missionaries; write a check.

One of my heroes is Peter Marshall, the former chaplain of the United States Senate. His prayers at the opening of Senate sessions are timeless. Peter Marshall believed in an action-oriented approach to Scripture.

> I wonder what would happen if we all agreed to read one of the Gospels, until we came to a place that told us to do something, then went out to do it, and only after we had done it ... began reading again? ...
>
> There are aspects of the Gospel that are puzzling and difficult to understand. But our problems are not centered around the things we don't understand, but rather in the things we do understand, the things we could not possibly misunderstand.
>
> This, after all, is but an illustration of the fact that

our problem is not so much that we don't know what we should do.

We know perfectly well ... but we don't want to do it.

Please don't misinterpret what I'm saying. Pray about everything. Then pray some more. But at some point, we have to quit praying and start acting. One of the great mistakes we make is asking God to do for us what God wants us to do for Him. We confuse roles. For example, we try to convict those around us of sin. But that is the Holy Spirit's responsibility, not ours. In the same sense, God won't do for us what we can do ourselves. And many of us get stuck spiritually right there.

We are called to pray about everything, but there comes a time when praying can be a form of disobedience, laziness, or negligence. We can't just pray like it depends on God; we also must work like it depends on us.

Action Verb

When Christianity turns into a noun, it becomes a turnoff. Christianity was always intended to be a verb — more specifically, an action verb. The title of the book of Acts says it all, doesn't it? It's not the book of *Ideas* or *Words*. It's the book of *Acts*. And if we said less and did more, I believe we would have the same kind of impact the first-century church had. And while we're on the subject, we should be more known for what we're *for* than what we're *against*.

Prayer that doesn't lead to action isn't true prayer; it's self-talk. When we talk to God, God will talk back to us. He will provoke us, rouse us, stir us, goad us, and prompt us. When we say "amen," inaction is no longer an option.

I'm always challenged by members of our congregation who leave everything they know to go to a mission field in another part of the world. They are the true heroes of the kingdom. A few years ago, Becky pursued her God-ordained passion halfway around the world to a little village in India. Why? Because she couldn't just pray about the injustice she had witnessed; she had to do something about it.

I went to India to work with women and children who were trafficked into sex slavery. Most of these women were Nepalese and ended up working as forced prostitutes in India's infamous red-light districts. Their children were literally born into brothels and knew nothing of life except violence, rape, and hunger. Although I wasn't able to rescue the women from their situation, I was able to offer hope and empowerment for the survivors and children. I led dance therapy sessions, helping to reconnect the survivors to their bodies and allowing them to see themselves as beautiful creations of God.

The area we were working in was devastatingly poor and malaria infested. And as an antitrafficking activist, I was in danger from the traffickers and brothel owners. My parents pleaded with me to leave, but I couldn't stay away. I could see God in each of their bloodshot, traumatized, beautiful eyes, begging me to touch, to comfort, to hug, and ultimately to love them.

If Christians believe that the image of God is in every person, why don't we act like it? Why do we turn our eyes from the poor, the widows, the orphans, and the prostitutes? Although prayer is necessary and helps bring comfort, it's not enough to truly alleviate suffering. God didn't send His Son to pray for us but rather to act for us. The only thing that upsets me more than downright evil acts are people who allow injustice to happen with their inaction. Jesus transformed God's message into action, and it should be our mission to devote our lives to similar action.

When everything is said and done, God won't say, "Well said, good and faithful servant." He won't say, "Well thought," "well planned," or even "well prayed." There is only one commendation He will give: "Well done, good and faithful servant."

Draw the Circle

Don't just pray about it;
do something about it.

A New Prayer

Sing to the LORD a new song.
PSALM 96:1

Spiritual growth is a conundrum. The key to spiritual growth is developing healthy and holy routines called spiritual disciplines. But once the routine becomes routine, we need to change the routine. Why? Because sacred routines become empty rituals if we do them out of left-brain memory instead of right-brain imagination.

Routines are a necessary and important part of life. Most of us practice a morning ritual that includes showering, brushing teeth, and putting on deodorant. On behalf of family and friends, please continue practicing those routines. But here's the catch-22: good routines become bad routines if we don't change the routine. One of the great dangers we face spiritually is learning how and forgetting why. Call it familiarization. Call it habituation. Call it routinization. Call it whatever you want, but when we learn how and forget why, we start going through the motions spiritually.

A few years ago, I came across a fascinating study indicating that we stop thinking about the lyrics of songs after singing them thirty times. I'm sure the numbers vary a bit from person to person, but the tendency is universal. And it has profound implications when it comes to worship. If we aren't careful, we aren't really worshiping God; we're just lip-synching. In fact, the lyrics can get in the way of genuinely expressing to God our own thoughts, our own feelings.

Can you imagine a marriage in which the only expression of love is through Hallmark cards? You never put your love into your own words; you just use someone else's words. That's how many of us worship God. We never go beyond the lyrics that someone else has written. Without lyrics on a screen, we'd have nothing to say, nothing to sing.

Six times the psalmist tells us to sing a new song. Evidently God gets tired of old songs. He doesn't want you to worship Him with just your memory; He wants you to worship Him with your imagination as well. Love isn't repetitive; love is creative. As love grows, you need new lyrics and new melodies. You need a new song to express new dimensions of love. If you express your love to your wife in the same way over and over again, she may stop believing you at some point. Why? Because it's a mindless expression of an old feeling.

Right-Brain Prayer

Left-brain worship doesn't cut it. Neither does left-brain prayer.

Jesus warns us, "When you pray, don't babble on and on as people of other religions do. They think their prayers are answered merely by repeating their words again and again.

Don't be like them, for your Father knows exactly what you need even before you ask him!"

It's easy to fall into a prayer rut. We repeat all the prayer clichés we know, followed by an amen! In the same way that we need to sing a new song, we need to pray a new prayer. We need a new vocabulary, a new methodology.

We tend to think and act in patterned ways. Our tendency to do things the way we've always done them is called a heuristic bias. It is an amazingly complex cognitive process, but the result is mindlessness. We do things without thinking about them. If we aren't careful, we pray without thinking — and that is just as destructive as thinking without praying.

A few years ago, I preached about overcoming our heuristic bias, and someone in our congregation was compelled to respond with a prayer experiment.

After your sermon, I decided to approach your challenge to thank God for the daily miracles we generally take for granted. Knowing the list of thanks could be infinitely long, I decided to focus only on the miracles I was receiving at the moment of my prayer. So I started praying. "Thank You, God, for aerobic respiration. Thank You for mitochondria, which right now are creating ATP. Thank You for ATP. Thank You for glycolysis. Thank You for pyruvate."

With a biology degree, I ended up having a lot of things on the list. By the time I got back to my place in Arlington, I was thanking God for each of the amino acids. "Thank You, God, for glycine. Thank You for leucine and isoleucine and tryptophan."

I started thanking God for the fact that all organisms that form amino acids have the same chirality so that my body can reuse the nutrients and cellular building blocks of the food I break down. I found myself in absolute awe of His creation.

I prayed while I took a walk outside, thanking Him for bones and ligaments and tendons. I also thanked Him that I somehow never took an anatomy course in college, because otherwise I would have felt compelled to thank Him for each bone by name, which would have definitely set me back even more in my quest to get through most of the miracles I was receiving at that moment.

I spent the day praying without ceasing! I literally didn't stop and just consciously kept listing things I was thankful for. I listened to music and thanked Him for my ear's cochlea. While I made dinner, I thanked Him for xylem in the plants I was preparing. I spent a lot of time thanking Him for the molecular properties of water. I thanked Him for the bacteria in my colon that helps me digest food. I thanked Him for the genetic recombination that made developing and cultivating cotton plants possible for the jeans I was wearing.

At around nine o'clock that night, I think God got amused with the futility of me trying to thank Him for everything. The Spirit finally hushed me, saying, "You can stop now."

Now that's a right-brain prayer!

God doesn't want all of us to pray the same way. We pray in keeping with our personality. So one dimension of my own prayer life is humor. We burst out laughing in the middle of prayer all the time because I'll bust out a joke. I know that sounds sacrilegious, but I love telling jokes. Why would I exclude God? And I can't imagine a relationship with someone where humor wasn't part of our conversational relationship. It would be downright boring. I'm not sure God laughs at all my jokes, but He's the one who created us with a sense of humor.

The next time you pray, try a new posture or a new time slot. If you typically verbalize your prayers, try writing them out. If you kneel while praying, try a prayer walk. Do something different. Get out of your regular routine, and pray a new prayer to the Lord.

If you want God to do something new, you cannot keep doing the same old thing.

Abide in Me

"If My words abide in you ..."
JOHN 15:7 NASB

In ancient Jewish culture, formal education began at six years of age. Jewish boys enrolled in their local synagogue school called *bet sefer* ("house of the book"). On the first day of class, according to tradition, the rabbi would cover their slate with honey. Honey was the symbol of God's favor. Then the rabbi would instruct his students to lick the honey off their slate while reciting from Psalm 119: "How sweet are Your words to my taste! Yes, sweeter than honey to my mouth." It was their first lesson and their most important lesson. It taught the students that nothing is sweeter than the Word of God. It taught them that the Bible is the land of milk and honey, the true Promised Land. By the time students graduated from *bet sefer* four years later, they had memorized the entire Torah. Every jot and tittle of Genesis, Exodus, Leviticus, Numbers, and Deuteronomy was engraved on their cerebral cortex via memorization.

After graduating from *bet sefer*, the best students continued on with *bet Talmud* ("house of learning"). From the age of ten to fourteen, students memorized the rest of the Hebrew Scriptures. For what it's worth, I think it's likely that Jesus attended *bet Talmud*. Scripture doesn't explicitly mention it, but even at twelve years of age, Jesus wowed the rabbis in the temple courts with his understanding.

After *bet Talmud*, a select few graduated to *bet midrash* ("house of study"). Those who didn't make the cut would typically go into the family business. Applicants asked a local rabbi if they could be his *talmidim* ("disciples"). If the rabbi chose them, he would extend a verbal invitation: *lech acharai*. Translation: "come, follow me." Inherent within that invitation was an understanding that it meant total surrender, complete devotion. It meant taking that rabbi's yoke on yourself. The yoke represented the sum total of the rabbi's philosophy and practice. It meant spending every waking moment with him. It meant going wherever he went, doing whatever he did, listening to everything he said.

The complete devotion of discipleship is sometimes described as being "covered in the dust of your rabbi." It was an allusion to the fact that disciples followed their rabbi so closely that the dust the rabbi kicked up with his heels would literally cover the disciples who followed him.

The Word of God

One of the surest ways to get into the presence of God is to get into the Word of God. If we get into God's Word, God's Word will get into us. It will radically change the way we think, the way we live, the way we love. But it requires more than a casual reading. In fact, the Bible wasn't meant to be read. It was meant to be memorized and meditated on. It was meant to be prayed and practiced. We have to abide in the Word of God and let the Word of God abide in us.

Words that are repeated throughout Scripture are repeated because they bear repeating. It's God's way of saying, "Don't let this go in one ear and out the other." These are words we need to pay special attention to. One of them is the word *abide*, which is repeated no less than eight times in John 15. In verse 7, John writes, "If you abide in Me, and My words abide in you, ask whatever you wish, and it will be done for you."

The word *abide* is a present imperative verb, which indicates a continual action. It's not something we start and stop; it's something we do for the rest of our lives. And we do more of it. The goal is to get closer and closer to God. And the way we do this is by abiding in His Word.

According to rabbinic tradition, every word of Scripture has seventy faces and six hundred thousand meanings. Each word is kaleidoscopic. And the word *abide* is a great example. Let me turn the kaleidoscope to reveal five reflections of meaning.

To stay overnight. Just like Jesus, who prayed well into the night on the eve of His crucifixion, sometimes we need to press into the presence of God a little longer. And if we linger in His presence, God's presence will linger on us. In my experience, God responds to extra effort with an extra blessing. It's those who spend the most time in God's presence that God can use the most because they are the people He can trust the most.

To hold fast. Every time we pray, we gain a position in the spiritual realm. The kingdom of God is advanced and the forces of darkness must retreat. And our most effective weapon is the Word of God. It's the same weapon Jesus used when He was tempted by Satan. Abiding in the Word of God is the way we take enemy territory and hold our ground. It's our best offense and best defense.

To stand still. Remember when the Israelites found themselves cornered between the Red Sea and the Egyptian army? The Lord spoke to Moses with these words: "Fear ye not, stand still, and see the salvation of the LORD." When we find ourselves between a rock and a hard place, we must stand on the Word of God and trust His promises. We will face some problems we cannot solve, some situations we cannot change. That's when we may feel like panicking, but it is the time to stand still and wait for the Lord's deliverance. No one likes being in those situations, but God often does His most dramatic miracles at those very times.

To be moved. The prophet Haggai writes, "The LORD stirred up the spirit of Zerubbabel." When the Word of God gets in our spirit, which is the spiritual womb, new passions are conceived within us. And inaction is no longer an option. We cannot abide in the Word of God and not be moved to action. We cannot sit on the sidelines. Like David, who ran to the front lines, we'll be looking for giants to conquer.

To tarry. This is precisely what Jesus told His disciples to do after His ascension. Just as they tarried in the upper room for ten days, we must tarry in the Word of God. Perhaps the spiritual disciplines of studying Scripture and engaging in prayer aren't two separate disciplines. One is the key to the other.

We're so busy trying to do something for God that we don't realize that the key to our success in any endeavor is letting God do something for us. We cannot do something *for* God if we aren't *with* God. We have to press into His presence. And the surest way to get into God's presence is by getting into God's Word.

Jewish kings were required to make a personal copy of the law in their own handwriting. They had to keep it on their person wherever they went. I've always found this fascinating. It's something like having a nation's president make a handwritten copy of the constitution and read it every day. So why did God require this of the kings? I think He knew it would force them to internalize it and personalize it. It also served as preventative medicine.

> "This regular reading will prevent him from becoming proud and acting as if he is above his fellow citizens. It will also prevent him from turning away from these commands in the smallest way."

I don't think you need to write out your own personal copy of Scripture, but let me offer one piece of advice that will help you personalize Scripture. Wherever you read the pronoun *you*, insert your name. It will help you take what you read more literally, more personally. It will also remind you that your life is a unique translation of Scripture. If people like what they read in your life, they might just want to pick up the Book that inspired your translation!

Reading without meditating
is like eating without digesting.

Spell It Out

"What do you want me to do for you?"
MATTHEW 20:32

More than a thousand years after the original Jericho miracle, another miracle happened in the same place. Jesus was on His way out of the city when two blind men shouted, "Lord, Son of David, have mercy on us!" The disciples saw it as an inconvenient interruption, but divine appointments usually come disguised. The disciples would have walked right past this "miracle waiting to happen." They had places to go and things to do. But Jesus stopped. Then He asked the two men a loaded question: "What do you want me to do for you?"

Is that question even necessary? They are blind. Isn't it obvious what they want? Yet Jesus forced them to define exactly what they wanted from Him. Jesus made them verbalize it. He made them spell out exactly what they wanted Him to do, but it wasn't because Jesus didn't know what they wanted; He wanted to make sure that they knew what they wanted.

What if Jesus asked you the same question: *What do you*

want Me to do for you? Would you be able to spell out the promises, miracles, and dreams God has put in your heart? I'm afraid many of us would find ourselves at a loss for words. We have no idea what we want God to do for us, and then we wonder why it seems like God isn't doing anything for us. The great irony, of course, is that if we can't answer this question, then we're as blind spiritually as these men were physically.

Most of us don't get what we want simply because we don't know what we want.

We've never made a list of life goals. We've never defined success for ourselves. We've never circled any of God's promises. And we've forgotten most of the prayers we've prayed before they are even answered.

If faith is being sure of what we hope for, then not being sure of what we hope for is the exact opposite of faith, isn't it?

Well-Defined Prayers

A few years ago, I read one sentence that radically affected the way I pray: "God does not answer vague prayers." I was immediately convicted by how vague my prayers were. Some were so vague that there was no way of knowing whether or not God had answered them. To be honest, I was subconsciously hedging my bets. My lack of faith didn't allow me to go out on a limb and lay my true request on the line. And because I was afraid God might not answer, I didn't even give Him a chance to answer!

The more faith we have, the more specific our prayers will be. And the more specific our prayers are, the more glory

God receives. If our prayers aren't specific, however, God gets robbed of the glory He deserves because we second-guess whether or not He actually answered them. We never know if the answers were the result of specific prayers or general coincidences that would have happened anyway. Well-defined prayers give God an opportunity to display His power in new ways. Well-developed faith results in well-defined prayers, and well-defined prayers result in well-defined answers.

Nearly two decades ago, Sergei and Aleona Isakov put their faith in Jesus Christ through the influence of American missionaries who served in Russia. Aleona turned her profession — fashion design — into her pulpit. She has shared her testimony with millions of people by means of televised interviews and live fashion shows in Russia, Israel, England, and Australia. A few years ago, Sergei and Aleona felt called to literally return the favor and move to D.C. as Russian missionaries to America. That's how they landed at National Community Church. In Aleona's words, "We believe that revival is coming to America, and we want to be part of it."

During our prayer challenge, Aleona spelled out six miracles. Their specific nature challenged and inspired me. First, she prayed that God would give her a platform at the National Prayer Breakfast to share her newest fashions. God answered that prayer with an invitation to speak to one hundred guests at the NPB, and one of those guests then invited her to speak at a conference in Norway. Second, they prayed that they'd receive their EB-1 visas, but God did them one better by providing green cards that allow Aleona to bring her entire fashion collection to the United States. Third, she prayed that God would heal her husband's six-month cough. No more cough drops required! Fourth, she prayed that her daughter and son-in-law would get American visas. They got them in two weeks' time. Fifth, she prayed that God would send her a new fashion photographer who loves Jesus. What she didn't expect is that the amazingly talented photographer would volunteer to shoot for free. And last but not least, Aleona prayed for a good job for her husband. Sergei started his job as an IT engineer at *National Geographic Magazine* two days after the prayer challenge ended.

Too often we rob God of the opportunity to answer our prayers because they are so vague. Don't worry about *when* God answers or *how* God answers. That isn't our responsibility. Our responsibility is to simply discern what God wants, and then humbly yet boldly to ask Him for it. And God will throw in a few holy surprises along the way because He may spell the answer differently than we spelled the request.

The Ladder of Success

Jesus is still asking the question: *What do you want Me to do for you?* And like the two blind men outside Jericho, we still need an encounter with the Son of God. We need an answer to the question. We need to identify our Jericho — the promise we are circling.

What promise are you praying around? What miracle are you marching around? What dream does your life revolve around?

What is your Jericho?

Jericho is spelled many different ways. If a loved one has cancer, it's spelled *healing*. If your best friend is far from God, it's spelled *salvation*. If your family is falling apart, it's spelled *reconciliation*. If you have a dream beyond your finances, it's spelled *provision*. But whatever it is, you have to spell it out.

It's easy to get so busy climbing the ladder of success that we fail to realize the ladder is not leaning against the wall of Jericho. Eternal priorities get overshadowed by our everyday responsibilities, and we pawn our God-given dream for the American dream. So instead of circling Jericho, we end up wandering in the wilderness.

What is your Jericho?

If you can't answer this question, stop reading. Get into God's presence and get an answer! Obviously, the answer to this question changes over time. We need different miracles during different seasons of life. We pursue different dreams during different stages of life. And we stake claim to different promises during different situations. It's a moving target, but we have to start somewhere.

Why not right here, right now?

Define your dream. Claim your promise. Spell your miracle.

Most of us don't get what we want because we don't know what we want.

Day 32

Get a Testimony

"... and by the word of their testimony ..."
REVELATION 12:11

Since the release of *The Circle Maker*, I've become a connoisseur of prayer testimonies. Hardly a day goes by that I don't hear a story that makes me want to cry or give God a round of applause. Those testimonies have lit a fire under my faith unlike anything I've ever experienced. Here's why: *If God did it for them, He might just do it for me.* Maybe that's why Revelation 12:11 places such importance on sharing testimonies. And maybe that's why the enemy wants us to keep our testimonies silent.

> "They triumphed over him
>   by the blood of the Lamb
>   and by the word of their testimony."

When God answers a prayer, no matter how big or how small, we need to share it. It's a stewardship issue. If we don't turn the answer to prayer into praise, it may very well turn into pride. Giving testimony is the way we give God all of the glory. But we also need to share it because others need to hear it. If we don't share our testimonies of how God is working in our lives, then others are tempted to think He isn't working at all.

Jesus triumphed over the enemy by His shed blood on Calvary's cross. He broke the curse of sin so we can break the cycle of sin. But the way we seal the victory is through our testimonies. Our testimonies don't just remind us that the victory has already been won; they also remind the enemy that he has already been defeated.

I wonder if the lack of awe in many churches is directly attributable to the lost art of the testimony. Churches that see people radically saved are usually churches that allow radically saved people to share their testimonies. Is it any wonder that what gets celebrated gets replicated? When a testimony of healing is shared, for example, those who hear it get an infusion of faith to believe God for healing in their own lives. Those testimonies double as prophecies!

When we share a testimony, we are loaning our faith to others. When we listen to a testimony, we are borrowing faith from others. Either way, the church is edified and God is glorified.

Hearsay

In the worlds of criminal law and academic research, we see a big difference between first-person and second-person testimony. A first-person witness is more credible because they actually saw it with their own eyes. Second-person testimony is hearsay. It doesn't mean it's not true; it just means it doesn't hold as much weight.

A testimony is powerful, in part, because we cannot argue with it. It's irrefutable and undeniable. A personal testimony is our secret weapon, and that's why the enemy wants us to keep our testimony a secret. It's not a testimony if we don't share it with others. If we don't share our testimonies, we are robbing God of the glory He deserves. And we aren't just holding out on God; we are holding out on those who need to hear it.

Our churches are filled with hearsay. What we need are witnesses with first-person testimonies. No amount of education can compensate for a lack of first-person experience. We don't get a testimony in seminary; we get a testimony by being tested. And if we pass the test, we get a testimony. That testimony is worth far more than any seminary degree can afford. And that first-person experience with God will override any of our inadequacies. Peter and John were described as "unschooled, ordinary men," yet the Jewish council was amazed at their boldness. It simply says that "they took note that these men had been with Jesus."

Nothing can compare to the power of first-person testimony. The most educated and erudite second-person testimony still can't compare with a first-person witness! So go ahead and get an education. Study to present yourself to God as one approved. But please don't just get an education; get a testimony! We don't change the world by going to graduate school or getting a degree. If we want to change the world, we must spend a lot of time with Jesus.

Remember the Samaritan woman who was totally transformed by a single encounter with Jesus at the well? She went back to her village and shared her testimony. That testimony sparked faith in those who heard, but their faith was secondhand faith. They needed their own encounter with Jesus, and that's exactly what they got. The transition from secondhand to firsthand faith is evidenced in their words: "Now we believe, not just because of what you told us, but because we have heard him ourselves."

We cannot live off of someone else's experience forever. Secondhand faith is as dangerous as secondhand smoke. We need a faith with our own name on it. We need to own it, and it needs to own us. We can't just know *what* we believe; we need to know *why* we believe what we believe. And it must be continually upgraded.

Don't be satisfied with simply going to church; get into God's presence.

Don't be satisfied with hearsay; get a word from the Lord.

Don't be satisfied with secondhand faith; get a testimony!

Crazy Prayers

One of my pastor friends, and a local hero, is Mike Minter. Mike is the founding pastor of Reston Bible Church, where he has served for nearly four decades. One day over coffee, Mike told me about a missionary friend named Jamie Winship, whose mission field is the Muslim world. Jamie travels to Baghdad frequently. He knows the Qur'an backward and forward. And he has led countless imams to faith in Jesus Christ.

Jamie is one of those guys who prays crazy prayers and

then crazy stuff happens. Divine appointments happen right and left. He'll be praying for a particular imam, and that imam will just happen to be on the same plane going to the same place or in the same restaurant at the table right behind him.

One morning Mike was scheduled to have breakfast with Jamie, so he prayed, "Lord, I'm sick of just hearing stories; I want to see one. Do something sovereign that is unmistakable." When they got in line to place their order, Mike noticed that the woman in front of them was wearing the traditional Muslim *hijab* with head covering. All they could see was the woman's eyes. Jamie greeted her in Arabic, which got her attention. Then he said, "I know you." Even though he could see only her eyes, he said, "I heard you speak at the University of Georgia a year ago" — to which she responded, "I remember you. You sat on the front row."

Not only was this woman one of the most influential Muslim women in the world, but Jamie had been praying for her by name. In fact, he had been praying that he would meet her, but he didn't know how to contact her. She happened to be in D.C. from out of town, and evidently God knew they both liked Panera Bread. As a result of the meeting, this woman contacted a number of leading imams, who met with Mike and Jamie to dialogue about faith.

I think Jamie's prayer, coupled with Mike's prayer for something sovereign to happen, collided at Panera.

That is a divine appointment of biblical proportions! And it reveals the power of two people praying. You never know when your prayer will collide with someone else's prayer and result in a miracle. But this is what happened with Mike and Jamie. They tag-teamed in prayer, and it resulted in a supernatural synchronicity. You can call me a simpleton, but I believe that God is still seated on His throne. And if God is ordering my footsteps, and I believe He is, then He is going to make sure I get where I need to go and meet whomever I need to meet.

I hope this testimony to God's sovereignty is encouraging, but it's also meant to be an exhortation. Mike wasn't satisfied with simply hearing someone else's story. Secondhand faith wasn't enough. There comes a point when you, like Mike, grow weary of hearing other people's stories. You need a story of your own. It's got to have your name on it. You've got to see it, hear it, taste it, feel it, touch it, and smell it for yourself.

You need to go get a testimony! Then you need to share it.

Draw the Circle

Most of us are educated way beyond the level of our obedience.

Prayer Covering

Aaron and Hur held his hands up —
one on one side, one on the other.

EXODUS 17:12

During my first decade of pastoring in D.C., I often felt like the Lone Ranger. I was doing my thing my way. I was so busy trying to build our church that I forfeited potential friendships with other local pastors. Then one day the Lord convicted me that it was easier for me to pray for a church four states away than a church four blocks away. So I started praying for area churches. We started investing in local church plants, and I started inviting local pastors to share their stories and their hearts with our team during staff devotions. Many of those staff meetings turned into prayer meetings. We would inevitably end up on our knees interceding for each other. Each time a local pastor did devotions, I felt the stronghold of territorialism being weakened.

I firmly believe we need many different kinds of churches because there are many different kinds of people. As long as a church is preaching the gospel, it's all for one and one for all. We may have different church names over the door, but there is one church and one Shepherd of the church. So I'm praying for revival in our nation's capital, but it doesn't have to start with National Community Church. I just want in on it.

In the last few years, God has blessed us with some tremendous pastor friends. Lora has cultivated friendships with four pastors' wives — Donna, Heather, Jill, and Taryn. And I've cultivated friendships with a handful of pastors whom I've grown to love and respect as brothers and fathers in the faith. Even pastors need pastors, and the Lord has blessed me with an Aaron and a Hur.

Bob Mathieu and Michael Hall have pastored in D.C. almost as long as I've been alive. Without my knowledge, they covenanted together to circle me in prayer every day. It's hard to describe what it means to have two seventy-something pastors praying for me daily, but I feel those prayers lifting up my arms.

Part of what makes these newfound friendships so meaningful is that they are the answer to a prayer I didn't even know was being prayed. A member of my prayer circle recently revealed that they had been specifically praying for God to strategically place older pastors in my life. Over the last few years, God has answered those prayers. The answers are spelled Michael, Bob, Amos, Mike, Stuart, Dennis, and Glenn, just to name a few.

Aaron and Hur

If we are going to intercede for others, we had better be sure that others are interceding for us. We need a prayer covering, especially when we enter an intense season of prayer and fasting. When we hit our knees, we pick a fight with the enemy. And the enemy will fight back. Make no mistake, there is a target on our back. The enemy wants to take us out, but he cannot touch us. He has no jurisdiction in our lives if we are covered by the blood of Jesus, but we also need a prayer covering.

Intercession is spiritual warfare. It's not for the faint or the feeble. By definition, praying hard is hard. There will be times when our hearts are breaking because of a prayer burden. There will be seasons when the labor pains become intense because the Holy Spirit is birthing something new in us. And there will be times when we feel the enemy launching a frontal assault on our family or business or church. That's when we need to stay on our knees and pray through.

Spiritual warfare can be scary and lonely, but I've always been strangely encouraged when I encounter increased spiritual opposition or oppression. It means I'm doing something right. It means I'm riling up the enemy. It's means I'm inching closer to the breakthrough. And just when the fighting gets fiercest, I know that God is getting ready to go to battle for me.

In Exodus 17, we find a blow-by-blow description of an ancient battle between the Israelites and the Amalekites. As long as Moses was lifting up his arms, the Israelites were gaining ground. But when Moses grew tired and lowered his arms, the Israelites lost ground. That's when Aaron and Hur stood alongside Moses and lifted up his arms until sunset.

Spiritual battles are fought the same way. The victory is

won with knees bent in prayer and hands raised in worship to God. The enemy cannot be defeated any other way. No victory has ever been won apart from prayer and praise.

We will have moments when we lack the ability, strength, will, or faith to pray for ourselves. That's when we need a prayer partner or prayer circle to hold up our arms, just as Aaron and Hur did for Moses. I'm so grateful for my personal prayer circle. There are a lot of people who pray for my family, but I have an inner circle that prays with a little more specificity, consistency, and intensity. I know they are on their knees interceding for me every day. I may unfairly get credit for the things I have done, but they get the assist.

Footnotes

The day after the Israelites defeated the Amalekites, I'm sure Moses made the headlines. But in the grand scheme of God's story, there is a footnote behind every headline. The footnote is prayer. And the true heroes of the kingdom are the Aarons and the Hurs.

In the words of Walter Wink, "History belongs to the intercessors."

Charles Finney was the most famous evangelist of his generation. He made headlines during the Second Great Awakening, but there is a footnote to the story. Finney had an "Aaron" named Daniel Nash. At the age of forty-eight, Father Nash quit his pastorate to devote himself to full-time intercession. Several weeks before Finney would visit a city, Father Nash would rent a room, recruit two or three intercessors, and begin laying a prayer foundation for the revival that would follow. By the time Finney showed up, the hard work had already been done. The victory had already been secured in the spiritual realm.

During one of his revivals, Finney was contacted by a woman who ran a boarding house in town. She asked him, "Brother Finney, do you know a Father Nash? He and two other men have been at my boarding house for the last three days, but they haven't eaten a bite of food. I opened the door and peeped in at them because I could hear them groaning, and I saw them down on their faces. They have been this way for three days, lying prostrate on the floor and groaning. I thought something awful must have happened to them. I was afraid to go in, and I didn't know what to do. Would you please come see about them?" Finney replied, "No, it isn't necessary. They just have a spirit of travail in prayer."

When public meetings started, Father Nash rarely attended. He stayed in his prayer closet pleading with God for the convicting power of the Holy Spirit to fall on the crowd and melt their hearts.

Shortly before his death in 1831, Father Nash recorded these words in his journal.

I am now convinced; it is my duty and privilege, and the duty of every other Christian, to pray for as much of the Holy Spirit as came down on the day of Pentecost, and a great deal more ... I have only just begun to understand what Jesus meant when He said, "All things whatsoever ye shall ask in prayer, believing, ye shall receive."

Father Nash is buried in a small cemetery near the border of New York and Canada. The headstone on his grave contains the following epitaph:

DANIEL NASH
LABORER WITH FINNEY
MIGHTY IN PRAYER
Nov. 17, 1775 — Dec. 20, 1831

Prayer is the pen that writes history. Don't worry about making headlines; focus on the footnotes. And if you focus on the footnotes, God will write the headlines.

**Draw
the
Circle**

***If you intercede for others,
make sure others are interceding for you.***

Day 34

Raise Up a Remnant

And the remnant shall yet again take root
downward, and bear fruit upward.
2 KINGS 19:30 KJV

In the eighteenth century, Count Nikolaus Ludwig von Zinzendorf formed a holy conspiracy called "the Order of the Mustard Seed." Members wore a ring inscribed with the motto "none live for themselves." They solemnly pledged to be true to Christ, to be kind to people, and to take the gospel to the nations. The secret order included such notables as the king of Denmark, the Anglican archbishop of Canterbury, the secretary of state of Scotland, and the eighty-seven-year-old Creek Indian chief Tomochichi.

On the evening before the order was formed, Zinzendorf called his friends to prayer. He held up the ring and said, "Brothers, we know why we are here. Tomorrow we will make our covenant, but tonight let us pray." Zinzendorf himself prayed all night. The next morning they pledged to use all of their gifts, all of their wealth, and all of their influence for the conversion of the heathen. Zinzendorf then laid hands on each member of the order and individually prayed for them.

The ceremony lasted a few minutes, but the covenant lasted a lifetime.

What was begun that day culminated in the Moravian Pentecost at Herrnhut in 1727. On August 27 of that year, a small remnant of twenty-four brothers and twenty-four sisters began praying around the clock. That prayer meeting was visited by the Holy Spirit, not unlike the 120 who prayed in the upper room on the day of Pentecost. Thus began hourly intercessions that would not stop for one hundred years! Even the children of the village formed prayer circles. And those prayers reverberated all around the world in one of the greatest missionary movements the church has ever known. Thousands of missionaries were called and commissioned. Some even sold themselves into slavery in order to reach their mission field.

Reformation

At critical junctures in history, God raises up a remnant to reestablish His reign and rule. It's rarely a majority. In fact, it's almost always a small minority. But all it takes is a faithful few to begin a reformation.

It's not a new discovery that sparks it. Reformations are birthed out of rediscovering something ancient, something simple, something true. In the days of Hilkiah the priest, for example, it was the rediscovery of the Book of the Law that sparked national revival. That one rediscovery brought a nation to its knees.

Every generation needs a reformation. Every generation

needs to tear down its idols and rebuild its temples. Every generation needs to repent of its sin and rediscover the ancient truths.

During our forty-day challenge at National Community Church, we felt we needed to circle one promise for forty days.

> "If my people, who are called by my name, will humble themselves and pray and seek my face and turn from their wicked ways, then I will hear from heaven, and I will forgive their sin and will heal their land."

If we circle the promises of God, God will deliver on them. It's not a question of *if*, it's only a question of *when*. But if we are determined to pray as long as it takes, revival will come. It's as predictable as the sun rising in the east. It's as inevitable as the sun setting into the west.

In the words of Charles Finney, "God is one pent-up revival."

And all it takes is a remnant rising up!

As a reminder of the promise, our church started gathering at 7:14 a.m. for corporate prayer. When the clock hit 7:14, we hit our knees. It became as instinctual as hunger pangs. Not getting on our knees felt like missing a meal.

It was at 7:14 a.m. on the National Day of Prayer that I felt as though the Spirit of God gave me a word: *I'm raising up a remnant*. To be honest, I was a little discouraged on that particular morning that we didn't have more people at our prayer meeting! After all, it was the National Day of Prayer. But that's when God reminded me that all it takes is a remnant. I stopped worrying about who had or hadn't shown up. I started focusing on the promise of exponential potential when just two or three pray in His name!

I believe there is a remnant within every church, within every city. It's time to rise up. It's time for reformation. The next great awakening won't be the result of a planning meeting. Just as it was for Pentecost, it will be birthed in a prayer meeting.

Since the National Day of Prayer, I've been circling 2 Kings 19:30. I believe it's a promise for our generation, for every generation.

> "Once more a remnant of the kingdom of Judah
> will take root below and bear fruit above."

We will bear fruit above! Heaven will be populated because of our prayers. But the root of revival is prayer. We've got to press into the presence of God as never before. Like the members of the Order of the Mustard Seed, we must covenant to seek God with all our heart and soul.

An Eviction Notice

In the 1950s, Argentina was a spiritual wasteland. According to Dr. Edward Miller, a missionary who spent four decades in Argentina, there were only six hundred Spirit-filled believers in the entire country. In his book *Cry for Me Argentina*, he describes the genesis of a revival that started in Argentina and swept across South America.

It began with fifty students at the Argentine Bible Institute who developed an intense prayer burden for the nation of Argentina. Dr. Miller said he had never seen people weep so hard or pray so long. Day after day, they wept and prayed. After hours of intercession, students would literally be standing in their own puddle of tears.

On the fiftieth day of around-the-clock intercession, there was a prophetic word. "Weep no more, for the Lion of the tribe of Judah hath prevailed over the prince of Argentina." Eighteen months later, hundreds of thousands of Argentines were flocking to crusades at soccer stadiums. The largest stadiums, seating 180,000 people, weren't large enough to handle the crowds.

Dr. Miller came to this conclusion:

> If God can get enough people in an area to reject the rulership and the dominion of satan, if enough of His people will reject satan's dominion in the right way — with humility, with brokenness, and in repentant intercession — then God will slap an eviction notice on the doorway of the ruling demonic power of that area. And when He does, then there is a light and glory that begins to come.

We never know how or when or where a move of God might begin. But if we hit our knees, God will extend His mighty right hand on our behalf. If we lay a foundation of prayer, God will build something spectacular on top of it. If we intercede like never before, God will intervene like never before.

*When the prayer meeting
becomes the most important meeting,
revival is around the corner.*

Day 35

The Longest Lever

"Do not despise these small beginnings."
ZECHARIAH 4:10 NLT

On July 1, 1857, Jeremiah Lanphier was called to be a city missionary in New York City. He soon felt led to begin a daily meeting where businesspeople in New York City could gather for midday prayer. The first meeting was held in September in the upper room of the consistory building of the Dutch Reformed Church in Manhattan. Only six people showed up. The following week there were fourteen. The week after that there were twenty-three. Eventually the prayer meeting expanded into the main sanctuary of the church and then outgrew the church itself. The prayer meetings began to multiply across the city until daily gatherings for prayer took place in almost every public building in New York City.

Commenting on Jonathan Edwards's call to "a visible union of God's people in extraordinary prayer," J. Edwin Orr writes, "When people are found getting up at six in the morning to pray, or having a half night of prayer until midnight, or giving up their lunch time to pray at a noonday prayer meeting, that is extraordinary prayer."

Horace Greeley, founder of the most influential newspaper of its day, the *New-York Tribune*, sent one of his reporters to investigate the growing revival. The reporter visited twelve prayer meetings in one hour on one day and counted 6,100 men fervently seeking God in prayer. At the peak of the revival, it is estimated that nearly 10,000 people were converted every week in New York City, roughly 1 percent of the population of one million per week!

I'd like to know who those six people were at the first prayer meeting. I can't help but wonder if they were discouraged that first week. Did they have any inkling they were starting something that would impact hundreds of thousands of lives? I have a hunch they had no clue. Very rarely does anyone know they are making history while they are making it. And that isn't our job anyway. But if we pray like the members of the early church did, Pentecost can happen anywhere. Our prayers have the potential to write and rewrite history.

Small Beginnings

In Zechariah 4, the Jewish remnant who returned to Israel are getting ready to rebuild the temple. It is an overwhelming undertaking. But the Lord encourages them with these words:

> "Do not despise these small beginnings, for the LORD rejoices to see the work begin, to see the plumb line in Zerubbabel's hand."

The plumb line was an ancient measuring tape. All they

had done at this point was measure! That's it. But God was already rejoicing over them. Like a parent that celebrates a baby's first step, our heavenly Father rejoices when we take the smallest of steps in the right direction. And those small steps become giant leaps in God's kingdom. If we do little things, God will do the big things. But we have to do the little things *like* they are big things.

We cannot worry about what we cannot do; we have to simply do what we can.

Oswald Chambers once wrote, "It is inbred in us that we have to do exceptional things for God; but we have not. We have to be exceptional in the ordinary things." And if we do the ordinary, God will add an extra to it.

Prayer is our plumb line. It's also the true measure of a person. No one is greater than their prayer life. Our potential is directly proportional to our prayer life. It is the single greatest indicator of our success in any endeavor.

The Lever

Archimedes of Syracuse is famous for his quip, "Give me a place to stand on, and I will move the earth." He was referencing the lever, one of six simple machines identified by Renaissance scientists. A lever amplifies the input force to provide a greater output force. Simply put, the longer the lever, the greater the leverage.

Let me borrow this simple statement and substitute one word: *Give me a place to kneel on, and I will move the earth.* In the kingdom of God, humility equals authority. Call it bold humility or humble boldness. That is our lever. If we try to exalt ourselves, God will find a way to humble us. But if we humble ourselves, God will find a way to exalt us. There is no leverage like kneeling in prayer. If we hit our knees in humble prayer, God will extend His mighty hand on our behalf. He will leverage us in ways that are humanly impossible.

One of our mantras at NCC is "stay humble, stay hungry." Humility is how we get out of the way of what God wants to do. And if we stay out of God's way, then there is nothing God cannot do in us and through us.

The first thing I do every day is hit my knees — a daily ritual that began the day we started our forty-day prayer challenge. At the end of those forty days, I was a totally different person. I have no idea why I wasn't kneeling every morning before that, but when those forty days concluded, I couldn't imagine starting my day any other way. There is nothing magical about kneeling, but there is something biblical about it. Posturing our bodies helps us posture our hearts. Bowing our hearts in reverence before God is what really matters, but I've found that it's easier to do if I'm in a kneeling position.

During our forty-day prayer challenge, God revealed his favor in amazing ways. We received the kind of news coverage that money cannot buy. *The Washington Post* ran a remarkably positive front-page story in the weekend Metro section. A few weeks later, the *Today Show* filmed one of our weekend services, and the segment aired on the last day of our forty-day prayer challenge. Coincidence? I think not. It had God's fingerprints of favor all over it.

Publicity isn't something to be sought, but it is something

we must steward. To be honest, it's a two-edged sword. The more publicity you get, the more you get pelted with stones. So on a personal level, I am inclined to avoid it at all costs. It just complicates my life. But if God can be glorified through it, then so be it. And I do believe that the good news ought to make the news. God was glorified through the *Today Show* segment that aired on Easter Sunday, and many unchurched folks have visited our church as a result. So praise God!

One of the unexpected blessings was ministering to the film crew. The reporter who did the story told me that her father was an atheist, but she had a praying grandmother. I gave Maria a copy of *The Circle Maker*. A few weeks later, she told me it was revolutionizing her prayer life. She even bought copies for some of her friends and family members. Who knows, maybe God is raising up a remnant at NBC!

If we do the ordinary,
God will add an extra to it.

Senior Partner

"Store up for yourselves treasures in heaven."
MATTHEW 6:20

I have a ninety-five-year-old friend named Stanley Tam. Actually, he's more than a friend; Stanley is one of my heroes. More than a half century ago, he made a decision to make God his Senior Partner. In one of the most unique corporate takeovers ever, Stanley legally transferred 51 percent of his business to God.

Stanley started the United States Plastic Corporation with $37 in capital. When he gave his business over to God, annual revenues were less than $200,000, but Stanley believed God would bless his business, and he wanted to honor God from the get-go.

At that point, most of us would have been patting ourselves on the back, but not Stanley. He felt convicted for keeping 49 percent for himself. After reading the parable about the merchant who found the pearl of great price and sold everything he had to obtain it, Stanley made a decision to divest himself of all his shares.

On January 15, 1955, every share of stock was transferred to his Senior Partner, and Stanley became a salaried employee of the company he had started. Since the day Stanley made that defining decision, he has given away more than $120 million.

Stanley spoke at National Community Church a few years ago, and afterward we shared one of the most memorable meals I've ever had. I ate up every word that came out of his mouth. The wisdom he dispensed in one hour will last a lifetime. In his matter-of-fact manner, Stanley said, "God's shovel is always bigger than ours." Translation: "We cannot outgive God." Stanley discovered the key that unlocks the joy of generosity: what we keep we ultimately lose; what we give away we ultimately get back. So Stanley said, "I just send it ahead by giving it away." Then Stanley threw out a one-liner that is more insightful than anything I've learned in the process of gaining three seminary degrees: "God cannot reward Abraham yet because his seed is still multiplying."

The same is true of Stanley. It will take quite a while to calculate his reward in heaven — not because of the amount given but because of the percentage. Stanley came awfully close to giving away 100 percent. As Stanley puts it, "A man can eat only one meal at a time, wear only one suit of clothes at a time, drive only one car at a time. All this I have. Isn't that enough?"

The Same God

Toward the end of our meal, Stanley shared one last thought that doubled as dessert. I'm not sure if it's *what* he said or *how* he said it, but it struck me as a simple profundity. Stanley said, "I've got the same God that George Müller has."

The same God who helped George Müller raise tens of millions of dollars is the same God who helped Stanley Tam give away tens of millions of dollars! And He's the same God who can accomplish the plans and purposes He has put in your heart. If it's God-ordained, it's inevitable.

Few things are as inspiring as seeing childlike faith in a very old person. That's Stanley Tam. He is the youngest oldest person I know. He simply takes God at His word. And when we take God at His word, God stands by His word.

One of the mistakes we make in reading history, whether biblical history or history in general, is thinking that those who lived before us were different from us. They weren't. If God did it for them, He can do it for us. And if we do what they did in the Bible, I'm convinced that God will do what He did. Nothing has changed. God wants to renew His deeds in our day. But we need to pray the price. Leonard Ravenhill put it this way:

> One of these days some simple soul will pick up the Book of God, read it, *and believe it*. Then the rest of us will be embarrassed. We have adopted the convenient theory that the Bible is a Book to be explained, whereas first and foremost it is a Book to be believed (and after that to be obeyed).

Legacy

I recently had the privilege of speaking at a conference hosted by a wonderful organization called Generous Giving. The focus of this annual gathering of some of the wealthiest Christians in the country is giving generously and strategically to kingdom causes. While there, I met some members of the Maclellan Family Foundation. They are among the most respected philanthropists in the world, and leaders in the generosity movement.

On June 7, 1857, a Scotsman named Thomas Maclellan made a covenant with the All in All. That covenant, made on his twentieth birthday, was renewed on his fiftieth and seventieth birthdays. More than five generations later, the seeds he sowed are still multiplying in the millions of dollars that are given away. But the genealogy of generosity traces back to one defining prayer.

> I now fall down before Thy throne and prostrate myself at Thy footstool ... O God of Heaven, record it in the book of Thy remembrances that from henceforth I am Thine forever. I renounce all former lords that have had dominion over me and consecrate all that I am and all that I have, the faculties of my mind, the members of my body, my worldly possessions, my time, and my influence over others, all to be used entirely for Thy glory and resolutely employed in obedience to Thy commands as long as Thou continuest me in life.

The greatest legacy a person can leave is a complete surrender of their life to the lordship of Jesus Christ. If we don't hold out on God, God won't hold out on us. Take God at His promise as expressed by the psalmist: "No good thing does He withhold from those who walk uprightly." And these good things will pass from generation to generation and become great things. God will answer our prayers in the lives of offspring we won't meet until the Father's family reunion at the marriage supper of the Lamb. But every prayer we pray, every gift we give, every sacrifice we make, and every step of faith we take is an inheritance left to the next generation. And our prayers live on, long after we die, in their lives.

What we keep we ultimately lose;
what we give away we ultimately get back.

Prayer Contracts

"Whatever you bind on earth
will be bound in heaven."
MATTHEW 18:18

More than a decade ago, I walked by a crack house on Capitol Hill, and God gave me a vision for a coffeehouse. It was a ridiculous prayer at that point because we had hardly any money and hardly any people. So we just kept walking around it the way the Israelites circled Jericho. Over the course of five years, we must have laid hands on it, stood on it, and circled it ten thousand times!

The owner's original asking price was $1 million, but the more we prayed, the more the price dropped. By the time we purchased it, we got it for $325,000. The amazing thing, however, is that four different parties offered more money for it than we did, including two real estate developers.

So how did we get it? My only explanation is Matthew 18:18: "Whatever you bind on earth will be bound in heaven." Our prayers were hyperlinked to that promise. We genuinely believed that our vision was given by God. Just as Jesus hung out at wells — a natural gathering place in the ancient world

— we wanted to create a postmodern well where the church and community could cross paths. And this piece of property — one block from Union Station, kitty-corner to the Securities and Exchange Commission, and right in the heart of historic Capitol Hill — was our Promised Land.

The word *bind* has a legal connotation. It means "to place a contract on something." This is precisely what happens when we pray in the will of God. Our prayers place a contract in the spiritual realm. So while February 7, 2002, is the date we put signatures on a piece of paper and took ownership of the property in the eyes of the government, the spiritual contract predates it by several years. The deal dates back to the first prayer circle we drew around the property.

Full Authority

I've emphasized a simple truth throughout this book, and I'd like to say it one more time for good measure: the purpose of prayer is not to get what you want; the goal of prayer is to discern what God wants, what God wills. But if your prayer is in the will of God, then it is backed by the full authority of the King and His kingdom.

A. W. Tozer wrote, "What comes into our minds when we think about God is the most important thing about us." So let me ask the question: When you think about God, what images come into your mind? The image that comes into my mind is a picture of Jesus with a lamb draped around his shoulders, because that is the painting that hung in my grandparents' house. For most people, I suspect the dominant image is Jesus hanging on a cross. That gruesome cross is the most beautiful picture of what true love looks like. But let me make an observation that may sound a bit sacrilegious. You aren't praying to a God who is hanging on a cross; Jesus is seated on the throne, and the earth is His footstool. All authority is His. And if you are His, then His authority is yours.

We grossly underestimate the authority that is ours because we are children of God. And we desperately need a vision like the one Isaiah had, who saw the Lord high and lifted up.

I think Tozer was right when he stated that a low view of God is the cause of a hundred lesser evils and a high view of God is the solution to ten thousand problems. Our biggest problem is our small view of God. God is so much bigger than our biggest problems. God is so much better than our best thoughts. He is infinitely wiser and more gracious and powerful than anything we can imagine.

Negotiate

In retrospect, I'm glad it took as long as it did to purchase our piece of our Promised Land. And I'm glad it was as hard as it was. Why? Because we learned to dream big, pray hard, and think long. It may sound redundant, but if it hadn't taken a miracle, it wouldn't be a miracle.

That experience didn't just teach us how to negotiate on a human plane; it taught us how to negotiate with God through intercession. It pushed our limits and stretched our faith. And now we're stewarding the miracle by believing God for even bigger and better miracles.

We tend to view the goal as the goal, but in God's economy, the process is the goal. It's not about *what* we're doing at all; it's about *who* we're becoming in the process.

It's not about doing great things for God; it's about God doing great things in us.

After explaining the binding nature of our prayers, Jesus explains the power of prayer circles.

> "If two of you agree on earth about anything that they may ask, it shall be done for them by My Father who is in heaven. For where two or three have gathered together in My name, I am there in their midst."

The concept of prayer circles is a double entendre. It refers to specific things we are circling in prayer, like the crack house that we turned into our coffeehouse. But when two or three agree in prayer, they are forming a prayer circle around the prayer circle. It's like double or triple circling!

The word *bind* means "to tie together." It's the same word used to describe marriage vows. Just as the two become one flesh, when we agree in prayer, the two become one spirit.

Something powerful happens when we agree in prayer. Our faith isn't just added together; it's multiplied. It doesn't mean we can walk down to our local car dealership and circle our favorite model with some friends. But if we are praying in the will of God and for the glory of God, then agreeing with someone in prayer is like getting our prayer contract notarized.

Finally, the word *bind* means "to chain." There are more than three thousand promises in Scripture, and according to the apostle Paul, all of them "are 'Yes' in Christ." Our most powerful prayers are chained to the promises of God. Don't just pray your words all the time; pray the Word of God because His word does not return to Him empty.

In the Old Testament, the idea of binding yourself to the Word of God was taken literally. The Word of God was kept in visible places and attached to body parts as a constant reminder. The Lord commanded the Israelites, "Thou shalt bind them for a sign upon thine hand, and they shall be as frontlets between thine eyes."

Chain it to your mind through memorization. Chain it to your heart through meditation. Chain it to your past, present, and future through prayer.

Agreeing with someone in prayer is like getting your prayer notarized.

Day 38

Climb the Watchtower

I will climb up to my watchtower
and stand at my guardpost.

HABAKKUK 2:1 NLT

Watchtowers served a variety of purposes in ancient culture — as built-in defense systems in the walls of ancient cities, as built-in pastures so shepherds could protect their flocks from wild animals, and as built-in vineyards for protection from thieves. Watchmen would climb into their watchtower, station themselves at their guardpost, and scan the horizon for enemy armies or trading caravans. The watchmen were the first to see, and they saw the farthest. So it is with those who pray. Intercessors are watchmen and watchwomen. They see sooner and see farther in the spiritual realm. Why? Because prayer gives us a unique vantage point.

My watchtower is Ebenezer's Coffeehouse. I love praying on the rooftop because I'm praying on top of an answered prayer. I often climb the ladder, pop the hatch, and pace back and forth in prayer. It's hard *not* to pray with faith when we pray in a place where God has already done a miracle.

I wonder if that is how Elijah felt as he prayed for rain on top of Mount Carmel. God had just answered an impossible prayer on that very mountain. Elijah defeated the 450 prophets of Baal in a sudden-death showdown on Mount Carmel. The God who sent *fire* can certainly send *rain*, right? That miracle gave Elijah the faith he needed to pray hard. And that is one of the by-products of answered prayer. It gives us the faith to believe God for bigger and better miracles. With each answered prayer, we draw bigger prayer circles. With each act of faithfulness, it increases our faith. With each promise kept, it increases our persistence quotient.

Geography and spirituality are not unrelated. That's why the Israelites built memorials in places of spiritual significance. During seasons of repentance, they would often return to those ancient altars to renew their covenant with God.

I have to believe that David revisited more than once the battlefield where he defeated Goliath. That Abraham made a pilgrimage back to the thicket where God provided a ram. That Peter rowed out to the place on the Sea of Galilee where he walked on water — and it renewed his faith. That Paul built a personal altar on the road to Damascus where God knocked him off his high horse. And that Zacchaeus let his grandkids climb the sycamore-fig tree where he had gotten his first glimpse of Jesus.

Going back to places of spiritual significance should be part of our spiritual rhythm. I occasionally go back to the cow pasture in Alexandria, Minnesota, where I felt called to ministry. I go back to the chapel balcony at my alma mater where I learned to pray. I go back to the places that remind me of God's faithfulness because they renew my faith.

For that reason, and a hundred others, *where* we pray is not insignificant. The Israelites pitched the tent of meeting outside the camp for a reason. Jesus prayed on mountains, by water, and in gardens for a reason. We need to find a place where we are free from distraction, where we get good reception, where we can focus, and where our faith is strong.

Prayer Targets

One ancient translation of Habakkuk 2:1 reads, "I will stand upon my watch, and station me within a circle." This Scripture inspired Honi to draw a circle in the sand and pray for rain. Honi stationed himself within the circle by kneeling inside it and praying the prayer that saved a generation: "Lord of the universe, I swear before Your great name that I will not move from this circle until You have shown mercy upon Your children." Honi was willing to die within that circle!

Once again, there is nothing magical about circling something in prayer, but there is something biblical about it. There are times when we have to mark God's territory. We have to pray a perimeter around a promise God has put in our heart. We have to be willing to go in and not come out until God answers.

Doing so can take a hundred different forms. Let me share a few examples.

I recently spoke at the weekly prayer meeting at Christ Tabernacle in Queens, New York. Michael and Maria Durso founded Christ Tab, a daughter church of Brooklyn Tabernacle, nearly three decades ago. Their three sons, Adam,

Jordan, and Chris, are on the pastoral staff, and they are one of the most anointed families I've ever met. This anointing is a testament to the power of prayer because all three boys were prodigals as teenagers. At times, it seemed as though their sons were lost beyond lost, but Michael and Maria would not stop fasting and praying for them. They literally purchased a shooting target, wrote their boys' names on the bull's-eye, and kept aiming their intercessions at their boys. That target was a tangible way of drawing a circle around them. It took years of circling, and they experienced seasons of discouragement, but one by one their boys came back to Christ.

One footnote.

When Michael and Maria were in their twenties, they were as far from God as a person can get. They lived from drug fix to drug fix, and they mocked anything remotely religious. They were on vacation when Maria mysteriously came under the conviction of the Holy Spirit. She wasn't in church. She wasn't listening to a preacher. She wasn't reading a Bible. The conviction came out of nowhere. What she didn't know is that thirty of her friends had gotten saved after she and Michael had left for vacation. The moment she came under conviction was the same moment that her friends formed a prayer circle and started interceding for her!

One more footnote.

For many years, the Dursos prayed for a youth group. What they didn't realize is that the youth group was right under their noses. They were raising the youth pastors in their own home. One day, God gave Adam a vision of young people lined up to get into their youth ministry the way people line up to get into nightclubs. Adam started a youth ministry, and Chris now leads it. And hundreds of kids line up around the block on Friday nights to get in.

Circle It

Since the release of *The Circle Maker*, I've heard amazing stories of the circles people are praying around the promises and promptings God is putting in their hearts.

The longest prayer circle may be a two-thousand-mile prayer drive around six New England states by my friend Josh Gagnon, who pastors Next Level Church. After reading about my 4.7-mile prayer walk around Capitol Hill, he felt compelled to pray a perimeter around their Promised Land. The five days that he and several staff members spent singing and praying in that car was such a powerful experience that they are making it an annual tradition at the beginning of every new year.

The most unique prayer circle happened right in my backyard. I don't necessarily prescribe it, but let me describe it. Through a dream and a prophetic word, a group of intercessors felt led to bury three thousand Bibles around the seventy-two-mile Beltway that encircles Washington, D.C. Armed with shovels and backpacks filled with Bibles, they circled the city over the course of ten nights and planted the Bibles in the ground forty paces apart. They second-guessed it more than once, but the Lord kept confirming it. Just as Ezekiel built siege works as a prophetic picture or sacred sign, they planted Bibles to stake claim to the nation's capital.

Over and over again we prayed, "God, soften the soil of D.C. and America, that the Word of God could be planted deeply again." We believed the Bibles formed a belt of truth around D.C. And we prayed Zechariah 2:5 — that God would be a wall of fire around Jerusalem and that His glory would be revealed within the circle. More than anything, we were circling the city to put a target on it for God Himself to pour out His Spirit.

Let me repeat, there is nothing magical about circling. It honestly doesn't matter whether it's literal or figurative. And it can be a circle, oval, square, or hexagon. The shape isn't the point. The point is this: if the Holy Spirit prompts us to pray, then we need to take a step of faith and mark God's territory.

Draw the Circle

Going back to places of spiritual significance can help us find our way forward again.

Holy Ground

"Take off your sandals, for the place where you are
standing is holy ground."
EXODUS 3:5

General Cecil Richardson is a retired chief of chaplains for the United States Air Force. While stationed in D.C., General Richardson attended one of our campuses and spoke to our men's ministry one weekend. As a Major General, he understands chain of command. So when the Holy Spirit gives marching orders, he salutes, falls into rank, and obeys orders.

That's what happened one Saturday when he was awakened at 5:30 a.m. with an inexplicable prompting to get new glasses. His wife had been telling him for years that he needed new glasses, but he had ignored her prompting. This new prompting was a strange one at a strange time. And the problem, of course, is that optical shops aren't open early on weekends. So the general had a long breakfast at Denny's and then visited the nearest vision center just as it opened.

When he got to the shop, Cecil felt led to tell the woman behind the counter that he was a chaplain. He resisted at first because he didn't want her to think he wanted a military discount of some sort, but he felt she needed to know. So he saluted the Holy Spirit and simply said, "I'm a chaplain." That's when this woman started trembling as tears filled her eyes. She said, "My husband is in the military and stationed abroad, and I just found out I have cancer. I have no idea what to do, so yesterday a friend and I prayed that God would send me a chaplain. And here you are."

These are the moments that give you goose bumps. These are the moments when you are reminded that God cares about every detail of your life. These are the moments when you take off your shoes, because you know you are standing on holy ground.

The Place

Tending sheep.

Can you imagine a more monotonous existence? And Moses did it for forty years. He must have felt that God had put him out to pasture. He once dreamed of delivering the people of Israel out of captivity, but that dream died when he killed an Egyptian taskmaster and fled the country as a fugitive. Moses spent the next forty years in spiritual exile on the backside of the desert.

Then God appeared to him in a burning bush.

I have a feeling that Moses got up that morning, put on his sandals, and picked up his staff, figuring it would be an ordinary day just like the day before, and the day before the day before, and the day before that. But you never know when or where or how God will invade the routine of your life.

Jewish scholars used to debate why God appeared to Moses in a burning bush. A thunderclap or lightning bolt would have been more impressive. And why the far side of the desert? Why not the palace or a pyramid in Egypt?

They concluded that God appeared to Moses in a burning bush for one simple reason: to show that no place is devoid of God's presence, not even a bush on the backside of the desert. So they gave God a name I've learned to love: *The Place*. God is here, there, and everywhere. So it doesn't matter where you are; God can meet you anywhere.

A few years ago, I heard author Ken Gaub share one of the most amazing prayer testimonies I've ever heard. He and his family were driving on I-75 near Dayton, Ohio, when they decided to stop at a restaurant. Ken's wife and children went right into the restaurant while he stretched his legs. As he walked past a nearby gas station, he heard a pay phone ringing. The phone kept ringing, and Ken thought it might be some sort of emergency, so he answered it. He heard the voice of an operator, who said, "Long distance for Ken Gaub."

Ken almost passed out. He said, "You've got to be kidding me. I was just walking in the middle of nowhere and heard this phone ringing." The confused operator said, "Is Ken Gaub there?" After making sure there weren't any candid cameras, he said, "This is Ken Gaub."

A voice on the other side of the line said, "Mr. Gaub, my name is Millie. I'm from Harrisburg, Pennsylvania. You don't know me, but I need your help." She went on to explain that she had just written a suicide note but had decided to give prayer one more shot. She said, "God, I don't really want to do this." And as she prayed, she remembered seeing Ken Gaub on television. She thought to herself, "If I could just talk with him, he could help me." But this was pre-Google, making it extremely difficult to track him down. As she prayed, some numbers popped into her head, and she wrote them on a piece of paper. She couldn't help but think, "Wouldn't it be wonderful if God were giving me Ken's number?" Then Millie said, "I decided to try calling the number, and I couldn't believe it when the operator said it was you."

Millie asked Ken, "Are you in your office?" When Ken said no, Millie sounded surprised. She said, "Then where are you?" Ken said, "You made the call. Don't you know?" She said, "I don't even know what area I'm calling. I just dialed the number on a piece of paper." Ken said, "You won't believe this. I'm in a phone booth in Dayton, Ohio." Millie replied, "What are you doing there?" Ken said, "Answering a pay phone!"

Ken went on to draw this conclusion:

I walked away from that phone booth with an electrifying sense of our heavenly Father's concern for each of His children. What were the astronomical odds of this happening? With all the millions of phones and innumerable combinations of numbers, only an all-knowing God could have caused that woman to dial that number in that phone booth at that moment in time.

When Ken hung up the phone, he walked over to the restaurant and sat down with his family. Still stunned, he said to his wife, Barb, "You won't believe this. God knows where I am."

Take Off Your Sandals

There are two moments in Scripture when God gives the same curious command: *take off your sandals*. The first one happens on the backside of the desert with Moses before God delivers Israel out of Egypt. The second one happens just before God delivers Jericho to Joshua. As Moses' assistant, Joshua had heard the story of the burning bush a thousand times. But no one can live off someone else's experience, someone else's story. We need our own epiphany, our own testimony.

So why did God ask them to take off their sandals?

I think it was an act of humility, an act of worship. It was a way of acknowledging absolute dependence on God. It was a way of removing any obstacle that could get in the way of God and Moses, God and Joshua.

In case you care, one of my idiosyncrasies is that I remove my shoes whenever I'm writing. I do it as a reminder that I need God's anointing. It reminds me that I'm fulfilling a sacred calling.

One last observation, because sometimes the obvious eludes us. The holy ground wasn't the Promised Land. It was right where Moses was standing. Don't wait to worship God until you get to the Promised Land; you've got to worship along the way.

This is holy ground. This is a holy moment.

Right here. Right now.

Take off your sandals.

The purpose of prayer is not to give orders to God; the purpose is to get orders from God.

Day 40

Prayer Alphabet

"Lord, teach us to pray."

LUKE 11:1

This past Easter, I attended the Easter Prayer Breakfast at the White House along with some two hundred religious leaders from across the country. Before breakfast, a seventy-six-year-old African-American preacher who had served alongside Martin Luther King Jr. in the civil rights movement offered a prayer. I was expecting a perfunctory pre-meal prayer, but it was anything but. To be honest, I usually pray short prayers before meals because I believe in eating food while it's hot. So I certainly wasn't expecting a pre-meal prayer that would make my entire prayer life flash before my eyes.

This seasoned saint prayed with such familiarity with the heavenly Father that I felt like I barely knew God, but it made me want to know God the way he knew God. And he prayed with such authority that it felt like he had just left the throne room of God. His prayers seemed deep-fried in the faithfulness of God. By comparison, my prayers seemed like weak sauce.

When this preacher had finished praying, I turned to two friends standing next to me, Andy Stanley and Louie Giglio, and I said, "I feel like I've never prayed before."

I wonder if that is how the disciples felt when they heard Jesus pray. I wonder if that's why they asked him, "Lord, teach us to pray." Jesus' prayers were so qualitatively different that the disciples felt like they'd never really prayed before.

Notice what the disciples didn't ask. They didn't say, "Lord, teach us to preach." They didn't say, "Teach us to lead," or even, "Lord, teach us to disciple." All of those endeavors are noble. But they have one request: "Lord, teach us to pray."

If we change the way we pray, everything changes. It changes the way we work, the way we parent, and the way we lead. It changes the way we prioritize and strategize. It changes the way we think, the way we feel, and the way we speak. Prayer changes everything from the inside out.

A New Language

When you've written a book on prayer, people tend to think you have everything figured out. The truth is, there is so much more that I *don't* know than I do know. I feel like it's the first day of school in prayer kindergarten. But I'm hungry to learn.

The word *prayer* often induces feelings of guilt simply because we don't do enough of it or because we feel inept when we don't know what to say. For the record, I've never met anyone who felt that they pray too much or too effectively! All of us fall short. But instead of feelings of guilt, the thought of prayer should induce unbridled excitement because nothing is more potent than kneeling before God Almighty.

While my prayer batting average is no better than anyone else's, I'm determined to get back into the batter's box because I can't get a hit if I don't take a swing. And if I swing enough times, I'll hit a few homers and accumulate a lot of RBIs. So quit worrying about striking out, and swing for the fences!

Don't beat yourself up over past failures or present struggles. Simply do what the disciples did. Ask Jesus to help you, to teach you. Let their simple request become your modus operandi: "Lord, teach us to pray."

It doesn't matter how much you know. Do you have a teachable spirit? Are you hungry to learn? Are you open to change? Wisdom is knowing how much you don't know. So you have to start there and ask God to teach you.

Not long ago, I went through a season of discouragement in my personal prayer life. I was using the same words over and over again because my vocabulary was so small. My prayers felt clichéd. So did my worship. If there weren't lyrics on the screen, I had nothing to say. And then it dawned on me that those lyrics are like greeting cards. I might like what they say, but someone else wrote them. Can you imagine giving your spouse a greeting card whenever you wanted to tell them you love them, but never expressing love in your own words? Yet this is what we do with God. A greeting-card relationship with God isn't enough.

One of the most meaningful worship experiences I had this year was in Ethiopia. The worship was in both English and Amharic. I enjoyed the English worship, but the Amharic worship was life changing because I couldn't understand it. I couldn't rely on someone else's words. So I started worshiping God in spirit and truth. I found my own words to sing. Sometimes lyrics get in the way of worshiping God because someone else is mediating our praise. God wants to hear your voice, your words, your praise.

One day as I was on my knees praying about praying, I felt the Holy Spirit lovingly and playfully asking, "Did you think this was going to be easy?" Learning a spiritual language is like learning Spanish, French, or German. We don't become fluent in a few minutes. Acquiring a prayer language is as arduous as learning a foreign language. Expanding our vocabulary of praise is as difficult as conjugating verbs in another language.

I love the story about the grandfather who walked by his granddaughter's bedroom one night and overheard her praying the alphabet, literally. "Dear God, a, b, c, d, e, f, g." She prayed all the way to "z" and said, "Amen." The grandfather said, "Sweetie, why were you praying that way?" The granddaughter replied, "I didn't know what to say so I figured I'd let God put the letters together however He saw fit."

Sometimes I feel that way too. I have no idea what to say when I pray. And that's OK. The first objective of prayer is praying about what to pray about. Prayer isn't about outlining our agenda to God; it's about getting into God's presence and getting God's agenda for us.

If you don't know where to start, or if you get stuck, go back to the Bible. Start reading, and God will start speaking. That's when you need to stop reading and start praying.

Words, phrases, or verses will jump off the page and into your spirit. You need to circle them in prayer. And don't be in such a hurry to get through the Bible that you don't get the Bible through you.

The Difference

My friend Ross Hill is the founder and CEO of Bank2, a community-owned bank in Oklahoma City. I don't believe I've ever encountered a businessman more devoted to the cause of Christ. The bank is his pulpit, and its customers are his congregation. Ross defines business as mission. And he's great at both.

When Bank2 opened its doors, its leaders literally anointed the doors with oil and prayed for every person who would walk in and out of them. Board meetings begin with prayer. Whenever new employees need to be recruited, prayers are offered for the process. And it's not uncommon for Ross to personally pray with customers or employees in his executive office. Prayer is the foundation of everything they do.

The bank isn't immune to financial challenges. In 2008, Bank2 experienced a large loan loss due to fraud. In fact, that one loss was larger than the cumulative losses that Ross had suffered during his thirty-five-year banking career. But in Ross's own words, "We prayed through it." And God answered. The very next year, *American Banking Journal* rated Bank2 the #1 community bank in the country. In 2011, they were the #7 mortgage operation in the country. And in ten years, they have loaned more than a billion dollars.

It doesn't matter what you do; prayer is the key to your business, your practice, your career. The anointing of God isn't limited to pastors who preach. The favor of God is for everyone. If you're an entrepreneur, you need innovative ideas. If you're a physician, you need the discernment to diagnose. If you're in politics, you need the wisdom to govern. If you're in entertainment, you need the charisma to perform. All of these things are manifestations of the Holy Spirit.

Whether we write lyrics or craft legislation, sell homes or teach classes, design spaces or open franchises, prayer is a critical part of the creative process. Don't just brainstorm; praystorm. Turn your classroom, boardroom, locker room, operating room, courtroom, and conference room into a prayer room!

Prayer is the difference between appointments and divine appointments. Prayer is the difference between good ideas and God-ideas. Prayer is the difference between the favor of God and the luck of the draw. Prayer is the difference between closed doors and open doors. Prayer is the difference between possible and impossible. Prayer is the difference between the best we can do and the best God can do.

Prayer is the difference between the best
we can do and the best God can do.

Notes

Page 10: *"If my people"*: 2 Chronicles 7:14.

Page 13: *"proved to be the most important forty days"*: Bill Bright, "7 Basic Steps to Successful Fasting and Prayer," www.cru.org/training-and-growth/devotional-life/7-steps-to-fasting/index.htm (accessed July 2, 2012).

Page 17: *"Whosoever will may come"*: Adapted from Revelation 22:17.

Page 19: *Remember when Moses got impatient*: Exodus 2:12.

Page 26: *"The world has yet to see"*: Quoted in William R. Moody, *The Life of Dwight L. Moody* (New York: Revell, 1900), 134; see Mark Fackler, "The World Has Yet to See . . . ," *Christianity Today* (January 1, 1990), www.ctlibrary.com/ch/1990/issue25/2510.html (accessed June 6, 2012).

Page 30: *"My Father, if it is possible"*: Matthew 26:39.

Page 30: *"I made a solemn dedication"*: Edward Hickman, ed., *The Works of Jonathan Edwards* (London: William Ball, 1839), 1:56.

Page 40: *"Delight yourself in the LORD"*: Psalm 37:4 NASB.

Page 45: *"Ask and it will be given"*: Matthew 7:7; Luke 11:9.

Page 48: *Like Noah . . . Israelites . . . Elijah*: Genesis 6:14–22; Joshua 6:3–21; 1 Kings 18:43–45.

Page 50: *"When you reach the banks"*: Joshua 3:8 NLT.

Page 53: *"I asked God"*: Sam Wellman, "Heroes of History: George Washington Carver," www.heroesofhistory.com/page11.html (accessed June 7, 2012).

Page 55: *low view of God*: A. W. Tozer, *The Knowledge of the Holy* (New York: HarperCollins, 1961), vii, 2.

Page 61: *"Everyone who's ever taken"*: Quoted in Pat Williams, *Go for the Magic* (Nashville: Nelson, 1998), 97.

Page 68: *"Being a first-class noticer"*: Warren G. Bennis and Robert J. Thomas, *Geeks & Geezers: How Eras, Values, and Defining Moments Shape Leaders* (Boston: Harvard Business School Press, 2002), 19.

Page 71: *"Surely the LORD"*: Genesis 28:16.

Page 73: *"Then God said"*: Genesis 1:11 NLT.

Page 73: *"I have observed"*: Quoted in *The Sabbath Recorder*, vol. 64 (Plainfield, N.J.: American Sabbath Tract Society, January 6, 1908), 738; see also William Jennings Bryan, "The Prince of Peace" (a lecture delivered at many religious gatherings), http://thriceholy.net/Texts/Prince.html (accessed June 15, 2012).

Page 74: *Jesus spoke of our faith*: Matthew 17:20.

Page 76: *But if we plant*: 1 Corinthians 3:7.

Page 79: *God owns the cattle*: Psalm 50:10.

Page 84: *He prowls around*: 1 Peter 5:8.

Page 84: *Jesus is the Lion*: Revelation 5:5.

Page 84: *"If God is for us"*: Romans 8:31.

Page 84: *"The one who is in you"*: 1 John 4:4.

Page 85: *"I can do all things"*: Philippians 4:13 NKJV.

Page 85: *"In all things God works"*: Romans 8:28.

Page 85: *"I will build My church"*: Matthew 16:18 NKJV.

Page 89: *"Contend, LORD"*: Psalm 35:1, 23.

Page 90: *They are circling us*: Psalm 32:7.

Page 91: *John Adams later recounted*: Charles Adams, ed., *Familiar Letters of John Adams and His Wife Abigail Adams, during the Revolution* (Boston: Houghton Mifflin, 1875), 38.

Page 92: *"O Lord, our heavenly Father"*: The Office of the Chaplain: United States House of Representatives, "First Prayer of the Continental Congress, 1774," http://chaplain.house.gov/archive/continental.html (accessed June 15, 2012).

Page 96: *"You do not have"*: James 4:2.

Page 97: *"You cannot tell"*: John 3:8.

Page 101: *word does not return to him empty*: Isaiah 55:11.

Page 101: *Every spiritual blessing*: Ephesians 1:3.

Page 101: *No matter how many*: 2 Corinthians 1:20.

Page 101: *No good thing*: Psalm 84:11.

Page 109: *They are a foundation*: 1 Corinthians 3:10–12.

Page 120: *"I'm giving you every square inch"*: Joshua 1:3 MSG.

Page 125: *When the angel addressed*: Judges 6:12.

Page 125: *"How can I rescue Israel"*: Judges 6:15 NLT.

Page 126: *"If you are truly"*: Judges 6:17 NLT.

Page 127: *"one of the great secrets"*: George Müller, *A Narrative of Some of the Lord's Dealings with George Müller* (London: Nisbet, 1886), 2:330.

Page 128: *"Let God be as original"*: Oswald Chambers, *My Utmost for His Highest* (Grand Rapids: Discovery House, 2006), June 13.

Page 132: *we're "busybodies"*: 1 Timothy 5:13.

Page 132: *"I have so much to do"*: Quoted in J. Oswald Sanders, *Spiritual Leadership* (Chicago: Moody, 1974), 76.

Page 132: *"go into all the world"*: Mark 16:15.

Page 132: *"Do not leave Jerusalem"*: Acts 1:4.

Page 134: *"Before I formed you"*: Jeremiah 1:5.

Page 141: *Laurie Beth Jones has stated*: Laurie Beth Jones, *The Power of Positive Prophecy: Finding the Hidden Potential in Everyday Life* (New York: Hyperion, 1999), ix.

Page 141: *"I grew up in an alcoholic"*: Ibid., xii.

Page 142: *"It is more noble"*: Quoted in Stephen Covey, *Principle-Centered Leadership* (New York: Simon & Schuster, 1991), 60.

Page 144: *"The time of business"*: Brother Lawrence, *The Practice of the Presence of God* (Radford, Va.: Wilder, 2008), 25.

Page 145: *"We try to call him to mind"*: Frank Laubach, *The Game with Minutes* (Westwood, N.J.: Revell, 1961).

Page 146: *"Don't worry about anything"*: Philippians 4:6 NLT.

Page 147: *"Last Monday was the most completely"*: Brother Lawrence and Frank Laubach, *Practicing His Presence* (Goleta, Calif.: Christian Books, 1973), June 1, 1930 entry.

Page 151: *I do a twenty-one day*: There are a variety of Daniel fasts. I recommend researching cookbooks before embarking on the fast.

Page 152: *"Couldn't you men keep watch"*: Matthew 26:40.

Page 152: *"The spirit is willing"*: Matthew 26:41.

Page 153: *"Jesus returned to Galilee"*: Luke 4:14.

Page 157: *"I wonder what would happen"*: Peter Marshall, *Mr. Jones, Meet the Master: Sermons and Prayers of Peter Marshall* (Old Tappan, N.J.: Revell, 1988), 143 – 44.

Page 161: *Six times the psalmist*: Psalms 33:3; 40:3; 96:1; 98:1; 144:9; 149:1.

Page 162: *"When you pray"*: Matthew 6:7 – 8 NLT.

Page 165: *"How sweet are Your words"*: Psalm 119:103 NASB.

Page 166: *Scripture doesn't explicitly mention*: Luke 2:46 – 47.

Page 167: *"If you abide"*: John 15:7 NASB.

Page 168: *"Fear ye not"*: Exodus 14:13 KJV.

Page 168: *"The LORD stirred up"*: Haggai 1:14.

Page 168: *This is precisely what Jesus*: Luke 24:49 KJV.

Page 169: *"This regular reading"*: Deuteronomy 17:20 NLT.

Page 171: *"Lord, Son of David"*: Matthew 20:30.

Page 178: *Peter and John were described*: Acts 4:13.

Page 179: *"Now we believe"*: John 4:42 NLT.

Page 185: *"History belongs to the intercessors"*: Walter Wink, *The Powers That Be: Theology for a New Millennium* (New York: Doubleday, 1999), 185.

Page 186: *During one of his revivals*: Cited by J. Paul Reno, *Daniel Nash: Prevailing Prince of Prayer* (Asheville, N.C.: Revival Literature, 1989), 8.

Page 186: *"I am now convinced"*: Ibid., 160.

Page 189: *"Brothers, we know why"*: Cited in Pete Greig, *The Vision and the Vow* (Orlando, Fla.: Relevant, 2004), 131 – 32.

Page 189: *That prayer meeting was visited*: Acts 1:12 – 17; 2:1 – 4.

Page 189: *In the days of Hilkiah*: 2 Chronicles 34:14.

Page 190: *"If my people"*: 2 Chronicles 7:14.

Page 190: *In the words of Charles Finney*: Cited in Leonard Ravenhill, *Why Revival Tarries* (Minneapolis: Bethany House, 2004), 138.

Page 191: *we must covenant to seek*: 2 Chronicles 15:12.

Page 192: *"If God can get enough"*: Quoted in Tommy Tenney, *The God Chasers: "My Soul Follows Hard After Thee"* (Shippensburg, Pa.: Destiny Image, 1998), 53.

Page 194: *"When people are found"*: Excerpted from a transcription of "The Role of Prayer in Spiritual Awakening," a talk given at the National Prayer Congress in Dallas, Texas, in October 1976 by J. Edwin Orr, www.prayerstorm.com/webinar_archive/The_Role_of_Prayer_in_Spiritual_Awakening.pdf (accessed July 2, 2012).

Page 195: *"Do not despise"*: Zechariah 4:10 NLT.

Page 196: *"It is inbred in us"*: Oswald Chambers, *My Utmost for His Highest* (Grand Rapids: Discovery House, 2006), October 21.

Page 196: *"Give me a place to stand on"*: E. J. Dijksterhuis, *Archimedes*, trans. C. Dikshoorn (Princeton, N.J.: Princeton University Press, 1987), 15.

Page 201: *"One of these days some simple soul"*: Ravenhill, *Why Revival Tarries*, 61.

Page 202: *"I now fall down"*: "Thomas Maclellan's Covenant with God," Generous Giving.org, http://library.generousgiving.org/articles/display.asp?id=16 (accessed July 2, 2012).

Page 203: *"No good thing"*: Psalm 84:11 NASB.

Page 205: *"What comes into our minds"*: Tozer, *Knowledge of the Holy*, 1.

Page 206: *vision like the one Isaiah had*: Isaiah 6.

Page 207: *a low view of God*: Tozer, *Knowledge of the Holy*, vii, 2.

Page 208: *"If two of you agree"*: Matthew 18:19 – 20 NASB.

Page 208: *all of them "are 'Yes' in Christ"*: 2 Corinthians 1:20.

Page 208: *word does not return to Him empty*: Isaiah 55:11.

Page 208: *"Thou shalt bind them"*: Deuteronomy 6:8 KJV.

Page 210: *prayed for rain on top of Mount Carmel*: 1 Kings 18:42.

Page 210: *Elijah defeated the 450 prophets*: 1 Kings 18:16 – 39.

Page 211: *"I will stand upon my watch"*: Habakkuk 2:1, quoted in *The Book of Legends: Sefer Ha-Aggadah*, ed. Hayim Nahman Bialik and Yehoshua Hana Ravnitzky (New York: Schocken, 1992), 202.

Page 213: *Ezekiel built siege works*: Ezekiel 4:2.

Page 218: *"I walked away"*: Kenneth Gaub, *God's Got Your Number: When You Least Expect It, He Is There!* (Green Forest, Ark.: New Leaf, 1998), chapter 1; "God Knows Where You Are," www.2jesus.org/inspstories/where.html (accessed July 2, 2012).

The Circle Maker

Praying Circles Around
Your Biggest Dreams and
Greatest Fears

Mark Batterson

According to Pastor Mark Batterson,
"Drawing prayer circles around our dreams
isn't just a mechanism whereby we accom-
plish great things for God. It's a mechanism whereby God accomplishes great things in us."

Do you ever sense that there is far more to prayer and to God's
vision for your life than what you're experiencing? It's time you
learned from the legend of Honi the circle maker — a man bold
enough to draw a circle in the sand and not budge from inside it
until God answered his prayers for his people.

What impossibly big dream is God calling you to draw a prayer
circle around? Sharing inspiring stories from his own experiences
as a circle maker, Mark Batterson will help you uncover your heart's
deepest desires and God-given dreams and unleash them through
the kind of audacious prayer that God delights to answer.

Available in stores and online!

The Circle Maker Video Curriculum

Praying Circles Around Your Biggest Dreams and Greatest Fears

Mark Batterson

This dynamic video curriculum helps participants understand what it means to dream God-sized dreams, pray with boldness, and think long-term. Four video sessions combine a teaching element from Mark Batterson with a creative element to draw viewers into the circle. Each session wraps up with a practical application giving the opportunity to put prayer principles into practice. Available as a pack, which includes one softcover participant's guide and one DVD. Participant guides are also sold separately.

Session titles include:

1. Becoming a Circle Maker
2. Little People, Big Risks, and Huge Circles
3. Praying Hard and Praying Through
4. Praying Is Like Planting

Also available: Curriculum Kit, which includes one hardcover book, one participant's guide, one DVD-ROM containing four small-group video sessions, a getting-started guide, four sermon outlines, and all the church promotional materials needed to successfully launch and sustain a four-week church-wide campaign. The curriculum can also be used in adult Sunday school settings, for small group studies, and for individual use.

Praying Circles around Your Children

Mark Batterson

In this 112-page booklet, Mark Batterson shares a perfect blend of biblical yet practical advice that will revolutionize your prayer life by giving you a new vocabulary and a new methodology. You'll see how prayer is your secret weapon. Through stories of parents just like you, Batterson shares five prayer circles that will not only help you pray for your kids, but also pray through your kids.

Batterson teaches about how to create prayer lists unique to your family, claim God-inspired promises for your children, turn your family circle into a prayer circle, and discover your child's life themes. And he not only tells you how, he illustrates why.

As Batterson says, "I realize that not everyone inherited a prayer legacy like I did, but you can leave a legacy for generations to come. Your prayers have the power to shape the destiny of your children and your children's children. It's time to start circling."

Available in stores and online!

The Circle Maker, Student Edition

Dream Big, Pray Hard, Think Long.

Mark Batterson
with Parker Batterson

Prayer can sometimes be a frightening thing: How do you approach the Maker of the world, and what exactly can you pray for? In this student adaptation of *The Circle Maker*, Pastor Mark Batterson uses the true legend of Honi the circle maker, a first-century Jewish sage whose bold prayer saved a generation, to uncover the boldness God asks of us at times, and to unpack what powerful prayer can mean in your life. Drawing inspiration from his own experiences as a circle maker, as well as sharing stories of young people who have experienced God's blessings, Batterson explores how you can approach God in a new way by drawing prayer circles around your dreams, your problems, and, most importantly, God's promises. In the process, you'll discover this simple yet life-changing truth:

> God honors bold prayers and bold prayers honor God.

And you're never too young for God to use you for amazing things.

Available in stores and online!

The Circle Maker Prayer Journal

Mark Batterson

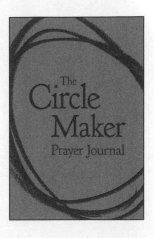

Discover the power of bold prayer and even bolder faith in God's promises. Based on Mark Batterson's revolutionary, bestselling book on prayer, *The Circle Maker Prayer Journal* features inspirational sayings and plenty of space to record your prayers, God's answers, and your spiritual insights. Learn to pray powerful words according to God's will—and see the amazing results! Gather your prayers so you can go back and see how God has been answering since you started your amazing prayer journey.

The Circle Maker Prayer Journal will be your guide to making your life goals a reality of answered prayers instead of merely fleeting wishes. This handsomely bound keepsake volume will become your written record for dreaming big and seeing God's answers.

Find Mark online at www.markbatterson.com,
on Facebook at www.facebook.com/markbatterson,
and on Twitter @MarkBatterson.

Share Your Thoughts

With the Author: Your comments will be forwarded to the author when you send them to *zauthor@zondervan.com*.

With Zondervan: Submit your review of this book by writing to *zreview@zondervan.com*.

Free Online Resources at

www.zondervan.com

Zondervan AuthorTracker: Be notified whenever your favorite authors publish new books, go on tour, or post an update about what's happening in their lives at www.zondervan.com/authortracker.

Daily Bible Verses and Devotions: Enrich your life with daily Bible verses or devotions that help you start every morning focused on God. Visit www.zondervan.com/newsletters.

Free Email Publications: Sign up for newsletters on Christian living, academic resources, church ministry, fiction, children's resources, and more. Visit www.zondervan.com/newsletters.

Zondervan Bible Search: Find and compare Bible passages in a variety of translations at www.zondervanbiblesearch.com.

Other Benefits: Register to receive online benefits like coupons and special offers, or to participate in research.

ZONDERVAN

ZONDERVAN.com/
AUTHORTRACKER
follow your favorite authors